C000183205

The Year of Liberation: a journal of the defence of Hamburgh against the French army under Marshal Davoust, in 1813, etc. By George Croly

Louis Nicolas Davout, George Croly

The Year of Liberation: a journal of the defence of Hamburgh against the French army under
Marshal Davoust, in 1813, etc. [By George Croly.]
Davout, Louis Nicolas
British Library, Historical Print Editions
British Library
Croly, George
1832
2 vol. ; 12°.
1055.e.11.

The BiblioLife Network

This project was made possible in part by the BiblioLife Network (BLN), a project aimed at addressing some of the huge challenges facing book preservationists around the world. The BLN includes libraries, library networks, archives, subject matter experts, online communities and library service providers. We believe every book ever published should be available as a high-quality print reproduction; printed on- demand anywhere in the world. This insures the ongoing accessibility of the content and helps generate sustainable revenue for the libraries and organizations that work to preserve these important materials.

The following book is in the "public domain" and represents an authentic reproduction of the text as printed by the original publisher. While we have attempted to accurately maintain the integrity of the original work, there are sometimes problems with the original book or micro-film from which the books were digitized. This can result in minor errors in reproduction. Possible imperfections include missing and blurred pages, poor pictures, markings and other reproduction issues beyond our control. Because this work is culturally important, we have made it available as part of our commitment to protecting, preserving, and promoting the world's literature.

GUIDE TO FOLD-OUTS, MAPS and OVERSIZED IMAGES

In an online database, page images do not need to conform to the size restrictions found in a printed book. When converting these images back into a printed bound book, the page sizes are standardized in ways that maintain the detail of the original. For large images, such as fold-out maps, the original page image is split into two or more pages.

Guidelines used to determine the split of oversize pages:

• Some images are split vertically; large images require vertical and horizontal splits.
• For horizontal splits, the content is split left to right.
• For vertical splits, the content is split from top to bottom.
• For both vertical and horizontal splits, the image is processed from top left to bottom right.

*Conserved under the
Adopt a Book Appeal*

No. e

M. Darmesteter (L. A.)
Cours de l'Schmidt.

THE

YEAR OF LIBERATION:

A

JOURNAL

OF THE

DEFENCE OF HAMBURGH

AGAINST THE

FRENCH ARMY UNDER MARSHAL DAVOUST,

IN 1813,

WITH

SKETCHES OF THE BATTLES OF LUTZEN, BAUTZEN,

&c. &c.

IN TWO VOLUMES.

VOL. I.

LONDON:

JAMES DUNCAN, 37, PATERNOSTER ROW.

MDCCCXXXII.

LONDON:
GILBERT & RIVINGTON, PRINTERS,
St. John's Square.

PREFACE.

———

THESE volumes contain a brief narrative, an episode, of the final year of the most eventful, brilliant, and influential period of modern Europe,—the great patriotic war of Germany.

The changes which have since passed over the European system, have all been the product of this extraordinary period. It is even difficult to look upon it but as the source of still greater changes to come. The working of the mine for good or evil is evidently far from being exhausted. The depth of oppression to which the greatest nations may be sunk, the buoyancy and invincible vigour that may lie hid in national resources, the facility with which the heaviest yoke of mere military domination may be thrown off, and the confusion, discontent, and spirit of misrule which may be summoned up in the midst of national victory, are lessons which have received an ampler development in this war, than in any equal period of the history of nations.

From this war eminently rose the fearful supremacy of Russia, which now threatens all independence ; and the not less fearful sense of popular power, which threatens all government ; the embodying of the principles of despotism and democracy, at this hour arming for a conflict, which, whenever it arrives, may cover the world with dust and ashes.

The rising of the people of Hamburgh against the French, was one of the most interesting incidents of the war. The present writer has described it as he saw it; with the opportunities of one on the spot, and the fresh impressions of the moment; impressions heightened rather than diminished by the twenty years which have been since interposed. He has found no record of the transaction from the native pen; and he has long felt an allowable anxiety that some memorial should exist of a public effort, which exhibited all the essential features of public virtue.

The general aspect of German affairs at the time, will be found occasionally observed.

The memorable men who gave a character to the war have now past away from the scene; Napoleon, and the conquerors of Napoleon, the multitude of warriors and statesmen whom the continent poured out from its bosom in this vivid and eager time, are gone,—"these our actors are but spirits;" the pageant which dazzled the eyes of all our generation, the most magnificent piece of witchcraft that the world ever saw, the FRENCH EMPIRE, is now vanished into thin air; in treading back upon those events, we tread every where upon the grave! But no date can be too remote for the attempt to do honour to the lustre of genius even in an enemy; and to the still higher claims of wise patriotism, manly labour of liberty, and the noblest qualities of human nature, exerted in its noblest cause.

CONTENTS.

VOL. I.

CONTENTS.

CHAPTER I.

THE PACKET.

THE general exclusion of the English from France, and all belonging to France, during the long interval from 1793 to 1813, had, like all other prohibitions, only sharpened public curiosity; and every one who had an idle week, or an idle guinea, was eager to expend them both on the continent.

With some, of course, the feeling was the mere love of novelty; but, with others, the objects were of a higher nature; and a rational interest might be fairly conceived, in seeing face to face, the men who had made themselves eminent in the memorable times of Europe, or in ascertaining on the spot the changes which the greatest of all wars had made, and which promised to be the parents

of changes that would outlast many a generation
to come. They were to traverse a continent, to
them not much differing from a new world, with
all the elements of creation or confusion still
struggling in every quarter; monarchy rising out
of the embers of revolution.

The peace of Amiens had done nothing to satisfy
this universal appetite. It was so brief, that it
could scarcely be called an interruption of the war.
Not one in a thousand of those who were on the
alert to penetrate all the secrets of the continent,
could avail himself of it. It had even rather
whetted public curiosity; for the few who crossed
the Channel could seldom go further than Paris,
where every thing was calculated, and calculated
on design, to give an exaggerated conception of
the power and brilliancy of France, and the
French empire. Napoleon's charlatanism, and from
the beginning to the end of his career, what was he
but the most dazzling of charlatans? was employed
to strike the senses of mankind. The stories which
reached England, of the pomp of his court, the
glitter of Paris, and the imperial exhibitions in
Paris, resembled nothing but the Arabian Nights.

To astonish the English, was an object of his especial policy at the time; and his levees and reviews, his balls and dinners, his public improvements, which undoubtedly formed a remarkable contrast with the old deformities of the streets of the capital; and his picture and statue galleries, which combined all the finest specimens of modern and ancient genius, made Paris, beyond question, of all cities of Europe, the best worth the eye of traveller, soldier, artist, or philosopher.

Napoleon himself, it would have been worth travelling round the world to see, merely as a living figure of war; but by the extraordinary vigour of his political course, and his surprising personal influence on European affairs, he had thrown a sort of *prestige*, a something little short of preternatural impression, over all belonging to him; his power had risen with the rapidity of magic, was sustained with the true mixture of splendour, subtlety and mystery, which established romance ascribes to the magician; and, however the feeling may be inexplicable to after times, and his enchantments may have since dissolved into thin air, nothing is more certain, than that, for his period, he singularly overwhelmed the understandings of mankind.

To see the great necromancer, was an achievement; and it was, from the circumstances of the peace, accomplished by so few, that they formed a privileged class, in whose presence their less fortunate brethren shone with diminished beams.

At last, however, the day for all was at hand. Napoleon played the desperate game of imperial vanity. The Scythian repaid the cropped laurels of the Austrian and the Prussian. The Cossacks hunted down the showy squadrons that had set off to hunt down every crowned head, from the Rhine to the Sea of Japan. The legions were left in the snow of Moscow. Napoleon was driven home, to make a second trial, at the expense of more French blood; the Russians and Germans were coming, full speed after him; Europe was struggling for deliverance in every quarter; and at length, Germany, to the great joy of all tourists, was declared to be open. Merchants, soldiers, scholars, men of science, artists, the mere loungers of Bath and Cheltenham, the infinite multitude who had any thing or nothing to do, crowded to the coast, gallantly dared the dangers of a summer navigation in a government packet, and migrated for the Elbe.

In whatever file the present writer is to be placed, he followed the general impulse, and early in 1813 embarked for Germany. The transit has since lost all the honours of adventure, and the cabin of a packet is at all times the least romantic of romantic things. But let due credit be given to heroism. The passage from England to the north was not then quite the unchivalrous affair that it has since become, by the help of steam and a general peace. Independently of the common sea-chances of being starved, or sent off by the shifting gales of the season to Spitzbergen, natural casualties, of which the steam-engine will soon wipe away the memory for all future ages; we might be picked up by a French lugger, and robbed, shot, or sent to prison, where the imprisonment lasted for life; and the danger was by no means imaginary. French privateering had been considerably restrained by our fleet on the Dutch station, yet the snake was but half killed, and no coast on earth could give finer opportunities for privateering than the coast from Dunkirk to

Cuxhaven, covered as it was with shoals, and running up into little creeks and rivers. The temptation was probably too much for even our Dutch friends; many a merchantman, " calmly slumbering on the ocean," in full security of British mastership of the waves, had been spirited away from under the bows of our showy frigates; and whether the exploit was to be performed by Frenchman or Dutchman, the difference to the plundered was not much a matter of importance.

Another and still stronger recollection was, that the French were yet in force, and that their abandoning the line of the Elbe to-day was no security against their retaking possession of it to-morrow. Some intelligence to the purport had been actually received, and it was well known that their troops, who, if they take a panic as soon as any other troops under heaven, yet often recover from it with extraordinary rapidity, and even grow more daring as they have been more frightened, were gathering in considerable numbers along the coast. Fiery proclamations, too, were flung out from Paris in quick succession, and Napoleon, the pasha of pashas, recovering his spirits and his style together,

was orientally threatening the insurgent cities with
the vengeance of heaven, and his recreant generals
with the loss of their heads. It was again beginning
to be treason to doubt of the eternity of the French
empire; and from the awe with which the continental
powers looked on their habitual conqueror, there was
sufficient probability that the first turn of fortune in
his favour would close the ports of our " most faithful allies" against us, or catch our hasty travellers,
as of old, in a French snare.

Our ship was luckily a different spot from that
usual receptacle of misery. The sea happened to
be remarkably serene, and we were thus not only
spared the scenes of the dead and dying, that
make all the recollections of packets intolerable;
but the passengers were enabled to know more of
each other; and the curious complexion of the
times had made ours a very varied and characteristic group.

Every man on board seemed to have some direct
and stirring object in his excursion. Some were
foreigners, who had broken away from trade in
London or Liverpool, to take up arms and join
the patriots in "liberated Germany." Some were

English military, or persons connected with diplomacy, and reappointed to the courts from which they had been driven by the French armies; we had among us merchants, couriers, Jews, dealers in contraband, eager to have the first-fruits of the opening mart; and, of course, ladies, who are, as they ought to be, every where.

The passage was tardy, and the waves through which the steam-boat now dashes in thirty-six hours, kept us dallying and dancing on them for a week; a time long enough to have cemented and broken again the most solid travelling friendships. But which, in return, gave us sufficient opportunity to study human nature, as it is at sea.

The Germans were soon exhausted, and after the first harangues on " freedom, hatred of Napoleon," &c. &c., grew common place, and sank into smokers. One of our fellow voyagers was a complete character, a young Englishman, handsome and well mannered, but wild as a roebuck. He had served for a year as cornet in a yeomanry corps, and, notwithstanding the severity of the service, " the marches and countermarches," as Major Sturgeon has it, " from Ealing to Acton, and from Acton to Ealing," the fatigue of the tavern feasts, and the harassing Sunday exhibitions of his epaulette, found himself so enamoured of war, that he had " determined to make the army his profession," and as the preliminary to a British ensigncy, was come to see campaigning on the scale of emperors and field-marshals. He was a fine lad, full of the reckless animation that makes the Scipios and Alexanders; a quality which, like the lion's or the tiger's taste for man, has, we may presume, its use in the scale of human things, however difficult it may be to discover that use, or inconvenient to come in its way. Here was a creature, with all the appurtenances, habits, and appetites, of one made to kill and be killed; gay, bold, active, and with no fear under the stars, but the fear of a general peace. He was now hurrying, loaded with letters, to the headquarters of the Prussian army, in the sole hope of reaching them before the next battle, of which he seemed to have no other idea than as an operation which, in one way or other, might put a too rapid close to the campaign. Yet all this was said and done in the simplest style imaginable. There was not a feature of the Thraso about him. Never was a being more palpably made to be shot, with less idea of his living for it in the mouths of men.

Another of our passengers, and a very intelligent and singular one, was the reappointed *charge d'affaires* to one of the little German courts, a rough-visaged and fierce-eyed old man, with a strong Northumbrian accent, but with the original ferocity of his manners curiously flourished and tesselated with diplomatic suavity. He conversed freely, and with every one, and nothing could be more amusing than the perpetual struggle of the native acid with the official oil.

Of England, and its councils and cabinet, for the time being, his opinions were screwed up to the highest point of official homage. Of the court to which he was accredited, no cross-examination of our's could extract from him a careless word. But, of the continent *en masse*, kings, courtiers, ministers, and people, his opinions were steeped in the very spirit of scorn. Of Vienna in particular, where he had spent some years, and probably had his memory sharpened by some of the slights that beset the beginnings of office, his descriptions were of the most unequivocal nature. " Its public men were

all either rogues, who sold the state for French
money; or fools, who did the business of France
without the trouble of bribing. Its generals were,
at best, but drill-serjeants; but the more frequent
case was, that they were not even drill-serjeants,
and then, they were but the fitter for the troops
which they had to command."

Some of the party on deck protested against this
sweeping sentence, and mentioned the great name
of the Archduke Charles. But the gallant archduke went the way of the rest, and was pronounced
to be the " one-eyed among the blind." Unfortunately the Austrian arms were not at that moment
in high odour with Europe. They have since nobly
redeemed themselves; but, for the time, we were
driven to make our stand on the proverbial hospitality and good manners of the higher circles. " Nothing can be better in a *fête* than both sexes," said
the diplomatist, "they dance almost as well as the
French, and dress better; they have brave men
among them, and beautiful women, and if you
neither play with the one, nor pay attentions to the
other, you may pass the ordeal tolerably safe. But
if you have either time on your hands, or money in

your pockets, your wisest plan would be to apply for your passports within the first twenty-four hours."

His wife was on board, a strong-featured personage, of whom the diplomatist seemed to stand in considerable awe, for those explosions of opinion were always delivered at a due distance from her ears. In her immediate neighbourhood he was silent and submissive. He acknowledged to us, that he carried her with him on all occasions; though whether as a protection to his portfolio or his purse, he left us to conjecture; his sagacity had probably discovered her use in his professional pursuits. It is remarkable how close a connexion exists on the continent between diplomacy and matrimony. " As dry as the despatch of a bachelor ambassador," is a proverb. On the continent, gossip is intelligence, as in the multitude of instances, continental intelligence is gossip. A dry despatch is the unpardonable crime. " Anecdote," as the Frenchman says, " is the delight of all mankind, and women are the proper officers for its collection."

Another of our passengers, and as peculiar as any of them, was a little German countess, of whose

French figure and fantastic step, we caught but the single glimpse that could be caught in her transit from the side of the packet to the cabin, into which she darted at once. Of her we saw nothing more during the voyage: for, though the sea was as smooth as a mirror, she remained continually below. It must be, however reluctantly, acknowledged, that the little countess's chief reason for keeping her cabin, seemed to be the opportunity which it gave of exerting matrimonial authority over her husband. The husband was a handsome, good-humoured Irishman, a captain in the Prussian service. They had been married a twelvemonth, and were now returning from a visit to the captain's friends. But formidable as the period may be to passion in general, the little countess's love was still so merciless, that she insisted on her husband's never being out of her sight for five minutes together. From dewy morn to dusky eve, she would take nothing but from his hands. The weather was beautiful, and the company on deck were lively and conversible; while the cabin was, what all cabins are, half-dungeon, half-hospital; yet there lay the countess, and between eating, crying, and complaining, she contrived to fill up the twenty-four hours very tolerably.

The husband was certainly a model of married submission. He now and then, when summoned away by a scream from below, to leave the fresh air and talking circle round him, for a plunge into the cabin, gave symptoms of the chain; but in general he dragged it along with all the good humour that could remain unground out of any man, by a twelvemonth of this ultra Algerine servitude. The men alternately laughed at and pitied him; but the ladies universally exclaimed against the barbarity of the little tyrant; for the Irishman had made great way by his showy figure and good manners; if not still more by his misfortunes, for compassion does much, and he certainly had occasion for all his philosophy.

We had soon drained the commercial men dry; Germans returning to begin their speculations anew, and English hurrying to take advantage of the opening of trade. But, beyond all comparison, the most characteristic of our crew was an Austrian courier, with a Vienna despatch box buckled to his back. It was not to be expected that the courier would be very prominent in the conversation; but his faculty of holding his tongue was scarcely less than miraculous; during the six days of our voyage, he did not utter as many words. When he wanted any thing, which was but seldom, for his pipe seemed to supply all his wants, mental and bodily, a sign accomplished his purpose. From morning till night he sat on the same spot of the deck, with his large blue eyes fixed on the same spot of the horizon, and his meerschaum in his mouth, pouring out perpetual fumes. Some of the passengers attempted to question him on the state of Germany, through which he had but just passed; but he was faithful to his meerschaum; dumbly shook his huge head, fumigated away with the same tranquillity, and completely baffled all curiosity by the mere force of smoke. At length they gave him up; naturally looking upon him as a well-contrived piece of mechanism, a *chef d'œuvre* of some modern Vaucanson, a human smoke-jack, a despatch-carrying automaton, of which tobacco was the moving power.

We had now been nearly a week at sea, and notwithstanding a civil captain, tolerable dinners, good society, and the marvellous absence of the landsman's misery, sea sickness, we longed to find ourselves on solid earth again. Every eye and every glass on board was turned to the point from which Heligoland seemed determined never to emerge. This anxiety, at length, grew ridiculously feverish. Columbus himself never watched the signs of sea or sky more nervously. The truth was, we were all intolerably idle; every soul weary of having nothing to do; all conversation flagged; all character flattened, and the Austrian courier was the only philosopher among us, for his smoke and his smile alone never failed. Every weed that floated by, gathered a concourse of spectators, who followed its career from stem to stern, and then hung over the ship's side looking out for a new arrival of seaweed and stimulus. An unhappy canary bird that had been blown out of some Dutch cage, and ventured to rest its weary wing upon our rigging, was a grand topic, and supplied us with conjectures for a whole evening. The Castle of Indolence lost the finest feature of all its descriptions, by forgetting the penalties of a *farniente* on board of a packet in an interminable calm.

But a less sentimental calamity now began to threaten us. Our passage had been so much longer than the captain's calculation, that we were in danger of being without provisions. We recommended the despatch of a boat to the shore, which was occasionally within sight. But the captain's official answer was, that " we might expect a wind every moment, which, from the length of the calm, would, in all probability, come in the shape of a gale; that the boat, in that case, must be left behind, and the mission, of course, be only so much thrown away; or that we must anchor, which might lose the ship, *besides* losing the gale, which could not now fail of carrying us to Heligoland in half a dozen hours, *provided* it blew fair."

The voyager even from Dover to Calais knows, by experience, that the captain, land-locked as he is, is sovereign; but on the actual ocean, with the eternal ice for his boundary, the sovereignty, as it spreads, becomes only the more inflexible. The czar or the sultan is tame to the despot of the helm. We had nothing for it, but submission; still we were fixed, tiding it on and off the shores of

Oldenberg, and still more embittering our situation by the knowledge that all the world were at that moment dancing, singing, or feasting; for, though we were starving, the sunsets were lovely; and if we were to perish, we should have had the consolation of finishing our mortal career in the finest weather imaginable.

Another of our vexations was, that though *we* were chained in the centre of a calm, there seemed to be wind enough in every other quarter. We frequently saw vessels threading the web of colours that covered the sea from the horizon to the spot where our shadow lay steadily asleep; then came the old inquiry of all the passengers at once, whether the sail was " not suspicious," and whether its ports, &c. had not very much the privateer look. However, in all instances, we were " quit for the fear." The privateer turned out to be some British merchantman, dragging its heavy load home; or one of our look-out frigates, sweeping down within a mile or two of us, like a colossal hawk, then suddenly checking its speed on making out our signal, and wheeling back to its station, with the ease of the hawk; commanding the breeze, while we could not wave a feather on the deck, and our pennant hung dead down the sail.

CHAPTER II.

HELIGOLAND.

BUT all things have an end. The sudden roll of
the vessel one midnight, and the immediate burst
of agony that rose from every corner of the cabin,
sufficiently told us that we had got a breeze at
last; which, as the captain had surmised, before
morning took the shape of a regular north-sea gale.
All *bienseance* was over for the time; and all who
could leave the place of suffering, hurried upon deck.
We had now wind enough, and on we rushed, dashing
and driving, bow-sprit under, and ploughing up the
billows, until the dawn showed us the brown top of
Heligoland in the horizon. The North Sea was angry,
and a whole wilderness of immense waves, topped
with yellow, bilious-looking foam, rolled furiously
towards the little half-drowned island, which con-

tinually escaped from us, and seemed as if it were swimming away for its life.

But rough as the gale was, it was luckily in our favour, we were hurled along like the foam itself, and, in the course of a few hours, we were abreast of the beach. The scene there was a very curious and peculiar one. All seemed on the smallest scale, and might have been sketched for Gulliver's first view of Lilliput. Heligoland is probably the smallest spot to which human life, adhesive as it is, ever thought of clinging. But, while we gazed, we were gazed at in turn; if we had been the Argonauts themselves, we could have scarcely excited a more marked *public* curiosity. We had our indulgence too; for instead of the aboriginal, half fish, half human, population of a little wild rock in the ocean, all before us was metropolitan! The *elite* of the London counting-houses were drawn out for our reception, and we looked upon a melange of morning gowns, white hats, Bath slippers, and gentlemen breathing the essence of " the latest newspapers from town."

Heligoland, like every other nook of this over-travelled world, has long since lost its ancient spell,

but it was then a novelty, and an extremely characteristic one.   Paley should have put it into his
chapter of " Contrivances."   It was impossible to
look upon it without recognising the original design of nature for the intercourse of nations; the
Plymouth Breakwater, or the Eddystone lighthouse,
is not a clearer evidence of intention.   Though it
had stood from the creation or the deluge, a solitary
point in the deep, the playground of the seamew
and the porpoise, for some thousand years, it was
yet as obviously placed for the uses of human kind,
when the low shores of Holstein and Hanover
should be peopled, as if it had been piled by a
Telford or a Rennie before our eyes.   Standing
about twenty-five miles from the mouth of the
Elbe, it is seen at the exact distance sufficient for
ships to make the land, without being entangled in
the shoals which line the whole shore of Germany;
its very form is that of the pedestal of a lighthouse,
and many a storm-tost blaze must have flared from
it to the squadrons with which Denmark and Sweden once paid such formidable visits to their more
opulent neighbours of Germany and England.

Its population, time out of mind, have been

13

pilots, and even in its name of " Holy Island,"
there may be found some reference to the sailor's
gratitude for his preservation. But things had
now, in the American phrase, prodigiously pro-
gressed; for the pedestal was not merely topped
with a huge lighthouse, glittering with reflectors
and all the improvements of modern art, but it
was enjoying that peculiar prosperity which, according to the proverb, in the worst of times, falls
somewhere; and being the first mark of all vessels bound for the Elbe, and just out of the reach
of Napoleon's talons besides, it had become a
grand depot of commerce; or to use a less dignified,
but truer appellation, of smuggling of the most
barefaced kind. Every spot was crowded with
clerks and agents from England and Germany;
many of them not improbably agents of more
important concerns than the barter of sugar and
coffee; for those were times when every feeling
of right, seconded by every dexterity of man, was
concerting the fall of the great enemy; and Heligoland was, perhaps, more nearly connected with
Vienna, and even with Paris, than half the cabinets
alive.

But all before us, was the merchant and his merchandize, bales of Manchester manufactures and bags of West India produce, and among them the busy Englishman stalking about, and the spectacled German following him, and each apparently too well employed to think of the fates of empires.

From our deck, the beach, which looked scarcely more than a hundred yards wide; and the rock itself, which did not seem half the number of feet high, gave the thickest picture of human swarming, that I had ever seen; the whole was black, restless, and buzzing with life, it had the look of an immense beehive.

The island originally belonged to Denmark; and, during the first years of the war, it had been quietly left to its employment of keeping up a lighthouse, and a supply of pilots, for the Elbe. But Napoleon's seizure of Hanover, and still more his war on British commerce, at length induced our statesmen to search for some point, from which, if the great Leviathan could not be completely hooked, he might be, at least, occasionally harpooned. Heligoland was obviously one from which this annoyance might be most happily administered; and an order was sent out to Admiral

Russel to collect his squadron, and take the island. The frigates of the squadron summoned the garrison, consisting of a company or two of invalids, and a militia of fishwomen, to give up possession in peace. The old Danish commandant made a speech *à la Française,* and swore " to bury himself and his gallant garrison under the foundations of the island." The admiral laughed at the heroism, and, not wishing to do any harm to the islanders, gave him a couple of hours to make up his mind. When the hours were out, a detachment of seamen and marines were seen getting into the boats to storm. The commandant having now satisfied all the calls of honour, hung out the white flag, and before sunset, Heligoland, luckily for itself, acknowledged the sway of his majesty George the Third.

All was thenceforth merriment and good fellowship. Feasting and the flow of British gold into the insular treasury, made every body happy. Denmark easily acquiesced in the loss, probably from the double motive, that while her little colony was sure to be grasped by either France or England,

there was no policy in exhibiting any fretfulness
on the occasion; and that wherever the English
touched, they uniformly left the people in a state
considerably fitter to assist the national exchequer,
when the day of drainage came.

The islanders, certainly, were not disposed to
murmur at the change. Never was the fidelity of
an ancient and loyal people in greater hazard of total
alienation. From a wild rock, rendered wilder, if
possible, by the aspect of its native stock, the island
was turned into one huge hotel, rude enough still,
but crowded with beings who must have seemed to
the natives something fallen from the skies; or,
at least, what the Spaniard might have appeared
to the Indian in the days of Columbus; the plunder excepted, which here was all on the other side.
They had not been left even to the common range
of English life. The London counting-houses had
poured out their most refined population; every
clerk assuming the dignity of a firm, and flourishing
away among the little lanes of wooden huts with the
fullest sense of the honours of trade. Every thing
that met the glance, was the " fashionable world."

Business was over soon after breakfast, the day was thenceforward for elegance and themselves, and the universal motto was " *Vive la bagatelle.*"

The touch of fashion too is always contagious, and the German clerks rapidly emulated the importance of their brothers from London. Unfortunately, their world was a narrow one; for the whole circumference of the island was not much more than a mile; and the principal street, if street it could be called, was but a few feet broad; the plan of the capital having been constructed on the principle of hiding it from the north wind, the first puff of which fairly threatened to carry it off, governor, garrison, traffickers, and all, into the clouds.

The usual exhibitions in which the *gens de boutique* of all lands equally delight, the handsome holiday displays of dog-cart and tandem, and the other vehicles of many names and effigies, which put pedestrians in bodily fear in the environs of a commercial city, were here out of the question; for the most capacious road in the island had never witnessed any thing beyond a wheelbarrow; there was not a quadruped in its circuit, above a cat; and the sole representative of the stanhopes, bug-

gies, and tilburies of wider regions, was a basket
swung on a pole between a pair of vigorous fishwomen.

Yet those were no great calamities to one who,
like myself, was sufficiently behind the civilization
of his age, to be a bad whip; and Heligoland was,
for its day, a most stirring and amusing little Island.
Even its condensed state of society, packed as thick
as its own bales, made it only the more eccentric.
We were squeezed together till the colour of every
man's character was forced to the surface. Our *table
d'hôte* was, it must be owned, at once homely and
dear; for the communication with Germany was
not yet sufficiently open to allow of higher luxuries than hung beef and stewed prunes. Why
such should have been the only contributions of
the great continent which we daily saw stretching
out its immeasurable brown sands and yellow
marshes before us, we could not conceive; unless under the supposition, that Germany produced no meat but beef, ready hung; and no fruit
but prunes ready stewed. We had, however, an
abundance of wine, calling itself by the hundred
titles, that cost so little to the wine merchant, and

so much to the consumer. Still, like soldiers in a besieged town, every man seemed determined to face his privations with the due fortitude; and if the art of inventing names for wine, and wine for names, was seldom more dextrously practised than among the rough natives of Heligoland; never was the art more patronised than by the gallant traffickers who daily lined the *table d'hôte.*

Some of those people, however, were ingenious and intelligent persons, whose activity and knowledge of languages had recommended them to their London firms, as agents for the very peculiar traffic carried on between the island and Germany.

It is now recognized that the main blunder of Napoleon was his attempt to ruin the commerce of England by his Berlin and Milan decrees. No man can be supreme in two things; and Napoleon's consummate soldiership necessarily disqualified him for all the triumphs of finance and commerce. The severity, abruptness, and prodigality of means, that make the principles of military success, are the antipodes to the principles of trade; credit flies at the sight of the sword, and a *coup de main* in commerce would be a folly, if it were not an impossibility.

The first exploit of Napoleon's system was felt in the ruin of his own resources. Germany had hitherto fed the French exchequer. The first blow of his sabre aimed at England, completely fell short, but it fell on Germany, and instantly cut off the conduit through which the German revenues had flowed into France. A more formidable result, than even the loss of revenue, instantly followed. The whole mind of the continent was at once exasperated against Napoleon. The passiveness of the people had been among the great causes of French victory. The resistance of armies, in all countries, is like the resistance of fortresses; the whole obstacle is seen at a glance, its strength is measured by the eye, and its fall becomes a matter of calculation. But the resistance of a people is made up of elements that elude the eye, defy the measurement, and defeat the calculation. And the period was not to be distant, when the genius of Napoleon was forced to lower its crest before the German peasantry. He was enveloped in a whirlwind of hostility; his armaments, and the world had seen none on a more stately scale, were broken down by the restless and multiplied hatred of the nation; until the armies that he had chased from one extremity of the continent to the other, recovered their strength and courage under the cloud of popular resistance, and issued forth to complete the overthrow of the common enemy of kings and people.

But the Berlin and Milan decrees, though tyrannical enough to stimulate the deepest national hatred, were singularly ineffectual for their peculiar object, the prohibition of English and German intercourse. They were opposed by all human interests, and against those, what brute power has ever succeeded?

The German merchant was tenacious of life; and English produce made its way through the double lines of the Douaniers. The quantity of bribery, perjury, and profligacy was enormous, but the revenue gained nothing. But it was when the French reverses in the north weakened the barrier, that the old traffic set in upon it with a tide which would have swept it away in its strongest days. Smuggling became universal. Colonial produce seemed to have suddenly become a necessary of life; and sugar and coffee were prizes for which the German often ran risks which far outdid his chivalry in the field. Where courage was essential, the trafficker played the hero; though where the business could be accomplished by dexterity, he spared his courage, and only outwitted the Frenchman.

The first French ordinances, whose military makers evidently conceived that sugar came in loaves from the cane, had been levelled only against " refined sugar," originally the chief object of importation into the French dependencies; for the famous Hamburgh refineries had perished. But the Heligoland clerks speedily gave the French lawmakers reason to know, that sugar might be found under other conditions, for they instantly poured in quantities of it in its raw state. The news reached Paris, and an ordinance was framed to arrest the unforeseen evil, by prohibiting all sugar in the " shape of grain or pulverization." The clerks were on the alert again; they dissolved the sugar, and inundated the French with barrels of this new *eau sucré*. Another ordinance made war against fluid sugar, followed by a succession of decrees, as the *savans* in the cabinet were enlightened by successive discoveries of the nature of this intrusive material. Until the clerks, wearied of torturing sugar, hit upon the idea of a wholesale system of *douceurs*. The new contrivance worked incomparably, and was found so congenial to the tastes of the custom-house people, and probably of their masters in Paris, that while Napoleon continued cannonading away at every *phantasma* of regular trade, the contraband went on flourishing with the happiest activity.

Trivial as such transactions appear, the memory of this period may form no trivial lesson to some future master of mankind. Cabinets and armies were found to be more easily disposed of than the coffee-cups of a region of slaves. The spirit of national resistance which left the ministers and generals, the whole embroidered aide-de-campship of the continental governments, to run their race of submission; took refuge, and revived, among the traders, in Germany, the smallest of generations; probably altogether forgotten by those stately functionaries, and certainly, for the first time, reckoned among the elements of war. Yet those traders were the men who gave the first blow to the uni-

versal conqueror; the gnats, who stung the behe-
moth to death; the Lilliputians who tied the man-
mountain to the ground.

Napoleon might have galloped his charger over
Europe, making her castles the dust of its hoofs to
the last of his days, but for his forgetting the spell
which, more than cannon or bayonet, fought for
the republic, the " *Guerre aux palais, paix aux
cabanes.*" He had now fallen on the *cabanes*, and
from that moment he was undone. The nations,
long discontented with their sovereigns, had seen
him trampling them down, and never moved a
muscle. But when they found his heel pressing on
the neck of every man alike, they sprang up, and
crushed him. Moscow or Leipsic, the snow or
the sword, may have been the direct instruments,
but the effectual reason lay in the prospect of
actual beggary. Alexander, Francis, and William
were but links in what a *savant* would call the chain
of *causality*. The ultimate cause lay in the fiery
hemisphere of sugar and coffee; and the spade of a
negro delving without a shirt in Jamaica or St.
Kitts, undermined the throne of the master of the
world.

CHAPTER III.

JOURNAL, &c.—1813.

THE ELBE.

April 4. The wind which blew us to this little island, has served us an ungracious turn, and threatens to keep us here. The whole *beau monde* are swept away from public view by the storm; and are now shivering over stoves, or buried between the piles of down, which the German calls a bed; but which never cover one extremity but at the expense of the other.

Yet the old proverb of the wind is, of all truisms, the truest here. This gale is the harvest of the Heligolanders; for it brings the crowd from England and the continent; and it keeps them imprisoned

c 6

here until they have expended their superfluities, for the benefit of the soil. By this morning's arrivals, too, the news is of rather a chequered description. The French hussars have been actually making incursions along the line of the Elbe; and the Douaniers are again threatening to establish themselves in their old haunt at Cuxhaven. Among the contingencies of this world, we may soon be attacked by some little swarm of rowboats; which the enemy contrive, by some dexterity, peculiarly their own, to have at all times ready at their bidding; and be carried off, bales and Britons, to the *depôt* in Bremen, to be thence consigned to one of the forty Bastiles of regenerated France. The island itself would be a prize to nothing but an army of seagulls; but it is now loaded with goods enough to excite the cupidity of any emperor of dragoons, from the equator to the pole.

────────

It blows a storm; and every wave that rolls in upon the little beach threatens to wreck our whole navy at its anchors. The man who " pitied idle gentlemen upon a rainy day," should have added to the rainy day, confinement upon an island a mile round, as flat as a bowling green, and with nothing upon it but a gathering of crazy huts, shaking in every limb, groaning in the wind as if they were groaning their last, and making it a doubtful point whether it were wiser to take the chance of being swept into the sea with them, or without them.

But the sea is magnificent: I now feel, for the first time, the full force of the words, " the *wilderness* of waves." As far as the eye can reach, the whole horizon is one moving mass of billows, rolling, foaming, and thundering on each other; sheets of spray suddenly caught up and whirling to vast distances, like the banners of the host of waters. Here are no chains of rock to fret the waves, no projections and promontories to break their mass, no distractions of the eye by the mixture of land and water: all is ocean, deep, dreary, and illimitable. With such an object before the poets of the north, well might they fill their imaginations with shapes of desolate power. Among the clouds which come continually rolling along the horizon, and almost touching the waters, it would be no difficult fancy even now to conceive some of the old pirate fleets, spreading sail from the Baltic, and sweeping down, with the lightning for their pilot, and the winds for their trump, to the spoil of Europe. All is wild, melancholy, and grand.

––––––––––

The *table d'hôte* again; more crowded, and more clamorous than ever; on the Lucretian principle, perhaps, of enjoying life the more within doors, the less we can enjoy it without. A flying skiff, too, from the mainland has just cheered us with the infallible intelligence that " Napoleon *has* fallen," though, whether by his own hand, the hand of the Parisian mob, or the hand of justice, the sender of the intelligence has kept to himself, *prudently* enough. But it is admitted on all sides, among our table council, that the Germans *must* beat the French, to the end of time; that Napoleon was *no* general, but merely a fortunate adventurer who came in, just at the lucky time to make use of the last impetus of the French Revolution; and, by a corollary touching our own incarcerated state in the island:—That it is a law of nature, that the day after the arrival of the packet, and as many days after, as it shall please the *table d'hôte* keepers, the wind *never* blows fair *from* Heligoland.

But the news of the French return towards the Elbe, has even added to the general festivity; for the island *lives* only by our exclusion from the continent; the clerks here too, could find no pleasure in the prospect of sinking from principals into subordinates again; and perhaps even their masters would not be peculiarly gratified by the opening of a market, which was open to all. With the Douaniers, on the opposite shore, the affair is now perfectly understood. The wheels of the contraband system have been so thoroughly oiled, that they run on without a sound; and though those Douaniers are so hated by the populace and peasantry, that in case of the fall of Napoleon, nothing but a levy of balloons and gryphons can carry them safe beyond the frontier; yet a new race, even of the German Douanier, would require so serious an outlay, that we prefer the old. The merchant, too, is any thing but a peace-loving animal; in all countries, the merchant loves war, so long as it leaves himself untouched. War is the dram-drink-

ing of nations; it makes them wild, ragged, and
mad; but it makes them drunk; and who then
cares for the chances of the world? If the eaters
of hung beef and stewed prunes round me ever
prayed, their prayer would, probably, be that of the
old Highlander; " Lord, turn the world upside
down, that honest men and Christians may get
bread out of it."

The dwellings of such a fragment of Europe
are scarcely worth speaking of, except as curious
evidences of the grasp which a predominant idea,
the sea, here takes of the mind; and as a model
of the general sea-coast habitations of the north.
The whole house is but a ship aground; its entrance is a porthole, and its rooms are the closest
resemblance that the architect, or rather the ship
carpenter, can frame to a cabin; yet for a bed
in this cabin, in the *prosperous* times of the island,
the landlord, I am told, has sometimes contrived
to charge a guinea a night. The tables are generally trunks, which probably have made many a
voyage. The lodger sleeps not in a bed, but in a

berth, in the side of the room, mortised into a hole five feet high up the wall, to which he climbs by a ladder, and where, when he awakes in the dusk of the morning, with the roar of the winds and the eternal dash of the waters in his ears, with the timbers of the house heaving and creaking round him, and the air filled with the smell of salt and seaweed, it requires some soberness of thinking, to doubt that the whole establishment has weighed anchor, and is going " right away before the wind."

The day after our arrival was Sunday, and all the female population were in full costume; my landlady, one of the *magnates*, may be taken as a model of the island *fashionable*. She is a complete Danish beauty; that is, she is short, round, and solid; with a face as round as her form, but a face which tells of boundless good humour and civility, and therein tells nothing but the truth. Fashion, in all lands, is preposterous; and the fashion of Heligoland, after all, is not much more opposite to grace and nature, than if it had been invented in the Rue Vivienne, or Bond Street.

May I be pardoned for the detail? She wore a vast

brown stomacher, probably bullet proof; over which the yellow fringe of what I believe was a kerchief of scarlet cloth, showed itself, in ample folds and flutterings round the very ample neck; the fringe being repeated round the knee; for, not much lower does the fashionable vesture of the island descend. Her stockings thus became important parts of the general display, as is indeed the case with all the northern peasantry; and those stockings, with the exception of most prodigally flowered clocks, were blue, " deep, beautifully blue." The head was not less attended to; the cap was Flemish, tissued, and clasped with some heavy golden ornaments, and fringed with a deep lace; from which shone out my landlady's handsome and florid physiognomy, surrounded by a whole flood of yellow curls; the entire strongly resembling the " glorious Apollo" that we see flaming with all his gilt ringlets round him, over the gate of an English inn.

As there was a church in the island, I went to it, though the language was Danish, and the service Lutheran; a practice which may be recommended to the traveller, wherever the service is not directly adverse to his feelings; if it were for no higher motive than that of standing favourably in the opinion of the people. Foreigners have universally an idea that the English are a Sunday-honouring nation; and they seem disposed to honour us the more for it; at least, nothing can be more indisputable than their surprise, and probably, their disgust, at our occasional compliances with their own levities on the subject. The Frenchman or the German, who thinks that, however Sunday may begin, it should finish with an opera or a *fête;* is very generally inclined to attribute the Englishman's appearance at either to a silly eagerness for foreign popularity, or rather to a vulgar abandonment of the national character. In all cases, the effect is paltry and unsuccessful; for let him do as he will, he never can effectually play the foreigner; and the alienated John Bull, instead of being welcomed as a proselyte, is generally received with the scorn of a deserter.

The church, like every thing else in the island, was modelled on a ship, so far as ship-timbers, ship-furniture, and gloom were concerned. Miniature ships in full sail and rigging were hung from the beams of the roof, and seemed to be considered

among the ornaments of the building. A large
cross suspended over the altar looked strange to
the English eye ; but the great reformer was somewhat of a monk to the last, and however he hated
the doctrines of Rome, he certainly had an old
affection for its relics.

The congregation were numerous, but chiefly
female, and wholly native. The fishermen were
probably resting after a night on the ocean, and
Messieurs les Négocians were as probably busy
about the important matters of smuggling, or the
London papers. The preacher, or prayer, for he
alternately read and declaimed, was as rude a specimen of the ecclesiastic, as his hearers were of the
human race. But his declamation seemed to be
perfectly in earnest. I was not prepared to find
the Scandinavian blood capable of such ebullition ;
he took his place in the chancel, and book in hand,
rushed and oratorized in all directions ; but his
audience listened with the most profound attention ; and what could eloquence do more ?

The wind has shifted round at last ; all is hurry,

to the heart of the little island; the Elbe carriers
are clamouring for their passengers to speed down
to the beach; a group of sea-nymphs are at this
moment contending for my baggage, in voices which
prove, at least, that they are not Syrens; and Heligoland bids fair to be depopulated.

We have been now six-and-thirty hours struggling up the Elbe. Our boat is one of the most
clumsy of river barges, an unwieldy hulk, with a
huge single sail, a stone for the anchor, and a wigwam raised on the deck for a cabin. We are wet,
cold, hungry, thirsty, and tired.

We left the island in great triumph, followed
by a jovial chorus of Amazonian voices, wishing
us all the good fortune that is compatible with a
passage by sea. The wind blew merrily, and with
a bulging sheet and a tossing keel, we soon saw
Heligoland dwindle down to a cloud, and then
drop into the deep: grew sea-sick, fell asleep,
and awoke in an hour or two, to learn, that the
wind had changed, that the tide was against
us, and that we must come to an anchor, and

spend the night rolling about at the mouth of the Elbe.

We had some Germans on board, who were returning to their country for the first time since the French conquest; and their delight, however patriotic, was among the annoyances of the passage. They sang and danced with intolerable vigour and uncouthness, till to sleep was as difficult as to smile; their gambols would have made capital illustrations of the story of the baron in Paris, who threw himself out of a window, and explained this extraordinary movement by " *J'apprends d'être vif.*"

Our thirty-six hours slowly dragged us along the sedgy banks, a sufficient time for a transit of seventy miles; but this is the land of primitive inventions. And in this tediousness must be included all the minor delays, which I think occurred as often as the stoppages of an English stage-coach. The captain was either compelled to wait the pleasure of some other lazy barge, that would not or could not get out of his way; or to wait the tardy will of the sentinels at the small posts established on either bank; where the barge was obliged to wait further, until the little commandants could rouse themselves to examine her passports; or finally to wait for the general sleep of the crew, who contrived to drop their anchor, and always find a wind or a tide for their purpose. However, making allowance for the excessive chill of the nights, which froze us through boots, blankets, and bags of horse-beans, the only couches of the " state cabin," and which gave us the nearest sensation to that of lying on the bare boards; for our being badly fed and badly housed; and for the whole host of evils included in the sights, smells, tastes, and touches of all navigation; our passage was a tolerable one.

As we sailed heavily along, the Hanoverian shore was a terrible trial of our loyalty. As far as the eye could reach it was a marsh, flat, yellow, and melancholy, for league on league : it is, perhaps, in the interior that we must look for the picturesque of the land of the Brunswicks. But the Danish bank gradually became elevated, though the tourist through the Alps may smile to be told, that its cliffs and promontories were sand, and their

loftiest pinnacles from twenty to thirty feet high;
but all things are majestic by comparison, and we
had hitherto floated through a region as level as a
billiard table.

By degrees we came upon the outskirts of life:
the hut, rude as the squatter's in an American
forest, was succeeded by the cottage, rudely decorated with a straggling vine, or a few stunted
shrubs: then came the little villas, peeping out
between the sand-hills, the outposts of being, that
tell us of the neighbourhood of the city, or rather
the offsets from the chief mushroom of the family.
Then hung afar off the cloud of heavy vapour and
yellow smoke, that even on the continent gives sign
of the city beneath. At last, to our great rejoicing,
towered in the distance the spires of Altona; then
rose the roofs of its ponderous and prison-like
buildings; then the masts of its barks and brigan-
tines; in short, we were in sight of our haven.

To our German fellow passengers all this was
magnificence itself; land, river, dingy ships, and dun-
geon-like houses, were all the triumph of nature
and art, and the world had no such exhibition as
this father-stream of their " father-land." The

less rapturous of the voyagers, however, had sufficient subjects for their contemplation in the remaining chances against their ever touching *terra
firma* again. Our pilotage was nearly in the original condition of the science; we were dragged,
run foul of, and only saved from being swamped
every moment, by miracle, I suppose; for nothing
of human interposition seemed to have any thing
to do with it. There were evidently, at least, as
many shoals as waves; our sea room was measured
by square yards, and we were continually in hazard
of being stranded against a furze-bush, or run down
by a floating Hanoverian milk woman and her pails.
At last, however, we worked our way, stepped from
one tottering plank of the half-swamped landing-
place to another, without broken limbs, and found
ourselves, to our great delight, quit of frost, famine,
and the Blankenese boat; and safe in the empire
of " the senate and people of Hamburg."

CHAPTER IV.

———

HAMBURG.

The first aspect of this famous old city gives the idea of opulence, as opulence displayed itself in the ancient days of Germany. It is not a French display nor an Italian; it is the gloomy, solid, and almost severe visage of the old Teutonic. Hamburg strikes the eye as a place where much money was made and much expended, and yet where it was both made and expended, by merchants, and those merchants republicans.

It is a curious circumstance, that all despotisms are great *decorators;* they are eternally putting up and pulling down, covering the ground with palaces, or sweeping away the old architectural disgraces of the land, always digging and delving for effect.

This at once amuses their own vanity, and is a bribe to their people. Their Lazarus is tenfold a beggar, but he is the most showy of beggars, and though they may not give him even the crumbs from their table, they will readily enough lend him the purple and fine linen. Varnishing and lackering, carving and gilding are among the first principles of " absolutism" all over the world. Who has such palaces and picture galleries as the " Autocrat of all the Russias ?" The Grand Turk does not build, because it is a law of Mahomet and nature that a Turk shall do nothing but decorate himself and his horse, and cut throats: but how magnificently does he decorate himself and his horse! he carries a king's revenue in his saddle. Louis le Grand painted and papered more walls in his day than any other master of the breaths and bodies of mankind; and he was to the full as tyrannical as the Grand Turk. Free Rome was a hovel compared with Rome when every man in it woke daily, as the Parisian said, wondering whether his head were upon his shoulders; and its first despot, a man of sound political experience, in other words, a man acquainted with all the vices and vilenesses of the human heart, wisely fixed his merits on having left the city marble, which he had found brick.

The theory is universal; all republics have a little of the *sans culotte* about them; or, as Paine observed of the Quakers, " If they had been consulted in the creation, what a drab-coloured creation they would have made of it." From America to Holland, from Holland to Geneva, and from Geneva to San Marino, the whole anti-climax are modelled on the same building principle. Athens and Venice are no exceptions; the one the *kingdom* of Pericles for forty years, and *decorated* as became a kingdom; the other a congeries of *kings*, a nest of royalties, shrined from the vulgar eye in silks and ermines, tiaras and jewels, on which it was high treason to look. But what is the fact, as shewn by our own architectural exploits? How do *we*, the opulent of the earth, succeed in public buildings? The plain deduction from the whole is, that wherever a man may wish to *live*, he should never attempt to lodge where there are any of the appurtenances or shows of freedom. Let him eschew the land of parliaments, presses, and trials by jury; or of any thing that goes more circuitously the way to keep the world in mind of its duty than the contrivances of old Louis himself, Bastiles and bayonets, regiments of Swiss, and squadrons of *gens d'armerie.*

But on our route through Hamburg, a city as difficult for a stranger as the labyrinth, we had an opportunity of seeing things better than its architecture; the honest, warm, and manly excitement, awakened in all ranks by the hope of throwing off the French yoke. Nearly every one was in uniform, or with some sign of preparation for soldiership; though the sign, it must be allowed, was not always of the gravest order. In some, the soldiership was exhibited in a regimental coat, while the rest of the person was left to the chances of the wardrobe; in others, the hero was demonstrated in a pair of scarlet breeches, finishing a figure whose upper man was brown canvass. In many, it lay in a prodigious *shako*, heaving with plumage, and overshadowing a countenance and dress, both indisputably and equally commercial; but the spirit was there. Old muskets, which, from their appearance, it might have required more heroism to fire

than to stand; halberts, and horse-pistols which
had probably slept since the wars of the Reforma-
tion, all were brought from their dormitories, and
flourishing on all sides. All was drilling and marching, the parade was the grand sight of the city;
and before I had crossed the dozen solemn streets
that led from the landing place to the hotel, in
spite of the funereal look of the houses, and the
gravity of the national girth and visage, I was fairly
trumpeted, drummed, and charged, out of all my
prejudices as to the possibility of German enthusiasm.

This was the carnival of the *tables d'hôte*; our
board was full. The company, amounting to thirty
or forty, seemed tesselated, through the whole
length of the table, like Burke's memorable description of the Chatham ministry, "a bit of black
here, and a bit of white there, all dove-tailed together;" and the whole, certainly, forming a curious
specimen of the veinings and colourings into which
continental society had been rubbed by the French
domination. However, many were intelligent and
accomplished men, such as are always to be found
in any considerable number of German gentlemen.

Our conversation was, like that of all *tables d'hôte*, miscellaneous, confused, and trifling, but the supreme topic was the war, and "what the cabinets intended to do;" decisions, which were provided for them with the usual fertility and certainty of coffee-house politics. The feature most amusing in all this, to an observer, was the extraordinary rush of the Germans into topics, from which, a month before, they must have shrunk as things utterly interdicted to man, temptations of the foul fiend alone, to betray them into Napoleon's claws. The bitter lesson so long and so strongly recommended by the French bayonets was now completely forgotten. The taciturnity of a dozen years was thawed in a moment; and like the sounds of Baron Munchausen's horn, the arrear of the frost was amply repaid in the burst of communication. Generals, ambassadors, and kings fell before them without mercy; nay, some had the hardihood to touch on the conduct of the corporation of Hamburg themselves, during the late French reign. Every man settled the world *à son gré*. Freedom of speech never asserted its privileges in a more unambiguous manner.

But, in the midst of those high concerns, the
English listeners made the discovery, and it was a
sufficiently trying one to travellers who had not
more frozen, than fasted, along the lazy Elbe;
that to enjoy a German dinner required a German
education. The epicure, who complained of his
friend's hospitality, that every thing at table was
cold, but the wine; and every thing sour, but the
vinegar; should have been placed here, for the
benefit of the comparison. All here was sour on
system. Every thing was drowned in vinegar, excepting the potatoes themselves, and even those
exhibited their affinity for the popular acid. That
any man living, with the power to procure any
other conceivable nutriment, to live with the
Russian on raw fish, with the Tartar on sodden
horse, or with the Swede on fishbones, should with
knowledge, and without duress of any kind, touch
sour krout, the most insufferable perversion of the
worst of vegetables, must seem one of the strangest
anomalies of our nature; but with my German
friends, the dish was ambrosia, to which vinegar
was the corresponding nectar.

A large part of this curious propensity must lie

in the construction of the German diaphragm, but something of it may be due to circumstances. The "colonies" supply the principal material of all that converts the culinary art into a *science*; but deprived of the mace and cinnamon, the allspice and the cayenne of east and west, the *cuisine*, that *cuisine* which had made so flourishing a branch of the fame of France, and had occupied so much solid .thought for ages in Germany, degenerated at once; and France and Germany exhibited tables, which, probably, made the nearest approach of modern times to the banquets of Dumnorix and Arminius.

The English fleet had done this; and the "gold of Pitt," and the "tyrants of the seas," were *sacréd*, and devoted to the evil gods, from morning till night, in every kitchen of the continent. Nutmeg, cloves, ginger, and a multitude of other essentials to the "*grande école*," had become non-existences to the hundred and fifty millions of continental Europe; the "proud islanders" had shut them out by barriers of cannon; beet-root-sugar, and vinegar alone were left; but the sugar was no favourite, for it was costly, tasteless, and above all, (for this justice must be done in all instances to the German) it was obnoxious, as a *protegé* of Napoleon; but vinegar was free from all those imputations, and it rose on the ruins of its rival accordingly; it became a patriotic principle, a shibboleth, by which the true man was to be distinguished; the " good German," from the secret hungerer after French politics and French pay. And into this strange condiment did they plunge every thing, fish, flesh, and fowl, from the sturgeon to the shrimp, and from the bustard to the sparrow. The re-opening of the gates of the world gives hope of some variety in their indulgences, and the younger generation will probably fall off in their allegiance to the national taste: but popular habits are stubborn things, and vinegar may be lord of the ascendant for another age.

In the evening, the sun, which had been as moody during the day as if he had been wrapped in the fogs of the channel, threw out a glorious gleam across our curtains; the German politicians were too busy in arranging the kingdoms of the earth, to move: but some of the English, who had been too much saturated with politics at home to care for them at the tenth hand abroad, left the party in high

debate, and sallied out into the streets: and as
Sterne says of the sentimental traveller, " they
had their reward."   The first sight that met them
was the one, which of all sights they had most
longed to see.   In turning the corner of one of the
little squares, we plunged into the midst of a pulk
of Cossacks; they were the true sons of the wilderness, as wild, brown, and barbarian, as ever couched
lance along the Ural.   The pulk disdained a roof,
and had taken up their quarters in the native style,
in the open air; eating, drinking, and sleeping,
without much question whether it were sunshine
or shower.   A party of them were at their
supper, which they devoured at a prodigious
rate (the city supplying their rations); others
were lying down, with their mats and blankets
thrown over or under them, as it might happen, and their packsaddles for pillows.   Some
were loud-tongued, and evidently not far from
being qualified to talk politics with my friends of
the *table d'hôte*, for the Hamburg brandy was
strong, and handsomely administered.   There was,
however, some look of military arrangement in
this Scythian festivity: the Cossack spears were

regularly planted in circles, and their little goat-looking horses were picketed.

Still, the packsaddle, bursting with all kinds of odd plunder, brought us back to the bandit again; the Cossack's trowsers being only the first recep-tacle, and, when the warrior's legs were surcharged with the watches, purses, and plate of his enemy, the packsaddle forming his " reserve magazine," until it was often nearly of the size of his horse.

But the pulk bore more distinguished signs of the " tug of war." There was scarcely a man of them who had not a French star, or ribbon, patched upon his rough coat; some had two or three, for the French vanity of orders, by multi-plying those baubles in the service, naturally brings with it its own punishment on the first reverse, and the *croix* fall in showers to the conqueror. Of those trophies the Cossacks were peculiarly proud, as marks of personal achievement; for they gene-rally contrived to let us know that the French wearer had fallen under their individual pike. They would seldom part with them for money; and they evidently intended to carry them back to the desert as proofs of their prowess in the " war of vengeance;" the favourite and striking name for the downfall of Napoleon.

———

I have just returned from a long tour of the streets. Hamburg improves upon acquaintance. Some of the public buildings are historic; and if they are superabundant in neither grace nor majesty, yet they occasionally have the look of times, when the Hamburg merchant could wield the battleaxe as well as the pen, and buckle on his iron coat against Swede and Dane. The front of the senate house, heavy and huge, is a gallery of civic heroes, all bronzed and gilded in full costume, and enveloped in wig and regimentals, " as a general ought to be;" the long line of trading gallantry from Charlemagne, or Nimrod. If Commerce ever sat for the portrait of Bellona, those champions of the desk might circle her car, as the attendant genii.

But, to my sorrow, Hamburg is all *pavé;* the streets were, of course, universal mire after the day's rain; as in sunshine they are universal dust; and the wonders of the city were not to be seen, without hazarding something little short of suffocation in public mud. It is odd enough, that this universal offence in the continental cities should arise not more from laziness, than luxury. " Thank heaven," said the French abbé, when he found himself on the flags of London, " a pedestrian's bones are worth something here ;" and this was the whole secret. In Paris, the pedestrian's bones were worth nothing ; for every man who was worth any thing rode in his carriage. The Hamburgers had been under the same circumstances ; the time was, when they were not compelled to know whether their streets were earth or water ; for such was the opulence of the city at the close of the last century, that there was scarcely a shopkeeper's family without an equipage and a country-house. The ladies of the firm seldom came into Hamburg but to purchase some finery of the day ; the gentlemen came in but to spend an hour behind the counter, hold open their hands for the golden shower that was literally pouring upon them from every corner of the earth, and then drive back to their villas, and luxuriate for the rest of the day among their lilies and roses. In fact, the life of the great English merchant *now* was the life of the little Hamburg trader then.

The French reformed this thoroughly; the marshals first cut down the opulence by a series of contributions, levied with the sabre; Napoleon gave the second blow by his " decrees;" but the final and the fatal blow was given by letting loose the swarm of French *employés* upon the unfortunate city. The rough men of the sabre trampled down the field; but it was the *préfets*, the collectors, and the custom-house officers, that played the part of the locust, and nipped every leaf and sprout of commerce out of the soil.

The landscape round the city is Dutch,—flat, quiet, and green, sprinkled with houses, looking not unlike those which sprinkled the suburb fields of London a hundred and fifty years ago; low, yet sometimes spreading over a considerable extent, sometimes showy, but, in most instances, ample and convenient. Hamburg itself is an inland Amsterdam, a huge mass of buildings, imbedded in a marsh on the side of a lazy river, and cut through in all directions with sullen canals. The citizens pronounce it a Venice, and a Venice it is, if we divest the Adriatic queen of her palaces, her squares, her skies, and her recollections.

CHAPTER V.

────

GENERAL MORAND.

WE had come at a fortunate moment to see Hamburg in its best spirits. A short time before, the city had been thrown into great tribulation, by the news that Napoleon, informed of its revolt, had ordered instant vengeance, in its most formidable shape, the march of a French army. All was utterly defenceless; the fortifications had not been touched by any implement beyond the spade, that planted their faces with turf, for the last century. Their armoury would scarcely have equipped a battalion of watchmen: their treasury was empty; and England, the universal ally, the *liberal*, in every penitential sense of the word, to whose passions and purse every hero and pauper in the circumference of the globe turns by instinct, lay with half a hostile continent between, while the French bayonets were already glittering on their borders. Of the clouds of Cossacks, whose reported advance had tempted the Hamburgers into *culbute*-ing the French *employés*, but a few troops had arrived; the rest lived only in the Russian bulletins posted on the walls. Those papers certainly did their duty superbly; on their showing, alarm of any kind was the most fantastic thing imaginable: they announced every morning such armaments in full march for the defence of the city, such regiments of horse and parks of artillery, such brilliant staffs and long-titled generals, that the " senate and people" of Hamburg must have been the most lily-livered commonwealth in existence to have felt a thought of fear.

But even the bulletins began to lose their charm. The experienced shook their heads, and sulkily reasoned, that no Chernicheff and no Kutuzoff appeared; that in spite of all head-quarter promises, the five or six hundred Calmucks and Bashkirs who had first bivouacked in their streets, were but five or six hundred still; and that the whole would inevitably take to their heels on the sight of a

regiment of French dragoons. And wisely they
would have done so, for if they waited for the meeting, they must have slept with their fathers. It
was equally clear that the volunteers of the city,
corps but just raised, scarcely armed, scarcely officered, and altogether undisciplined, must have been
a mere sacrifice in the first encounter. Marching
and countermarching as they were from morning
till night, drilling and driving, loading guns and
charging bayonets, fearful experiment for burghers!
nothing but madness could propel them against a
French line, as nothing but miracle could bring
them back to tell the tale.

The times were gloomy; a powerful French division lay in Magdeburg, armed with all the muni-
tions of vengeance, and openly and hourly threatening the city, from which its commandant St.
Cyr had been so ignominiously ejected. A whole
army lay in Hanover, giving intimations of its
wrath by furious tirades in the journals, movements
towards the frontier, and the general robbery of
the friendly country, as a specimen of their future
exploits in the culprit one; but, while the public
eye was watching for the thunderbolt from Saxony

or Hanover, the true storm was grimly rolling on from behind.

A French division from the north, whose existence had probably been forgotten, was in full march for Hamburg. The intelligence was alarming; and all was natural anxiety for a few days, until it was ascertained that the division, which report had magnified into an army, had suddenly turned off, and was moving up the Elbe. But the good news was as suddenly dashed, for the next intelligence was, that Lunenburg was taken by the French, who had established themselves there as a preliminary to an advance on Hamburg, and had commenced by shooting the inhabitants, as usual.

The case of Lunenburg was exactly a case in point: for it had turned out the French *employés*, and let in the Cossacks, had declared itself German again, and had even the measureless insolence to shut its gates against a squadron of hussars, who came for the express purpose of plundering the city. By those acts the people had forfeited all hope; for, as Napoleon had declared the whole country a portion of France, all resistance was thenceforth not war, but rebellion. Morand, the commander of the

division, was a fierce ruffian of the revolutionary
school; and no man could have been more fitted to
clip the wings of rash patriotism. He had been
left with the remnant of the French garrisons in Pomerania, from which, on the evacuation of Berlin, he
had moved, carrying the French civil establishments
with him, and determined to revenge himself where-
ever he could. His first object was Hamburg, rich,
helpless, and patriotic, to the full measure of high
treason. He had three thousand men, and eighteen
pieces of cannon, which would have robbed and
slaughtered to the most complete extent. On his
advance, too, he had met the expelled garrison and
Douaniers; and with this reinforcement to his
strength, and probably to his indignation, for a
Frenchman stripped of his office is as little likely
as any individual on earth to bury his sorrows
in his bosom, Morand hurried on to chastise the
contumacious territory.

But he found an unexpected obstacle. The
Danish government remembered that Altona was
within sight of Hamburg, and that a French force
was at all times a hazardous neighbour. Trifling
and tardy as the Danish politics were, the govern-

ment could not willingly see Hamburg in the hands of a French brigade. A message was accordingly sent to Morand, intimating that the city would be *protected*. He had then turned off to Lunenburg, blown in the gates, seized the principal inhabitants, and without an hour's delay, ordered them to be brought before a military tribunal. The law of the drumhead is expeditious, those gentlemen were found guilty on the spot, and before set of sun they would have been where tyranny could touch them no more, but for the Frenchman's desire for a spectacle. They were ordered to be shot next day at noon, in the principal square, in the presence of the troops and people.

Yet the man of blood is sometimes disappointed; and there are few instances of thwarted atrocity more striking than the fate of Morand. The next day all was anxiety and melancholy, of course, among the inhabitants; and the condemned, whose friends had in vain made the most strenuous applications to the Frenchman's mercy, were already ordered out to stand in front of the fatal platoon; when, suddenly, the report of musketry was heard outside the ramparts. Morand and his staff, who were getting on horseback to attend the execution, rode off to ascertain the cause. The scene of murder waited for the general's return; but he still delayed; the firing grew heavier, and in various directions. It was soon evident from its approach, and from the number of wounded who were continually dropping back into the streets, that the city was attacked in force by the allies. What must have been the feelings of the condemned men and their families, while the struggle was going on, which to them made the difference between life and death! At last, an aide-de-camp rode in, crying out that the general had fallen, and ordering the last troops to move to the gates. The affair was now acknowledged " to be serious;" and though the French officers ridiculed the idea of their being beaten by the " ragamuffin Cossacks," their soldiers took good care to prepare for all contingencies, by packing up all the plunder that they could carry. But it was too late; after a short and desperate conflict, the allies carried the gates; a hurrah, a rush of the French battalions back into the streets, and a crowd of Cossacks and Russian dragoons coming pell-mell after them, and cutting them up in all quarters, fully explained the story. All was now triumph; the condemned were brought to their homes with acclamations, and Lunenburg was once more free and German.

It is extraordinary how much a brilliant little exploit of this kind tells in a war. The movements of the main armies are on too large a scale to interest any but the tactician. A great army is a machine; and who but the machinist can take an interest in the springs and pulleys that move a hundred thousand men at a time? it is in the minor actions, in those movements of the small corps, where man finds room to distinguish his individual activity and enterprise, that the spirit of man follows with perpetual curiosity, or more than curiosity, with the animating and lofty interest which we are constituted to feel in all remarkable displays of human energy. The capture of a sloop from under the guns of a French battery, has often braced the spirit of the British tar, as much as the victory over a fleet. The battle of Maida, though, in its numbers, scarcely more than a skirmish between two advanced guards of continental armies, instantly took off the cloud from the British name in Italy; decided the question of physical superiority between the British and foreign soldier for the rest of the war; roused up the fallen courage of the continent; and was incomparably felt, in the new popularity of the service at home, and the new confidence which enabled its lamented commander-in-chief to remodel and invigorate its whole system, to a point not far short of military perfection.

In Germany, where every province was arming expeditionary troops, Morand's fall was of great importance; for it shewed what could be done by small corps, conducted with activity and skill. As to the victors themselves, it elevated their crests prodigiously; they towered among their less lucky brethren, like Titans; every musketeer a hero, and every dragoon, according to the old established rule, something more. The enemy, too, felt its effects, in a corresponding fall of that self-satisfaction, which, in common life, carries so many smoothly through the world; but which, in soldiership, is absolutely an essential of success. The new-raised partizans now ran upon them wherever they were to be seen; and the moral of the whole is, that, in a war of insurrection, every thing ought to be attempted.

The narrative of this remarkable rescue is the *beau idéal* of partizan triumph. For some weeks before, Chernicheff, an aide-de-camp of the Emperor Alexander, and distinguished for his alertness and intrepidity, had been roving at the head of a few squadrons of dragoons and Cossacks, to keep the front of the allied army clear, and protect the young insurgency of the north. Doernberg, the Hanoverian, who had been busily collecting recruits from the scattered Hanoverian army, and had succeeded in forming a light corps of some hundred men, all sufficiently indignant against the enemy, and all capital soldiers, joined the Russian on his arrival on the Elbe; and they thenceforth proceeded down the river, laying a heavy hand on the marauding parties which the French officers, strangely unsuspicious of their own situation, sent loosely through the country.

While they were thus threading the enemy's posts, and sometimes recovering the pillage of the unfortunate peasantry, they heard of Morand's march; this recalled them to a higher class of operations at once. The French mode of treating German cities was well known; a moment was not to be lost, and the two corps marched straight to the rescue of Lunenburg. This march itself was an extraordinary instance of what may be done by troops when their hearts are in the cause. A part of the force was infantry, which of course held back the dashing riders of the Ukraine; but the whole, cavalry and infantry, contrived to wade through five-and-forty miles of German mire and sand, and there are no roads on earth where mire and sand are in such perfection, in little more than twenty-four hours.

But on arriving within sight of Lunenburg, their labour seemed to have been in vain; the French were already in possession, and had even got before them by an entire day. They had now nothing to do but to lie by in the environs, and pick up patrols in the old way: they were soon roused by the intelligence of the intended massacre. From the peasantry they had learned nothing but exaggerated accounts of the French force, which, combining with the strength of the walls, and the nature of their own, without guns, and almost without any of the means of assault, would, in all probability, have determined them to withdraw. But by dawn, some of

the frightened townspeople stole out and gave information of the scene that was to ensue. It is grati-
fying to our common sense of justice to find villiany
thus working its own punishment. The two officers instantly and gallantly decided to attempt the
assault, cost what it would. They had but two weak
battalions of infantry, and two thousand irregular
horse; yet with those they dashed at gate and
rampart. Morand had been strangely negligent
of the neighbourhood of his active enemy, and,
in fact, appears to have been completely blinded
by his own presumption. However, the French are
soon on the alert, and on this occasion they fought
well; but on the breaking open of the gates, the
affair was at an end; the cavalry burst in, sabreing
on all sides, until the enemy threw down their
arms. Nothing could be more brilliant than this
success. Morand's whole division were taken, infantry, guns, baggage, staff; all were in the power
of the Cossacks before evening; and last and most
welcome prey, was a whole *possé* of custom-house
officers, who, to a man, expected to have their heads
cut off, for their manifold sins against the peasantry.
Two thousand two hundred privates were taken, with

E 2

one hundred officers, a most unusual proportion in
the continental armies, but in this instance, probably
made up of the wreck of some of the battalions in
the Moscow campaign.

But the chief prize was the murderer, Morand
himself; his fate had been exchanged with that of
his intended victims; he had been desperately
wounded in the assault, and was found at the gate,
bleeding to death; he was brought back into his
quarters, but his wounds were evidently mortal,
and in a day or two after he expired.

Every man concerned in this dashing business
received a strip of red ribbon, as a distinction;
with, I believe, some slight gratuity from the citizens of Lunenburg, both of which he well deserved.
Some of them were pointed out to me in the
streets immediately after, and they seemed very
proud of their blushing honours.

CHAPTER VI.

─────

THE HANSEATIC LEGION.

April 7. Thunder, lightning, and rain; spring gone, winter come back in his ire, and the French coming; the worst news of all. The whole day has been a perpetual public fever; expresses galloping through the streets; the Cossacks ordered out, peering along every road for miles; the walls placarded with new exhortations to popular courage, and new promises of the arrival of Russian troops, bad signs of both; and the commandant Tettenborn and his suite riding about, cloaked up to the foreheads, and leaving us in doubt whether they, and the train of baggage-waggons drawn up before head-quarters, are getting ready for a flight or a battle.

Tettenborn's appearance to-day is universally

E 3

regarded as an ill omen.   Our physiognomists read disaster through all the little of the human countenance shown through a German warrior's mustachios.   We could scarcely have recognized the gaudy and handsome hussar, who used to flourish through the streets with stars and crosses on his breast enough to have decorated an emperor, or a hero of melodrame, in the stern personage who now led his forlorn hope to the gates; the whole shrouded in long grey mantles, and the whole, as they moved away through the fog and rain, looking not unlike a patrol of ghosts.

Tettenborn's own story is thoroughly *continental;* gallantry, good luck, adventure, promotion, and all of a rapidity that might move the bile of our tardy service.   The peace principle is nearly the same every where, grumbling, *ennui*, and half-pay, in Germany, half paid; but in German war the Dalgetty principle carries all before it.   Tettenborn, at the beginning of the year, was a simple half-pay captain in the Austrian service.   Nothing was to be done there, for Austria had been so completely eviscerated by the French, in her last experiments in the field, that her policy was pacific per force.

Tettenborn offered his sword, according to the custom of the country, to the Russian emperor, then rushing upon France with the impetus gained by a march of a thousand miles through the snow. A crowd of German officers had already done the same; but the demand was overmatched by the supply; and when Captain Tettenborn presented himself, even the emperor had nothing to offer him but a handfull of Cossacks. Nothing could seem more unfortunate, nor be more lucky. Another hero, accustomed to the pomps of the regular cavalry, would have scoffed at the Bashkirs, torn up his commission, and finished his history by putting a pistol to his head. But Tettenborn was wiser; he took fortune in whatever shape she came, mounted his horse, determined to ride at every thing, fell on the French without ceremony, became a favourite of his Bashkirs, who found the productiveness of following a " lucky officer," and, from mastering their rugged souls, became a favourite of the emperor, who was, to the last, half a Tartar himself.

The Cossack makes *reconnoissances* of two or three hundred miles ahead. On the news of the expulsion of Carra St. Cyr and his Douaniers from

Hamburg, Tettenborn was sent forward with his pulk as the advanced patrol of the grand army at Berlin! At Hamburg he was received with rapture, and at Hamburg he lived in the first style of the Dalgetties. The simple Austrian captain was suddenly the governor, the commander-in-chief, the king of the whole senatorial territory. Thus exalted, he now loftily disdained to look like a Cossack: he had the handsomest coat, the handsomest horses, and kept the handsomest table that ever dazzled the republican eye of Hamburg.

The French are actually in motion again. The morning's report, which shapeless as it was, was sufficient to " fright the land from her propriety," has been since confirmed on even better authority than the firmest denial of our bulletins. A conflux of frightened landholders along the Elbe have just brought intelligence that a large French force has rapidly advanced in the direction of Lunenburg. Melancholy tidings for the unfortunate Lunenburgers, who will have to pay the price of Morand's defeat; and scarcely better for this city, which will undoubtedly be the next point of attack, and unless a few corps of volunteers can work the miracle of beating a regular army, the next object of possession.

Evening. The Jungfersteig, the after-dinner Rialto of Hamburg, was crowded; every one of the crowd a furious politician, and every one with his own version of affairs. But all agreeing in the main fact, that the French, irritated by Morand's defeat, are in march, with Davoust at their head, brimful of rage. This is a double charge of calamity; for of all the French marshals, Davoust is notoriously the most violent, and he has a long grudge to repay besides. For the sins of the city he had been put in command of the department of the Hanse Towns, where he contrived to render himself so personally obnoxious to the citizens, that his name became a bugbear, until neither hope nor flattery could bring the people to offer any show of civility to him.

In one instance this was strikingly shown. As he sat on his horse at a review, a gust of wind blew off his hat; not one of the populace would step forward to hand it to him. His aides-de-camp were in another part of the ground, and the furious marshal was left to sit bare-headed, until an officer rode out, picked up the hat, and restored it to its position. The contrast of this military ruffian's insolence with the manners of his predecessor Bernadotte, threw him still more into the shade. That brave man, without relaxing the discipline of either the troops or the city, rendered himself an equal favourite with both. His honest secret was justice gently administered. The Hamburgers early predicted that he *must* be fortunate, and when they heard of his adoption as Crown Prince of Sweden, they seemed actually to take a personal interest in his extraordinary elevation.

Night. All in confusion. Certain intelligence has arrived at last. A dragoon has just brought in a dispatch, stating that the advanced guard of Davoust's army are within a day's march of Lunenburg; that the Hanoverian partizan corps are ordered to retire, and that the whole of the Russian light troops and patrols have been withdrawn to the right bank of the Elbe. Here are tidings for a huge, crowded, and utterly defenceless city. Well may England rejoice in her sea; that noble ditch, which costs her nothing to keep it in repair, which no enemy's spade can turn off, and no drought can dry. But who can have patience with our war amateurs? belligerents in their easy chairs; heroes in their night-gowns and slippers! Here is the rough reality. The French are coming, the men who have already marked their way through Germany with fire and sword! and formidable as the announcement must be at any crisis, it is doubly so, when they are hurrying forward, with open vengeance, to a city from which they had been angrily expelled, and where they are coming, not to conquer, but to extinguish; not to fight the fair battle of soldier against soldier, but to scourge and crush a population of rebels.

When I saw the distress and dismay painted in every face round me, high and low; the people packing up their little property for flight, or rushing to their doors at the sound of every waggon that drove by, as if they expected to see the enemy's cavalry charging through the streets; I could

E 6

have wished for Aladdin's lamp, or any other means
of transport, for the lovers of the romance of war;
and still more for those " gentlemen of England,
who live at home at ease," and find the world and
their breakfast dull, without "news from the armies;" get through the day only by the help of the
list of killed and wounded, and sleep in the faithful
hope of a " remarkable" conflagration or a " merciless" massacre by morning.

Here, at least, the amateurs would find stimulus
enough; for the news, various as it is, all coincides
in one centre; the enemy are at hand! though
whether within thirty miles, or as many furlongs;
or whether Hamburg is to atone for its premature
disloyalty, by fire or sword, by pillage or the dungeon, or by the whole four, are questions which
no one yet feels himself qualified to resolve. They
would supply the quidnunc with the degree of uncertainty essential to his comforts, and in the doubt
whether he was to be shot or sabred in his first
sleep, he might lay himself on his pillow in the
full enjoyment of all the picturesque of actual
hostilities.

In this state of things I asked a clever friend,

long resident in the city, " what he would advise strangers to do;" his answer was, " to get out of the scrape as fast as they can."

This pithy advice deserves some consideration; and I feel perfectly disposed to take it, *provided* that it does not require my leaving the city. Happy is the man who has others to decide for him; and I should rejoicingly surrender my liberty of choice into the hands of the first seer who could tell me what is likely to become of this famous city before a week is over. But to one whom the place interests, odd, old, and ugly as it is; who has so far fought his way through the language as to be able to decypher the commandant's placards on the corners of the streets, a sort of peripatetic lesson, which has the double spur of curiosity, and easy scholarship; and is, beyond all question, the smoothest way of *getting down* so indigestible a language; Hamburg, even in its paroxysms, has some charms. There is something in the tumult and chances of its wild life; in the certainty of being within a few leagues of a real field-marshal, a genuine, existing figure in the history-piece of the conquest of Europe; in the chance of seeing a pitched battle ; in the chance of having to fly for our lives; nay, in the chance of being shot. After all, the great misery of life is monotony; else why do our squires break their necks over five-bar gates, our nobles plunge into party, and our merchants speculate into the gazette? But here, round me at this moment, the world is all motion, busy, elastic, and insane; five hundred thousand human beings are rushing from their firesides, to cut each others' throats, and leave their limbs to the dogs and kites; Napoleon against the world! and what am I, in the midst of this universal whirl, that I alone should stand steady? in this universal frenzy, that I should be sage? in this supreme race of folly, and royal dance of death, that I should gravely rebuke mankind?

The town chimes were striking midnight, and sweetly ringing Luther's hymn, as my council of war broke up: and, unlike that of any other council of war on record, its decision was *against* running away.

CHAPTER VII.

———

DIPLOMACY.

APRIL 8. Deeper and deeper still! Reports of disasters in all directions have formed our news of to-day; crowds have remained since morning in front of the Russ colonel's quarters; obviously in expectation of seeing his farewell; and even the bulletins on the walls endeavour to cheer us, by stoutly declaring, that the French army corps under Davoust are still "some days' march" from our catastrophe. But whatever the bulletins may say, our telescopes tell a different tale; there is an evident bustle at Harburg, lying, as it is, under our eyes on the opposite side of the river, and our chief point of communication with Hanover. The peasantry, the customary heralds of all military movements, are flying from their homes; and those who conceive themselves most in the secret, reckon the enemy at fifty thousand men. True, there is no arithmetic equal to that of fear: but the news of the advance is confirmed, for the Correspondenten "doubts it altogether."

This morning supplied us with a new example of the truth of Oxenstiern's famous apophthegm. As the world is all covered over with the diplomatists of England, she has a *chargé d'affaires* here. From the sullen look of affairs, and the utter impossibility of dividing the truth from the falsehood, under any form of the public documents; some of his countrymen thought proper to wait upon this minister, simply for the purpose of receiving any advice which he might have to give; it being naturally presumed, that from his information, he must be a better judge of the actual state of things, than those who depended for their proceedings on the newspapers. Even an opinion of the propriety or security of remaining in Hamburg at this time, might not have been too much to expect from the affability of our diplomatic friend.

But the *chef* himself was either absent, or too conscious of his elevation to trouble himself on the subject; he was invisible. As the next resource, the secretary was asked for; the party were then shewn into the ministerial *salon;* whose appearance certainly nullified all the guilty luxury so often imputed to our agents abroad. Nothing could be more Spartan; but it was only the more in character with the attendants, and even the *chargé d'affaires* of the *chargé d'affaires,* the secretary himself. They expected in this man to find, at least, an Englishman; they found a squalid German, scarcely speaking English, utterly uninformed upon the matter in question, and perhaps upon all other matters; but pert and pragmatical beyond even the secretary species, an ultra-puppy of the *attaché* breed. From this ape of envoyship they could get nothing; whether the French were a hundred miles off, or within the next furlong; whether any intelligence on which the safety of the mass of English merchandize in the city might depend, had reached the minister, or whether the minister himself was on the earth or under it, all were points on which this grave baboon " thought it his duty," "*garder le silence,*" until the party, disgusted with this display of third-rate diplomacy, shook off the dust of their feet against his " Excellency's"

gates, and resolved one and all to keep themselves
out of the way of the whole dynasty of clerks for
the rest of their lives.

Evening. Another change of fortune: our
troops have had a brush with the enemy, and
triumphed too. As I was returning from the
table d'hôte, I was roused by huzzas and the
trampling of horses; the populace were shouting
in honour of a party of the Hanseatic cavalry,
who had come into contact with the French, and
had *come back!* The troop amounted to forty or
fifty; they looked tired enough, but they responded
gaily to the congratulations of the crowd. The
corps to which they belonged had been posted a
dozen miles up the Elbe, to watch Davoust's movements, which were presumed to menace the fords
there; but finding that the French patrols had not
yet showed themselves in their front, they ventured
to feel the enemy a little more nearly, crossed the
river, and had the fortune to fall in with some companies of conscripts scattered among the farms,
foraging, as they delicately term it, but as the
indignant Germans pronounced it, and with good
reason, robbing and ruining every where. The

Hanseatics gallantly gave them chase; the Frenchmen rallied, and the affair rose to the dignity of a skirmish, but at last the enemy broke, and our city troopers had the honour of catching some of Napoleon's youngest thieves.

This was not much, but it was only our beginning, the first sprouting of our laurels, and we are right to cherish the growth: for it has instantly made heroes of us all. The people are every where grouping in the streets, perfectly secure for this evening, that Davoust must shrink from walls which inclose such defenders; and that Napoleon shows his wisdom in fighting only kings and emperors a hundred miles off, up the Elbe.

Our weather would make a fitting accompaniment to worse news. It has suddenly changed from a soft spring temperature to a bitter autumnal mixture of gusts and rain. But drench as it may the patriotism of the populace, it cannot drive them within doors. This however is common. The foreigner will bear hail, rain, or snow, the whole " spite of winter," to convince the world that he has the finest of all possible climates: the climate makes a silly source of national pride, and he is soused for it, just as he deserves. The Englishman alone is not fool enough for this folly; and accustomed as he is to acknowledge the worst of his weeping sky, he indignantly finds himself half-frozen and half-drowned in the " perpetual spring" of *bella Italia*, and the "eternal summer" of *la belle France*. There are months of cold in "fair Florence," that would be worthy of the Polar circle; and months of rain in fairer Paris, that might compete with the monsoons of the Malabars; still the foreigner will persist in his boast, and point to the peasantry sitting shivering, with the frostiest gusts of winter howling round them, as a proof of his "early spring;" or drenched from top to toe at their doors, as an answer to all doubts of his enjoying the most serene temperature under the moon. It must be confessed, however, that the German populace are singularly unsusceptible of the inclemency of their very inclement climate; they seem waterproof, body and soul. The tempest that drives an English grenadier to his sentry-box, leaves the sons and daughters of Germany reading their little blurred newspapers, making their markets, gazing at nothing, or knitting their rugged stockings, all alike, *sub Jove*.

The Hanseatics required some laurels to over-shadow their formation; for a more ill-judged contrivance for raising an effective force was never discovered. The only principle was to raise a sufficient number within a sufficient time; the nature of the force entered into no man's calculation. The expedient was, however, not to be charged upon the citizens, it was altogether Russ: Russ in its conception, its execution, and its failure.

A few days after Tettenborn's entry, he had issued one of those proclamations with which the officers of the Czar were furnished, to raise the German levies by the magic of *words.*

" Citizens of Hamburg,—you abolished the authorities existing under the French government, before the Russian troops entered your territory, and you established the ancient magistrates. This manly and worthy act, by which you have begun the work of your deliverance, and made yourselves an example to all Germany, renders you worthy of the approbation of my august monarch, and of the esteem of the Russian nation. You introduced us

not into a French but into an old German city;
and only on those terms could we greet you as
brothers.

"Your transports on our entrance into the city
have deeply affected every one among us. Yet,
Germans and brethren, your joy will not be declared in its full force, until you take an active
part in the great work of the deliverance of your
country. To arms, then, all who feel oppression
as infamy! to arms for your country and justice!
The work of deliverance is not yet effected, and
therefore let no one dwell till then on recreation
or enjoyment. The most honourable employment
now is to draw the sword, and drive the invaders
from the soil of Germany, who have been already
pursued fifteen hundred miles by the victorious
Russian armies.

"Shame and infamy, therefore, to every one who
can sit with his arms across at this eventful period,
when the first of human rights are contended for.
Once more then, to arms—to arms. Under the
protection of my august sovereign, you will assem-
ble round your own standards; and I rejoice that

it has been reserved for me to be the first to lead you against the enemy, and the first to witness your valour.

(Signed,) "BARON VON TETTENBORN,

"Colonel in the service of his Majesty the Emperor of all the Russias, and commander of a corps of the army of the Count Wittgenstein."

"HAMBURG,
"*March* 19, 1813."

This was an unfortunate paper; for, by urging the formation of a military force, especially connected with the city, it invited the wrath of Napoleon on the first reverse; and by declaring the overthrow of the French influence in Hamburg to be the direct act of the citizens, it left them without the plea of having been compelled to it by the allies. The policy of thus urging the city to defy France and its formidable and vindictive master, was, at this moment, infinitely rash. The Russians should have reflected that all was not *couleur de rose*, even in the allied camp; that Napoleon was advancing with a force which the Russians and Prussians together could not meet; and that they had no troops to detach to the assistance of the unlucky city, in case of an attack from the left bank of the Elbe.

But war has not much time for consideration; the immediate purpose was to stir up the north of Germany, at whatever risk; and the measure which, if delayed for a fortnight, would probably have saved a vast quantity of spoliation and misery, was unhappily expedited with an eagerness and want of care which must have defeated a much more salutary design.

On the day after Tettenborn's proclamation, a decree of the senate appeared, announcing in consequence, the formation of a body of troops; consisting of levies from the three Hanse towns, Hamburg, Lubeck, and Bremen. It must be acknowledged that no measure could have been more amply met by the public with enthusiasm. The Germans are nationally brave, and the insults and oppressions of the French had inspired Hamburg with the strongest determination to resist. All the principal families either sent their sons, or gave large pecuniary assistance to the new corps; the ladies worked colours for it; some gave jewels and watches as contributions, and made large quantities of clothing for the service. Even the maid-servants of the city insisted on offering their especial contribution, which was said to amount to upwards of 500*l*. sterling.

But whether from the haste with which the plan was carried into effect, or from French intrigue, which seldom sleeps, and which on this occasion was wide awake to the whole of the proceedings; the fabric of the legion was speedily vitiated; its being recruited from all quarters, and all kinds of character, left it open to the enemy; the French, finding that all who offered would be received, took good care that it should not want recruits of their own choosing; and there is no question now in the public mind, that, at least in the first establishment of the corps, a considerable number were actually in French pay. A French spy had nothing more to do than to offer himself, and he was a German and a patriot on the spot. This confidence went so far, that known Frenchmen, and even some who had been public *employés* under Napoleon, were suffered to hold commissions in the legion. The more prominent instances of this extraordinary abuse have been rectified; but there can be little doubt

that the consequences will be felt in the first
action*.

Our Burgher guard, however, is on another construction; it is more on the plan of the English
volunteers, and consists of respectable townspeople, officered by their own election. But here,
too, Russian legislation was busy; for, once come
in contact with martinet diplomacy, and men eat,
drink, and sleep only by general orders.

On the 26th of March, a rescript from the senate
had summoned the citizens to *volunteer* per force.

" The senate announces to the inhabitants of the
city and its territory, that by order of Baron Von
Tettenborn, colonel in the service of his Majesty
the Emperor of Russia, a Hamburg Burgher Corps,
of six battalions, for the city and territory, shall be

---

* There was, unluckily, too much fact in this conjecture; the
Frenchmen ran off to their own countrymen, after doing, as might
be presumed, all the mischief that they could. The vagrant
Mecklenburgers, Prussians, Saxons, and nondescripts, speedily
followed the example, and eloped in all directions. The corps,
however, was purified; and finally served under Bernadotte with
some distinction, and took an honourable share in, I believe, the
battles of Juterboch and Leipsic.

formed, in which all the inhabitants between the ages of eighteen and forty-five, are *bound to enrol themselves !*

"The senate, while it acquaints the public with this regulation, expects at the same time that every citizen and inhabitant will pay due regard to this order; the object of which is the defence of the city; and will conform to the further regulations to be made to this effect."

This ukase is only one instance among a myriad of the ill-luck of a stranger's meddling in personal concerns. A month ago there was not a man in Hamburg who would not have rejoiced at the opportunity of having a shot at the French. But men like to do things in their own way; the ukase fairly extinguished the merit of volunteering, at a word; and it is easy to foresee that not one of the six battalions will ever parade its 1200 men, nor the half of its 1200 men. The numbers come in laggingly already; and though their hatred of the enemy is not diminished by a grain; and there is, probably, not a pauper within the walls who would not die, musket in hand, as stoutly as any janissary on earth; yet the burgher guard will now never do more than what they are doing now, with great assiduity I own, learning the goose step, drumming and trumpeting through all the streets at all hours, and going in the glories of war to church. Had they been left to themselves, the result might have been otherwise. But, right or wrong, there is now no time for them to learn their new trade. The French are coming! and the French will come, before they know the difference between the muzzle and the breech of their muskets; before a month is out, their clarionets will be disloyally converted to the Napoleon grand march; their new blue coats will be embezzled for the profit of Napoleon commissaries; and their goose step will be no more.

CHAPTER VIII.

THE COLLIER.

APRIL 15. A London December morning; foul, frostnipt, and unwholesome. The sky a " congregation of pestilent vapours," and the ground, what the ground of every continental city is after the first half hour's rain, a quagmire.

The morning was appropriately whiled away over the crabbed characters and still more crabbed paragraphs of the Correspondenten, the famous gazette of Hamburg. Such is the passion of mankind for hearing of each other, that this paper sold forty thousand copies a week, in " the good old times;" and even now, with the Russian hook in its nostrils, it is the oracle of every coffee-room of Germany; thence diverging, if we are to believe Hamburg report, until it makes the tour of the

F 3

universe, and comes up at breakfast with the coffee
and cigars of the Incas, the tea of the Emperor of
China, and the betel of the great Mogul.

The Correspondenten is undoubtedly in great
request, though it is as puzzling as the sphinx, and
has exhibited as many fashions in its day as a
French *marchande de modes*. France, Prussia,
Denmark, England; France again, Russia, all
have found it a faithful depository of their notions,
for the time being. And the German sovereignties have often pored over it, as the criminal does
over the judge's report. The paper might well be
of importance that let the reader into such news,
however in the shape of enigma. Another source
of its influence was the conflux of little diplomatists from the little states, which made their nest
in Hamburg from time immemorial. For this too
there were reasons many and strong.

By some law of nature, no king, even to the
highest condition of kingship, ever has any ready
money. As Burke said, " all the king's cheese
goes in parings." The German revenues were
absorbed in epaulettes, orchestras, chasseurs, and
maids of honour. And Hamburg was the mart

where Gentile craved of Jew, and where Jew fleeced Gentile. Every little court kept a minister here, who, on the smallest salary that ever sustained a laced coat, did the grand business of state, and brokered for the necessities of empire. Intelligence, in return, flowed broadly from this fount. It was impossible that among half a hundred agents, perpetually mingling together, political secrets should not make their escape from time to time; or that the *table d'hôte*, between the heat of controversy, the willingness of all men to show that they have a secret to tell, and the natural softness of the human heart, after an hour's circulation of the bottle, Rhenish and astringent as it was, should not witness communications, which Harpocrates himself could not have kept in hand. Those, of course, made their way direct into the Correspondenten; and the world was suddenly enlightened by decisions, which left their framers as much in the dark as ever. In some instances, this communicative faculty was turned to good purpose, and sovereigns felt their way at the rival courts of St. Petersburg and Paris by the simplicity of a paragraph. The stocks had their influ-

ence too, for Hamburg was the ruler of the
exchanges, the supreme arbiter of agios, per
centages, and the price of ducats; the " Lady
Company" of the subahdars and rajahships of the
northern land of gold.   Even the intricacy of its
style added to the charm; the politician studied
it with the triumph of one developing a cypher;
the simple quidnunc delighted in finding at least
one work that might give him something to do or
suffer from morning till night; and the philosopher,
if philosophers ever read newspapers, amused himself with seeing one half of the paragraphs con-
tradict the other, or finding despair at the loss of a
fiddler fill as large a space as the fall of a dynasty.

News has arrived of some kind or other, for the
people are all hurrying through the streets.   A
crowd in London is nothing, or the mere result of
an over-drove ox or a captured pickpocket.   But
here it is every thing.   The French are n every
man's thoughts, and the first impulse on the first
murmur in the streets is to draw on one's boots, put

the travelling expenses in the purse, and sally forth
in fighting or flying order. The rumours now are
enough to satisfy the most voracious love of intelligence.—An English fleet in full sail up the Elbe.
—An army-corps under Wittgenstein in full march
for the city.—Davoust and all his *braves*, who, if
ill-wishes were culverins and mortars, would have
been blown to the moon long ago, in full march
too for the city, preceded by terror and followed by
Nemesis.

However, some news *has* arrived, of considerable
value, if it be *true*, (an important qualification in all
continental intelligence,) that a treaty has been entered into between England and Denmark. The extraordinary interest attached to this most doubtful
piece of information is another proof of our distance
from London; there a treaty with Denmark might
not have excited a much deeper sensation than a
treaty with Madagascar. But here Denmark
amplifies into the most important dimensions of
sovereignty, for its *empire* is within half a mile of
us; we daily see with the naked eye the dun-
coloured red of its troops waving in long lines
outside the gates of Altona; and with the Danes

against us on one side, and the French on the
other, the soul and body of our large, fat, and
helpless city must be crushed like an olive in the
press.

New exultation: the people, great and small, are
crowding down to the harbour. Woe be to him
who now dares to doubt of the treaty; for a ship
direct from England, (the fleet has dwindled to
this already) is running up the Elbe, and all the
world knows that she could not pass the guns of
Gluckstadt without Danish permission; *therefore*
" Denmark has signed a treaty offensive and defen-
sive with England."   The conclusion is rapid; but,
as to dispute it would probably occasion the sceptic's
being thrown into the river, it is carried without a
dissentient voice.

Evening.   We have had at least one afternoon of
national cheerfulness.   The sun is at this moment
sinking in a glorious sky over Hanover, flooding the
sands, cottages, and river, with inimitable crimson,
and giving rosy complexions to all the sallow artizans
of this industrious and dingy-featured city.   But the

ship *has* arrived. After some parleying under the Gluckstadt batteries, she came up the Elbe in full sail, dextrously threading all its shallows, and ploughing the quiet river into billows that terrified the native navigators, and threatened to send the whole buttertub fleet to the bottom. Repeated cheers saluted the sailors, who seemed highly amused by those marks of public attention, which the style of their equipment was so little in the habit of receiving at home, for the vessel was simply a Newcastle collier.

Yet sooty a representative as she might make of the British flag, she did no discredit to its seamanship, and after all she could not be blacker than the navy of Hamburg. On dropping her anchor, she covered the shore with her jovial-faced crew, and filled the coffee-houses with news and newspapers from the centre of the world, England *.

---

* It turned out that the rumour of the Danish negociations was true, though the *facts* were false. Chiefly with the object of rescuing Hamburg, the English government had offered terms to Denmark; but the little monarchy was too angry and too short-sighted to exhibit common sense on the occasion. The Danish minister selected a middle policy, the habitual refuge of simpletons.

The collier was not to be the only wonder of the day. Another current of the people carried me to one of the landing places, where I found as the *nucleus* of a crowd of admirers, some companies of soldiers in the British uniform, the genuine men of red. A sentimentalist would here talk of recollections and *ranz de vaches*, but I at least shared in the popular feeling, if I did not take personal credit to my country for their soldierly look, and capital style of equipment.

The illusion received a slight shock from their answering my enquiries in the roughest tongue of Teutchland. They were a detachment of the German Legion, just arrived from England, yet with no conceivable purpose, except to be thrown away, for they amounted to but a couple of hundreds. However, if the men were German, their appointments and their discipline were British; and still more unequivocally British were their guns, two light six-pounders of the most finished construction. A group were gathered round them too, evidently, from their dark visages and massive limbs, blacksmiths, some of that race of armourers who once formed one of the boasts of

Hamburg. They looked over these toys of war with an air of evident science, and were full of Cyclopean admiration.

To bewilder us still more, Count Walmoden Gimborn has just come thundering through the streets from the "grand head quarters;" though what his business is remains a secret of state. The people have decided at once that he must be the forerunner of an army. Thus, with "fifteen thousand English troops, including the guards and household cavalry, which are immediately to follow the German legion; and forty or fifty thousand men from the emperor Alexander," we promise to be handsomely provided for. The English fleet certainly has rather fallen short of our expectations; but for the present we can do without it.

The continent is, after all, the place to see the high style of soldiership. An English general officer, with his aide-de-camp and couple of grooms, makes a most diminished figure beside your true continental brigadier; with his three or four britchskas, his crowd of aides-de-camp, valets, and secretaries, and his half dozen led horses; and all those but a moderate provision for him.

He lives by billet wherever he goes; all post-masters open their stables at his bidding; he feasts, and every body round him feasts, with no more care for the morrow than the fowls of the air; he is clothed, fed and lodged, with no more trouble to himself than one of his own chargers; and when he rolls with his suite through one of the German cities, the thunder of his wheels over the aboriginal pavement prepares the world to expect an emperor.

———

April 20. More good news: Lord Stewart arrived this morning; reviewed the Burgher guard, admired their discipline, said "that he had never seen any thing *like it*," for the time, and having finished his dextrous compliment, and bade them beat the French wherever they met them, galloped off on his way to the Russian head quarters. His Lordship's Peninsular fame gave due weight to his words; and he left us all with the impression that we are the very material for heroes. After this, who would be cold-blooded enough to doubt the arrival of the fifteen thousand English?

I went in the evening into the fields; the weather was once more calm, and the citizens were
enjoying it, *more suo*, sitting cooped up in coffee-
houses, smoking like furnaces, diluting their satur-
nine souls with *eau sucrée*, flat beer, and brandy,
as hot and empyreumatic as if it were intended to
burn the drinker alive; it might have been boiled
in the crater of Vesuvius.

In one of the fields, some old men and boys were
gathered about a piece of cannon, which had, I
suppose, been *forgotten* by its artillerists at their
last field day. It was now affording practice to a
veteran, ragged, tipsy, and oratorical. The grand
difficulty with him was how to make sure of the
bore; for the rammer was perverse, and always
missed it, with malice afore-thought; luckily there
was no powder in the case, or the patriot's promises
of annihilating Napoleon must have finished in
sending himself and the boys round him piecemeal
into the elements. The old hero, after having
exhausted himself in vain endeavours to get the
rammer down, offered it to some of an English
party on the ground, probably, as a national compliment; it was declined, to his great surprise, for

foreigners give us credit for doing every thing; and an Englishman who could not ram a cannon must be, at best, a degenerate Englishman.

I remarked the genuine German physiognomy of the boys. The French had been masters of Hamburg for ten years; their lawless ideas are well known, and yet nothing is so rare among the rising generation, in either Hamburg, or any other part of Germany which I have seen, as a French face. The truth is, an army is thoroughly *Malthusian*. It has been said, that in the best regulated service on earth, and the British may be taken as the example, a regiment scarcely rears children enough for its own fifes and drums. The two millions of Frenchmen who, since 1804, have quartered on Germany, have not remoulded a feature of the original barbarian. So much the better: for, who would not prefer the quiet, spectacled forehead of the German, to the restless impudence of the Frenchman and his eye-glass; the fair, flat visage of the Goth, piscatory as it is, to the bilious, pug-dog physiognomy of the Gaul?

CHAPTER IX.

THE HAMBURGER BERG.

APRIL 23. This has been a day of gala; last night news arrived from the Upper Elbe, which, unless mankind are all in a conspiracy to deceive us, must be true. The allied sovereigns, moved by our hazards, or their own, have at last turned their eyes upon M. Davoust, and talk of cutting him up for the birds of the air. The report ran, that Napoleon had some idea of wheeling his host into line upon the Elbe, and after making Hamburg a redoubt for the *appui* of his left wing, bursting forward to overwhelm Bernadotte, who has yet but a few troops, and seems sufficiently afraid of dipping his foot too far in our waters of strife. The next step was to be his joining the garrisons in the north, sweeping

Landstorm, Landwehr, patriots and partizans, all
before him ; and then pouring down in a tornado of
gunpowder and bayonets on the backs of the allies.

The project is so far deemed possible, that an
allied corps has actually touched the Hanover frontier; Montbrun, the Frenchman, who had taken
possession of Lunenburg, to the great terror of the
inhabitants, who expected to pay dearly for the
lopped laurels of Morand, has set off in too great
haste to allow him to kill any body, though he had
levied contributions in a most military style; and
the French patroles have now been beaten on so
many occasions, that the sound of a German bugle
seems enough to set their whole army in full movement to the rear.   All this is glittering enough,
and to give it something like official confirmation,
Tettenborn's pen is *en état d'activité*, and the following report is issued, evidently, from the commandant's bureau.

" Major General Tettenborn prosecutes with
unabating zeal, and constant activity, the work so
happily begun, of restoring to our city its old rights,
and at the same time of providing the means of
vigorously asserting those rights.

" Under the direction of his excellency, and by the co-operation of the inhabitants, who cheerfully fulfil and do their utmost to anticipate the generous wishes of the general, the formation of the Hanseatic Legion is advanced so far, that above 3000 infantry, and several squadrons of cavalry, well provided with every requisite, have attained by their daily exercise no common degree of steadiness, and full of ardent zeal for the cause of their country, are ready to follow the call of their leader to battle.

" At the same time the greatest attention and the most active care are employed to ensure the security of the city. The general surveys, almost daily, the works on the ramparts and in the suburbs. All the breast-works are ready, and Hamburg can already await, without uneasiness, a considerable hostile force; the Burgher Guard is to be augmented to the number of 7200, and will soon be completed; the troops are daily exercised in arms, in order, if the enemy should venture to approach our territory, to oppose him with ability, and successfully to defend their families, their properties, and their homes. The formation of the Burgher Guard will,

indeed, in the sequel, be of incalculable advantage
to the city.

" The same judgment and wisdom in directing
the good-will of the inhabitants; the same libe-
rality in employing the resources of the other
countries, to which the victorious arms of Russia
and the allies may penetrate, as are here shown
under the direction of the general, will ensure the
triumph of the good cause, and the speedy and
happy termination of the contest in which we are
now engaged.

" According to accounts which may be relied on,
the Russian light troops, under the command of
Lieutenant-Colonel Von Benkendorf, are advanced
within a mile of Bremen.   In this expedition they
have taken some prisoners, among whom are three
officers.   The Hanseatic cavalry have had an
honourable share in those combats."

———

This has been a day of gala; and as, though we
have not had any opportunity of distinguishing our
personal prowess, we have done all that we could,

in the preparation for heroism; we proceeded to-day to sing our Te Deum, by anticipation. We had a church service, to consecrate the five handsome banners which the ladies have embroidered for the Legion. The ceremony was, as usual, noisy, showy, and half heathen. The commandant and his whiskered staff made a conspicuous figure among the laced caps and ruddy cheeks of the Hamburg belles; the senators looked all that senators ought to look, ponderous and well powdered; our volunteers, brilliant with new coats and feathers; and our populace, with their working physiognomies put off, and their faces washed once in the seven days. The service was performed in the great church, where the pastor, Raimbach, preached the consecration sermon. It was thoroughly patriotic *; but, in all other points, as comprehensible as might be expected from a man at least ten

* This was an unlucky sermon for poor Raimbach; the circumstance, of course, reached Napoleon's ears instantly, as every thing among us did; and on the subsequent entrance of the French, this highly respectable man was compelled, at the age of 80, to fill out the gin from morning till night for the workmen employed on the fortifications.

years past the time which David has pronounced to be the limit of the human understanding.

———————

Evening. After as agreeable and interesting a day as I remember. Our party dined at the house of an old and opulent merchant, and thus had an opportunity of seeing the old German manners, simple and primitive as they are, combined with the enjoyments, and some of the graces of modern life; the old school for the foundation, the new one for the *façade.* Our table did honour to the opulence of our entertainer; for this was indispensable in the " old school." The Hamburg empire is bounded by a few leagues, yet within those leagues it once enjoyed the reputation of as much good living as was comprehended in half the continent besides; not yielding even to that colossal gourmand, London itself.

One reason was, that the Hamburgers were all merchants; and who is entitled to be a better judge of tastes, than the man who is perpetually supplying the cinnamon and cloves, the claret, and

13

turtle-soup, of all mankind? another was, that it had a plethora of wealth. From the year 1793, when Holland paid for her republicanism by being beggared, as she deserved; and Amsterdam paid for her especial absurdity and ingratitude, by being turned into a French barrack; Hamburg became the only channel for the German and English commerce, and became a second Tyre.

All the old famous depots of German trade now bowed their heads before her, or were rejoiced to be on her list; Leipsic was but her pamphlet seller; Frankfort but her haberdasher; Bremen and Lubec, once her rivals, were now proud to be her maids of honour; the Rhinegau was her butler, and all the world her cook; she was the lady-mayoress, the portly civic queen of northern bodies corporate.

Her sudden accession of wealth was astonishing; and it was rendered still more obvious, from the narrow space in which it was concentrated; it was not, as in England, where wealth has room, and the golden shower is absorbed like a shower in the desert. In Hamburg, the shower fell into reservoirs, and every drop *told;* the wealth came into

the hands of her conspicuous class, her merchants;
and it fructified instantly, and before the eye, in
more showy equipages, more pearls and plumes on
the heads of their wives; more laced lacqueys, more
villas, and more dinners, balls, and suppers.

It was, however, in the table, that the national
pride disdained a competitor. " Breakfast in Scot-
land, sup in France, but _dine_ in Hamburg," was
the adage.—" You may go to London, for liberty;
to Paris, for the opera; or to St. Petersburg, for
the knout;" was the undisputed saying of the German Apicius and Crœsus in one : " but it is only
in Hamburg that you can order two and thirty
wines from your merchant, and have them all
good."

But those were the rosy hours; and for some
years past, the ancient dinner glories of their state
are spoken of as having fallen formidably into
eclipse; time and taxes are rapidly levelling, and
what will they not level? those culinary honours
which the Hamburger once valued, as the Silesian
baron does his pedigree; and the " Grande Science"
is fast sinking into the degraded simplicity of
three courses and a dessert.

Our table was full; for the old man had gathered, as is the good and graceful custom of his country, all the branches of his olive round him; sons, daughters, sons-in-law, and daughters-in-law, with a rising circumvallation of grand-children, who, it must be acknowledged, did not suffer themselves to be considered the least important of the party.

Yet, after all, has life many better things than this? Johnson's maxim, that if wedlock has many troubles, celibacy has no enjoyments, is unquestionable, if the celibacy be *old* celibacy. For it is the time that settles the argument. The paradise of bachelorship is youth, when life is enjoyment in itself; the purgatory is old age, when every thing instinctively grows tasteless. It is when man is the wearied traveller, the *satur conviva*, the struggler with the natural infirmities of years, that the superiority of marriage is felt in those simple supports and consolations, which make us forget our decline; those deep and faithful attachments, which have exchanged the ardour of passion, only for the fidelity of a bond of nature. The old man is then no outcast, miserable, if he does not flutter in younger society, and ridiculous, if he does; no friendless and objectless hanger-on upon life, he has friends and occupation in his children; in their variety of mind, acquirement, pursuit, success, he has a living study of the heart, a revival of gentle thoughts and consecrated memories, cheered and animated by the still higher consciousness, that he has given pledges to his country, that he has bequeathed the noble gift of life and mind, to those who will honour his memory, when he is gone; that he has added to the virtuous, the intelligent, and the lovely, among mankind. It is surely worth more than the chance of some anxieties, to be able to say, when the world is closing on us, that we have not lived altogether in vain.

Our way home was through some of the villages skirting the Hamburg territory, where the people were enjoying the hour with great delight. The storm had passed away, and left sunshine in its room; and the sunshine was now passing away, and leaving the skies, far and wide, full of the lights and lustres of one of the finest of fine evenings. I turn a deaf ear to the nonsense of the Italian, raving about his perpetual blues and crimsons. His tale is *not* true, and if it were, the

genuine charm of climate is in its variety. If the
sky were orange from pole to pole, and from one
end of the year to the other, it could not give half
the delight, the true, fresh, animated delight, that
speaks in every countenance, and sings in every
bird, and I had almost said, springs and breathes
in every bush, at this break of sunshine, this golden
smile of an upper world, through our cloudy and
distempered sky.

We all know with what delight the Englishman
feels the first touch of summer: but there is more
provision for its popular enjoyment in Germany.
Even in the neighbourhood of Hamburg, by no
means the most sensitive corner of the world, there
is almost a public carousal, in the shape of a fair, on
every day of tolerable weather. This evening the
gates are crowded with vehicles of all kinds, from
the donkey chaise, to the ponderous stuhlwagen,
the Hamburg "Dilly, carrying twelve insides;"
pouring out a citizen swarm, a true *émigration
boutiquière*, into the sands and shades, the gardéns
and coffee-houses, for ten miles round. In the
Hamburger Berg, an open space near the city, all
is festivity, if not of the most refined nature,

yet very well for the purpose. Round-abouts are
heaving up the portly citizens to heights that
enrapture their children, astonish themselves,
and perhaps delight their wives with the near
prospect of liberty. Monkeys are rope-dancing,
jugglers tossing up their knives and balls, fiddlers
and harpers *troubadouring* it in every corner, and
some of them tastefully enough; those universal
travellers, Punch and his wife, with their cracked
trumpet, cracked, as it should seem, by statute all
over the globe; wooden horses in endless gallop, on
which our citizen cavalry learn to charge, lance in
hand, and fearlessly carry off the turbans of Turks
and Moors; all are in their glory, in the midst of
singing, trumpeting, drumming, and the grinding
of barrel organs innumerable.

I might justly object to the day, as intended for
graver things. The robin, too, and the thrush,
might be more congenial melodists to the hour,
and to the sweet and luxuriant verdure that the
rain has revived in such living emerald. But national taste is imperious, and there is no contending against the habits of a Hans Town, and a
thousand years.

CHAPTER X.

—————

THE BATTLE OF JENA.

THE extraordinary efforts of Prussia to prepare for the present campaign, which must lead to her final liberation or her grave, have already raised her to a high rank in the German eye. Nothing is talked of in general conversation but Prussia, past, present, and to come. The following sketch of the fatal battle of 1806, in which her fortunes were overthrown in a day, alludes to the catastrophe of a wing of her grand army.

—————

A Hussar Sketch of the Jena Campaign.

*　　　*　　　*　　　*　　　*

" If I take up the pen, it is neither to abuse the enemy, nor to praise our poor Prussians: enough has been done on both points by others. The

French are capital *soldiers*, and that is enough.
Thank Heaven, I have nothing more to do with the
cuirassiers of Milhaud, or the *chevaux légers* of
Murat, or any other *sabreur* of them all.

" If I escaped being shot—or what was much
worse, lying half a dozen years in a French prison; it
was by the simple good fortune of being put under
the orders of a brave madman, who galloped with
us every where, for no reason on earth, that I can
tell, except to get himself sabred into a hundred
pieces.   I commanded a regiment of hussars under
Prince Louis, as bold a hussar as any in Prussia,
and as fit to command a division of cavalry as a
new born child.   He was clearly half lunatic, but
so was every body at the time: for, if a whole nation
can be mad together, Prussia was certainly mad by
wholesale in 1806.   Statesmen, generals, nobles,
army, and populace, all were raving alike.   The
nation was craving for war, though it had seen the
French breaking the armies of Europe like glass, and
though it was notorious that Napoleon asked nothing better than a summer's promenade to Berlin.

" The populace were mad with the Parisians, for
laughing at our bad French, and our ambassador's

coach. Though, considering the class of diplomatists whom we sent there, on the faith of a hussar,
I do not know what else they could have done,
were they the gravest people on earth. Our diplomacy would have convulsed the muscles of a
Chinese. I was a little surprised, I own, at their
sneers at Lucchesini, whom I had known in early
life, and mixed with a good deal, as we both got on
in our services, and who certainly was no fool at the
table, whatever he might be in the bureau. And
I still think my own opinion the right one, for
Napoleon got rid of him as soon as he could.

"That universal genius was actually spoiled by
his taste for war. He would have been master of
Europe more surely, if he had never fired a shot.
His plan was the simplest imaginable. He always
asked for an ambassador, and we may rely on it,
that he never asked for the most stubborn, nor the
cleverest man, about court. He loved a goose that
he could pluck, a pack-saddle that he could ride on,
a footstool, a carpet, a pillow, of a man. When he
found him, he had him made ambassador, brought
him to Paris, and there taught him diplomacy after
his own fashion. When the pupil was finished, he

asked for another, sent the old one back, and only
requested that he should be made first minister at
home.   In a dozen years every minister in Europe
would have received his education in Paris; and
Napoleon took care, in one way or another, that
the interests of the master should never slip out of
the mind of the pupil.   But he spoiled all, by being
in too much haste to be emperor of the world.

"Our last ambassador was the best dresser in
Paris, and while he was dressing, they told him that
the emperor was going with his 250,000 " *braves*,"
on a hunting party, or an expedition to the mountains of the moon—and he believed them.

"Our old generals were mad with nonsense
about " *Le grand Frédéric*," the Prussian tactics,
and the battle of Rosbach.   Our whole army was
mad, because armies are made up of men; and
men, ninety-nine out of a hundred, require nothing
but a stimulant,—love, money, brandy, or politics,
to make them fit for strait waistcoats in any month
from January to December.

"Our king was always good, brave, and with
more brains than half the people about him; but
then he was but a boy: he was in the hands of his

cabinet, and his cabinet was mad, if ever madness took up its billet in the skull of any cabinet since the deluge. It had lost its senses from the beginning, had quarrelled with every ally that we had in Europe,—England first, then Russia, then Sweden; and finally, despising Austria, which was willing enough to give us some help, rushed into war a complete month before our tardy friends, the Russians, to whom we had cried in our extremity, could stir a step. Next, as if to make the national blunders complete, instead of retiring, to shorten the distance between us and the Russians; we rushed headlong over the Saale, leaving our magazines behind us at Nuremburg, totally exposed, of which Napoleon took good care in a day or two after; and pushed ourselves into the very muzzles of the enemy's guns, with nothing certain but our being either shot or starved. But, as if we had not done enough to be ruined, we finished the business by making the Duke of Brunswick generalissimo of the Prussian army—a man, who, whatever his soldiership might have been fifty years ago, was too old at seventy-two, to beat Napoleon at thirty-six.

" However, to war we must go. We were 'the predestined deliverers of Europe;' the Brandenburg eagle was to fly from Potzdam to the Tuilleries; and, in short, we were to do what we liked. Of course, we made every possible blunder. We marched, to save the French the trouble of marching; and our first attack was upon our own friends. We threw ourselves across the Saale into the territory of Weimar, where the first twenty-four hours swept every pound of bread, flask of brandy, and bundle of forage, from the face of the land. Weimar, always poor, was, in a moment, as naked as the deserts of Arabia. It then occurred to our generals, for the first time, that we had left our magazines a week's march behind. A brigade of cavalry, in which was my regiment, was now sent off at full speed to clear the country for the waggons to bring up supplies for our starving troops. Off we went, delighted to get as far as we could from the learned beggary of Weimar; and before we took up our quarters for the night, we had to break through Ney's whole cavalry, which were already in rear of our line, and burning and plundering for ten leagues round.

" We now began to feel that we had got into a

trou de rat. However, on we galloped, till on reaching a height half a league from Hof, we saw Soult's division, of at least 30,000 men, marching at their leisure through the plain, in the direction of Nuremburg; and at night we had the advantage of the blaze of our own magazines at Hof, to light us on our way home to the grand head-quarters.

" We there received the news, that if the general did not fight within the next twelve hours, the army must run away; for on the spot where we were there was not provision enough for a sparrow. Our prince naturally longed for a battle. He was as brave as a cannon-ball, and with as much brains. He had distinguished himself from boyhood in the true Prussian style: first he was a *roué,* then he was a Voltairist, and then he was a republican. The whole meaning of this is, that he was nothing. We called him the Prussian Orleans. But he certainly had spirit in the field, as his division soon found to their cost. He was now put in command of the advanced guard of the corps of Hohenlohe, and his business was to keep the French hussars from passing the Saale. We marched accordingly, and waited by the river's side,

eating grass, and raw turnips, when we could get
them, for two days; while the French were pillaging
Coburg, and the whole range of little towns, before
our faces, and feasting like emperors.

"On the memorable morning of the 10th of
October, as the fog cleared off, we saw them coming, brigade by brigade, up the plateau in front
of our position. Half a dozen regiments of their
hussars advanced to *feel* us, while we were at our
morning's meal of turnip-tops. A few shots from
our battery at the bridge of Saalfeld, sent them to
the right about; and the prince, in the glory of
the moment, ordered us to follow and cut them
into a thousand pieces. Away we went. But
the Frenchmen had been feeding better than we;
and all soldiers know that the main-spring of victory is in the stomach. They made head against
us, and after making a few prisoners, we wheeled
about to take up our old ground; but we had now
other matters to think of, for as we came out of
the forest, we saw the road between us and the
bridge completely blocked up by a column of
cuirassiers. We might as well have attempted to
force a wall of iron. We tried it, however, and

were soon brought to a stand. Escape was the next object; but wherever we turned, we found another evil-looking column of cuirassiers or lancers. In short, the whole cavalry of the division of Lannes was upon us. The result may be easily imagined : we were broken into fragments. Their light artillery came up, and the affair was decided. The enemy were fifty to one ; and every man who still had a horse was off at full speed. This was our last sight of the prince. After riding up to my regiment, and ordering us to make the best of our way ' back to Hohenlohe,' he galloped off; and we heard afterwards, that in attempting to make his way over some ploughed ground, his horse stuck fast, he was overtaken by a party of the enemy's dragoons, to whom he refused to surrender, and by one of them was brutally shot.

" All that happened thenceforth was the mere common story of a broken army ; a scattered mob, where every man shifted for himself. In the course of the night I gathered some of my regiment, a league or two from Saalfeld, and, after following the French example of plundering, which however, was actually necessary for our existence,

we attempted to reach the grand army at Auer-
stadt: but the French were there and every where;
and finding all the roads blocked up, we turned
sulkily enough towards Magdeburg.

" Here we had news indeed ! We were scarcely
inside the gates, when the tidings came that the
king had been seen on the road to Berlin, and that
the army was totally dispersed.   It was clear that
the day of Prussia was over, at least for this time.
Magdeburg was a place of horrible confusion, full
of wounded, starving, and dying: then, hour after
hour, we were crowded with aides-de-camp, engineers, generals, and the whole flying staff of the
army, riding in as if the French dragoons were at
their heels, cursing each other, and the duke, and
the French, and the weather, and their ill-luck,
and ready to cut their own throats, and every one's
else.

" The absurdity of the plan of campaign had
been such, that there was actually no point of retreat
marked out in case of a check; and thus the wreck
of an army of 150,000 men all ran back upon
Magdeburg.   True, the city was strong enough to
keep out the French for a year; but the old fatality

was there again: it had not provisions for a week. As if our councils had been divided between Momus and Mammon, a spirit of economy had come upon us just when we were going to throw away millions in an unnecessary war: Magdeburg, the strongest place in all Prussia, the citadel, in fact, of the kingdom, to save a few thousand rix dollars, had been stripped of its magazines. Every thing had been sent to the field, and every sack of grain there was in the enemy's hands. Never was any national misfortune at once so ludicrous and so complete. The garrison, of 10,000 men, were half starved already; and when Hohenlohe, with the Prussian guards, and a multitude of remnants of corps, to the amount of, at least, 30,000 men, came rushing in upon us; in twelve hours more we must have eaten each other. If a French patrole had appeared that night, we must have surrendered, without giving his Highness of Berg's lancers any further trouble.

" I was lying at midnight on some straw in a bastion, and thankful for my straw, even on the pavement; when I received an order to attend Hohenlohe, who had just come in wounded, look-

ing tired to death, and surrounded by a staff that
had suffered terribly. The rooms in the governor's house, through which I passed, were filled
with wounded officers crying out for the surgeons.
The sight was horrible; they covered the stairs
and every spot where a man could be laid; but
there was no time to think of those things. The
patrols came in thick, with reports of the advance
of the French, of which indeed we could see sufficient proofs in the fires that began to start up on
every rising ground for leagues. All the fugitives
were now to be cleared out of the city; and with a
hundred and fifty hussars, the *débris* of my corps,
I was turned loose, to find what quarters I could
on the glacis, in a night as black as the bottom of
the Elbe, with the rain coming down in torrents,
and the wind rooting up the trees of the esplanade.

" My men grumbled a little at the turning out;
yet a hussar is seldom better off than when he gets
out of the way of walls and generals. I promised
them luck in the exchange, and offered my last half
dozen dollars to the first man who should find us
quarters.—In half an hour I was sitting at a roaring fire, in a palace, with my officers round me, at

a sumptuous supper, with every man of my troop bottle in hand, and our horses up to the neck in hay and corn.

"We had got into his excellency the governor's villa, where he had intended to entertain the king on his return from 'annihilating the French.' But as matters were now altered, and the French would have had the feast if we had not, we had nothing to do but keep our own secret, and sit down without scruple to his majesty's supper.

"There, for two glorious days, we fed on the fatness of the land, and drank champagne and johannisberg like contractors. But this life was too good to last. One of our fellows got drunk, and revealed the secret to a straggler from the town; he let it loose to a woman, and she, of course, let it loose to all the world. A furious order was instantly dispatched from the governor, threatening to hang us all up, and so forth, for 'robbing his cellar.' But this was no time for hanging hussars; we laughed at the threat, dismissed the orderly who brought it, with good cheer enough to disqualify him from bringing any more messages for the day; and it was not till the fourth day

of our carouse, that, hearing the French guns opening on the gates of Magdeburg, we got into the
saddle, and coolly loading a couple of waggons with
his excellency's chambertin, and other trifles which
might be useful in the campaign, we moved off at
two in the morning, in the quietest style of hussars; which, it must be acknowledged, is not much
unlike the quietest style of thieves.

"The world was now before us; and as we had
heard that Hohenlohe was making some attempt
to gather the army again, we rode in search of him.
On our way we had another brush with the French
dragoons, a regiment of Murat's division, who, like
us, were looking for Hohenlohe; and at whom we
rode like furies, and scattered them through the
fields in a moment. The governor's feeding had
done this: the French were now eating the turnip-
tops. In war, every thing depends upon the
stomach.

"Towards evening we fell in with Hohenlohe.
Heavens, what a sight! what an army! What had
become of the superb troops that, but half a dozen
days before, seemed fit to march over Europe?
Where were the guards; the fine regiments of the

line; the incomparable cavalry; the tiger hussars, and a hundred others! I saw nothing before me but a mob of beggars: brave still, and, to do them justice, longing to have vengeance on the enemy; but starving: all rags, famine, squalidness, and rage. I grew ashamed of our late feasting, while those noble fellows actually had not a morsel of bread to put into their lips. His excellency's chambertin flew among them, and it could not have done more good if it had been swallowed by a general congress.

"The army, if that could be called one which was made up of fragments, and mere fragments, from every corps, was in march for the Oder. But the French were upon our heels, and I well knew the consequences of a pursuit: our 40,000 men had neither guns, nor ammunition, nor bread; it could not hold together for twenty-four hours; and this too, with 20,000 French cavalry thundering upon our rear.

"But we had abundance of recrimination; and if scorn upon every thing that bore the name of minister or general, could have helped us along, we might have defied Murat and his 20,000 dragoons to overtake us till doomsday.

" There were a hundred versions of the story of the battle, agreeing in nothing but that the whole was like a work of magic or infatuation. In the first place, the French were allowed to choose their ground, and to seize, out of the three passes of the hills in front of our position, notoriously the most important one; one which, before nightfall, cost us eleven different attacks, and the whole eleven, failures. In the next place, one half of the army knew nothing of what the other half was about. But, while all was confusion among us, the French were under arms from before daylight, with all their attacks arranged at the first dawn. The Prussian left was suddenly attacked by Davoust, and paralyzed for the day; here 40,000 of as fine troops as any in the world, were thrown away upon the rocks and bushes of defiles, which a half battery of field guns, and a little common foresight, would have made impregnable against ten Davousts. The centre was then attacked by Soult, with the French centre, and all the reserves : there we fought with some reputation, and the enemy had hard work of it; but there we had our ill-luck still; the position was badly chosen for cavalry, in which was our strength; they sat in columns in the rear, and had scarcely an opportunity of drawing a sabre during the day. The French guns, too, were more numerous than ours, and better served; their batteries moved at the head of the columns, and their fire was ruinous. The Prussian guards still fought desperately, but as the enemy's artillery advanced, pouring in showers of grape, they lost so many men, that to hold their ground was impossible. At this critical moment the reserves were not to be seen; the men stood only to be mowed down; and there seemed no hope but that of retreat, under protection of the rear-guard, commanded by Saxe-Weimar. But even this was speedily settled, by the appearance of the whole French cavalry of the centre, emerging from the flank of the wood, on which Soult had till now *appuied*. Their charge decided the day. The Prussian centre, of nearly 80,000 men, was broken, and all the rest were put to flight. An hour after this crash, the right wing came up, for what conceivable purpose can be known only to its general; but with the natural effect of being instantly charged, and sent to follow the centre. Then we had the rear-guard to retire

upon; and the heads of battalions went rambling
in all directions to find his highness' troops; but,
the pen almost drops from my fingers as I write it,
the rear-guard had not moved an inch from the
spot where it was drawn up the day before; and
that spot was exactly thirty miles from the field of
battle. Never was there any thing like it. How is
all this to be accounted for, but on the principle
that preternatural blindness sometimes falls upon
a people, or that some mocking spirit is allowed,
now and then, to play tricks with our wise men?
But the result was indescribable. Prussia was
ruined. The losses of the army were not to be
ascertained; all that we knew was that the kingdom had now neither general, nor soldier, nor
fortress, nor government; neither man, money,
nor king. We had lost, on the lowest computa-
tion, from 50,000 to 60,000 men in the field;
nearly all our generals, artillery, staff, were killed,
wounded, or prisoners. Never was there so complete a dislocation of a country; it was a breaking
down into the dust, or up into the clouds—a chaos.

" Now began the harassing part of the business.
The enemy, having nothing more to fear in the

field, hunted us like hares; wherever we turned, we were sure to find a French column on the road behind or before us. We sometimes made them repent their vivacity; but success was of no use; we had not strength to follow them a league. Every day was thus spent in fighting, and running on; and every night in freezing in the open air, or plundering, to keep soul and body together.

" Our march was now a race for Prenzlau, where some depôts of bread and beer had been laid up. The weather had become dreadful: perpetual storms, the country a morass, with all the rivulets turned into torrents; but the enemy were before us again; and after cutting our way, in the fury of hunger, through a division of Lasalle's dragoons, and topping the position above Prenzlau, we had the mortification to see Murat's whole cavalry drawn up below, our march completely brought to a stop, and the town in the hands of half a dozen battalions of the imperial guard. Hohenlohe himself came up about mid-day, and, though the attempt was desperate, he ordered the enemy to be dislodged. By a movement on Murat's flank, we contrived to alarm him sufficiently to get him out

13

of the way into a plain on the left, where he continued manœuvring his horse, until our battalions forced the town.

" But this bold attempt finished the prince's campaign. In the town we found nothing. The French returned in overwhelming force; and the 28th of October saw him, after gallantly sustaining a variety of attacks, and with the hourly sight of columns coming up from the grand army, surrender at the head of 20,000 men: just half the number with which he had set out from Magdeburg.

" There ended the war of Prussia: the rest was the mere struggle of a few brave hearts, to keep up the honour of the Prussian name, and, if they must fall, fall like gentlemen. But all was over; Prussia was a province in the hands of Napoleon. As for my own share of the transaction, I was furious, but tired to death; resistance was so utterly hopeless, and I was so sick of the campaign, that I was by no means sorry to find that I had some chance, at last, of lying on a bed, and getting something to eat: and homely as such considerations may be, let me tell those who have never slept for a fortnight together in a German ditch in the month of October, nor fasted for forty-eight hours at a time, that they are natural.

"I was *not* a prisoner. Easily foreseeing the result of affairs at Prenzlau, I had made my way out of the gates on one side, as the French négociators came in on the other; dismissed my brave fellows on the glacis, recommending to them to make their way home as fast as they could, received a parting cheer, and saw them gallop off to all points of the compass.

"I was now alone, like Adam before he had found his Eve, or like Robinson Crusoe, left to his own contrivances. I turned my horse's head towards the north, as the least molested by the enemy's patrols; buried my sword in its sheath, was roused from my meditation by the sound of the cannon, which announced the hoisting of the French colours over the last quarters of the last army of Prussia, saw the cursed tri-colour flaunting and dancing in the sun, as gaily as if it had been inhabited by the spirit of a Frenchman; and, with a feeling more melancholy than I now wish to recall, went my solitary way."

CHAPTER XI.

―――

THE BATTLE OF LUTZEN.

MAY 7th. Intelligence *has* arrived at last. The first blow of the war has been struck, and the Berlin papers announce a complete victory on the part of the allies. The city is in great exultation, and with some reason, on its own account; if the reports be true, that an army is to be detached from the field to clear the Hanoverian side of the Elbe. We are all prodigiously anxious to send Davoust back to France after his master.

The evening has brought further news. Napoleon was, for the first time, *not* the attacking party, though his force was computed at 130,000 men. His loss is at least 10,000 in killed and wounded: the allies are even said to have out-manœuvred him,—to have thrown themselves across the line of his march, and *forced* him to fight. The battle was at Lutzen, and nearly on the ground where Gustavus fought his last famous battle. There are great rejoicings in Berlin; for the young Prussian volunteers fought like lions, charged the French repeatedly with the bayonet, and always drove them off the ground. The allied loss is comparatively slight; they remained on the ground, and at the close of the action celebrated their victory by a general *feu de joie*. Another exploit like this, and the world will be at rest again. We are all now looking for the opening of the road to Paris, if not for the sacking of that showy capital!

———

The war engrosses every one; and even if we were less anxious to know how soon the houses may be set on fire over our heads, or we may have the burning of the enemy's tents and waggons at Harburg—either of which events may happen in the course of the next twenty-four hours—there is nothing here to attract the lover of quieter topics: literature, the drama, and the concert, are equally

fled.   France boasts of patronizing the whole conclave of the Muses and Graces, but all the Muses
that she suffered to exist here, were the Moniteur
and the Bulletin, and all her Graces were the pupils
of the drill-serjeant.   The city possessed some distinguished *litterateurs* previously to her seizure ;
but, let the world smile as it will at the subser-
viency of literature, she is not by nature a slave ;
and while many a louder champion of rights and
privileges was content to eat the bitter bread of
French menialism here, the men of literature
withdrew to spots where they were at least out of
the clanking of the chain.   *Soirées*, and those con-
versational meetings, which make the stranger
" free of the commonwealth," are at an end ;
and there is no possible intercourse with the more
intelligent ranks, except what may be found in an
occasional dinner, at a club, or a coffee-house.

Under such circumstances the Englishman's
habits are of use to him ; for, be it known, that
the Englishman is the only inhabitant of Europe,
who, between the hours of dinner and sleep, *can*
stay at home.   Be the weather wild as Boreas and
Eurus together ever made it, the sun-loving Italian

steals to his casino; the Frenchman rushes out into the whirlwind, to yawn for three hours in the same coterie where he has duly yawned every night for the last fifty years; the Dutchman finds a moral impossibility of smoking his pipe at home, and goes to enjoy it in the Harmonie; the Spaniard's lemonade is tasteless unless he can sip it in the accustomed Caffeteria; and the German's *schnapps* and newspaper cannot go down, except in the Guinguette atmosphere of brandy, lamp-oil, and the most pestilent tobacco fumes that ever nauseated the lungs of man.

This anti-home propensity accounts for half the phœnomena of foreign life; for the rarity of affection where it ought to be, and the universality of attachment where it ought not;—for the wretched profligacy of private life, and, as a consequence, for a good deal of the very scandalous corruption of public; for the crowding of the theatres, the prosperity of the gaming-tables, and the general propensity to suicide.

The Englishman, on the contrary, *can* sit at home, and bear to look at his wife and children, without grudging the moments given to either, as

so much lost to sentiment, and the billiard-balls.
Yet his domesticity is severely tried in a huge old
German town; with society cut up root and branch;
with nothing in the newspapers but eternal soldiership; and nothing on his table but Gesner, sillier
than his own sheep; or, *Die Edelfrau von Bosenstein*,
five endless acts of the blackest letter and spirit,
and leaving the indefatigable head that could toil
through it, nothing to dread in Arabic or Sanscrit.

Yet Germany is the land of tragedy; and now
the only land. The attempt to naturalize her legends
in England failed, after a few years of desperate industry. Monk Lewis, and his followers, rode their
Pegasus to death; but the breed, as rough, hardy,
and prolific as its own black-forest ponies, is still
a hereditary product of Germany. What historian
shall impeach the veracity, for instance, of the " Life
and death of the Margraff of Klagenfurth; his having
won the most celebrated of Saxon beauties; his
being assassinated in the church at the moment of
bridal; and the horrible fate of his brother, the
Count, by whose jealousy he fell; and whose spirit
appears once a twelvemonth on the Elbe, for the
purpose of being carried off again," &c. &c.

The Night of Klagenfurth.

HERE were hundreds yesternight,
Maiden smiles, and glances bright,
Sounds of infants at their play,—
All was laugh, and love, and May.
Now I hear my lonely tread,
As o'er chambers of the dead.

Yet, on yonder turrets old,
Klagenfurth, thine ancient hold,
Gilding all their time-worn seams,
Shoots the sun as lovely gleams;
Sheds the rose as soft a balm,
Flows the dimpled stream as calm;

And the mountain melts from view
Into skies as holy blue;
And with living emerald,
Is the mead as richly palled;
And the valley of the vine
Smiles as sweet in day's decline.

'Tis the night, the dreaded night,
Signal of the peasant's flight;
Sin and terror of the·year!
When upon a bloody bier,

By a brother's desperate hand,
Lay the chieftain of the land!

Hark! a fearful minstrelsy!
Swells it from the earth or sky?
Like the sounds of troubled sleep,
Joy might at its anguish weep;
Yet, as rolls its wondrous flow,
Mirth might mingle with its woe.

Where are gone the breezes, springing
As if flowers the air were winging,
Where the sounds that lulled the soul?
In their stead the thunders roll.
Bursts the river, chill and strong,
Raves the sudden gale along.

Day is plunged in sudden night;
Every star has lost its light;
Like the ocean on the shore,
Heaves the wood's mysterious roar,
Things unholy seem to ride
O'er the torrent wild and wide.

But, the scene has found a change!
All is calm, yet all is strange,
Sounds, so melancholy sweet,
That the heart forgets to beat.

Sights, that check the living breath,
Shapes of beauty, anguish, death!

Elbe, upon thy waters glance
Flashes of the helm and lance;
Elbe, thy crested waves between
Forms in silk and gems are seen.
Foremost, loveliest, side by side,
Walk a chieftain and his bride.

Elbe, upon thy glossy breast
Seems a mighty pile to rest;
Rich with sculptures old and quaint,
Gilded martyr, marble saint;
While beneath its arches dim
Come the chaunt of harp and hymn;

And the blushing bride is crown'd,—
And the tie of ties is bound!
Ha! a shriek, a flash of steel;
See the gallant chieftain reel;
Hark! the wild soul-piercing cry
Lips can give but once—and die.

Bleeding, breathless, side by side,
Sink the bridegroom and the bride!
But a gleam above them plays—
Now it reddens to a blaze,

Now, a pyramid of flame,
Glows the temple's mighty frame.

Chief and pile are blood and ashes ;
But above the sinking flashes,
Leaning on his sabre bare,
Stands a figure of despair.
He who fir'd that holy hall,
Now he has his vengeance—all !

What beholds the homicide ?
Dust that once was beauty's pride ;
Who's the gore, a brother's gore ?
Fearful was the oath he swore,
That before the sun was down.
His should be land, bride, and crown.

Murderer, thou hast now thy prize ;
But what visions round thee rise !
Shapes of sorrow, wild and dim,
Hollow eye and wasted limb :
Things on fiery pinions borne,
Round thee sweep the dance forlorn.

" Come, to die, yet never die,"
Rings their voice of agony :
" Shedder of a brother's blood,
Come, to be our serpents' food,

Come, and by our scorpions torn,
Curse the hour that thou wast born."

" Yet," they cry, " thy soul to smite,
Ever on this evil night,
Yearly shalt thou come, to gaze
On the pomp, the blood, the blaze."
All is gone! that parting ban
Never rose from mortal man!

CHAPTER XII.

———

PRUSSIA.

ALL is trouble again. The course of politics seems, like the " course of true love," destined never to run smooth. The Danes are coming to *protect* us; an ominous sound, which has put us all in commotion. The tale of the day is, that the Swedes and Danes, hitherto as amicable as two bears in fear of the same hunter, and making common cause not to be eaten, are about to quarrel for Norway. And this French trick has so far succeeded with the two fools, that the envoys on both sides have demanded their passports; and so the snows of Sweden and the green of the Baltic are to be incarnadined for a spot of earth, of which neither can make a sixpence; a wilderness of rock and fen, on which a rational Indian would scarcely build a wigwam, and whose national luxuries are saw-dust and fish-bones.

But the most intolerable part of the transaction is, that those Scandinavians will not be content to grind each other into their kindred sand, but Hamburg must be torn to pieces between them. Its name has certainly entered into the negociation, though, whether Sweden has insisted on laying its claw upon us, or Denmark has determined, in right of proximity, to be the first plunderer, are matters that still lie in the profound of the cabinet bosom. One thing is certain, that regiments are moving through Holstein, and the garrison of Altona is replenishing without beat of drum. The " delirant reges, plectuntur Achivi," has been true from the days of Troy, and many an age before ; and the squabbles of a Goth and a Vandal for a morass, are now to involve the for tunes of a great European city in utter ruin. For, let them clip the wings of commerce as they will, she still retains enough of them to fly away; and a year of either sovereignty would see Hamburg a barrack or a poor-house. The citizens would go off with their goods and chattels to some other corner of the

river, or of the world; build the republic of Cuxhaven, or of some equally obscure quicksand; dry
up the commercial glories of the usurper, and
leave him bankruptcy for his prize.

Prussia is all exultation.   The battle is acknowledged to have been " a drawn one," merely the
first trial of the *national* war ; but it has given such
unequivocal proof of the gallantry of the Prussian
levies, that the country feels all the sensations of
victory.   She has redeemed her pledge ; she has
thrown the weight of shame off her heart, and she
now stands upright again ; and if human feelings
are good for any thing, she will yet see the French
to the Rhine, and perhaps beyond the Rhine.

The French have to thank themselves for this
passion of hostility.   In other countries their conduct was comparatively mild.   War, at the best of
times, must be a horror.   But the continent is prepared to see its plunderings ; there must be requisitions and robberies ; requisitions for the
soldiery, and robberies for their masters.   But
in Prussia, the national suffering was envenomed

13

by personal insolence. Napoleon, though of captains the greatest, here showed nothing of the great captain's generosity. He was bitter and malignant, and took a personal pleasure in trampling on a fallen enemy. His troops, of course, imitated their hero. Germany abounds with the most revolting statements of the insults which the highest and lowest Prussian families alike underwent from the French free-quarters. The French military once carried the manners of their nation into the field, and certainly no military had ever added more to the grace and courtesy of the code of war. But the republic changed all this; crowds of their officers have risen from the ranks; all republicanism is rough, and even affects roughness; the natural violences of war might have kept up the republican habit even under the monarchy; but Napoleon's native bitterness sustained and envenomed it by licence of all kinds.

The French requisitions were intolerable. Poor as the country was, and worn out by war, they extracted from her the enormous sum of four millions sterling. It may be conceived what the private extortion must amount to, with 100,000

Frenchmen let loose through the land for four years. With what delight every eye in Prussia must have followed the misfortunes of the Moscow retreat, and read the memorable official list in which Alexander announced that he had captured the whole surviving army, its "41 generals, 1,298 officers, and 167,510 soldiers, with 1,131 pieces of cannon." This was the work of six weeks, down to the 26th of December, 1812. A more astounding list has just appeared; the number of the dead found on the thawing of the snow, amounts to 300,000! Europe has never yet seen destruction on so colossal a scale, nor so visibly marked by infatuation and frenzy on earth, and the fury of the elements, as the vengeance of a Superior Hand.

From the hour of the retreat the French felt the ground shaking under their feet in Prussia. It became notorious that the people were preparing arms, holding meetings by night, and from time to time making seizures of the requisition cattle and stores. All those symptoms increased with the approach of the Russians. Large bodies of the people were now known to be exercising on the heaths. The sound of horns, and signals by musketry, were heard through the whole winter's night. The French had many a weary march after those gallant insurgents, but they were generally either eluded or beaten; until the service became too harassing for their diminished numbers. The land was now teeming with insurrection. Fires were seen on the hills; horsemen were heard flying through the dusk, none knew where; the French proclamations were torn down, and Prussian proclamations put up by invisible hands, even in the enemy's garrisons. Letters denouncing speedy vengeance were poured in heaps upon the French authorities. Prussia rang with national songs; the national spirit was raised from the grave; and, for the honour of human nature, we may rejoice that such a spirit was never raised to be waved down again by the sword of an usurper.

Then came a succession of thunderclaps. D'Yorck marched over to the Russians with 15,000 men! Schwartzenburg drew off his 40,000 into Galicia! In January, the king suddenly broke away from Potzdam, and appeared in his Silesian capital! On the 17th of March he issued his celebrated proclamation, declaring the necessity of resisting France to the last man, and pronouncing that upon this effort depended the existence of Prussia as a people!

" We bent," said this manly and feeling paper, " under the superior power of France. But peace, which deprived me of half my subjects, brought no blessings. It was more injurious even than war."

Of all the pictures of society, the most noble and the most instructive, is that of a nation rising against the tyranny of an invader. The voice of the king was instantly echoed by every bosom in the land. The distinctions of ranks, the ordinary occupations of life, professional habits, personal feelings, were all forgotten, or all merged into one great current of patriotism, all fused into the one fiery stream of vengeance, now swelling round the enemy.

The tale of those times will pass away like others, but it well deserves to be remembered; even for its evidence that there is no public calamity beyond the reach of national courage, and that there is no nation which cannot right itself in a just cause. It must not be forgotten, too, in honour of a sex whom all are bound to honour, that the women of Prussia shared all the patriotism of their brothers and husbands. They contributed largely to the equipment of the troops, and even brought their jewels and plate, and laid them at the foot of the throne. In return, they were delighted to receive the little rings and patriotic emblems supplied by the Prussian iron manufactories. To every woman who brought a contribution, was given one of those emblems, which will be long treasured as memorials of the heroic time of Prussia. History furnishes no instance of a nobler traffic, and the Prussian women may long exult in the illustrious improvidence which exchanged gold for iron.

There was but one blow more to be struck, for the liberation of the country. Beauharnois still had his head-quarters in Berlin. The French, exhausted by the campaign, or, like Napoleon, infatuated, seemed to have forgotten that there was an enemy in the field. Wittgenstein now threw out a body of cavalry to seize the slumbering viceroy; and nothing was ever nearer being successful. The news of Wittgenstein's movements had evidently reached the people, and the French might have seen, in the ill-concealed joy every where round them, that they were in danger. But the viceroy was immoveable, until his videttes came galloping in with the tidings that the Cossacks were in sight in all directions. There was, of course, not a moment now to be lost. The French garrison would have been prisoners in twelve hours more. They fled at midnight, on the 3rd of march, and the Russian patroles were in triumph at the gates next morning. Thus proudly closed the greatest campaign within the memory of man; that campaign which, as Kutusoff said, had " only *begun* at Moscow." Thus proudly, too, closed Kutusoff's career. Excepting our own great Nelson, no chieftain ever died a death more congenial to the wishes of a fortunate warrior. His last hours came in the fulness of renown. Kutusoff died at the close of a march of perpetual victory, from Moscow to the Elbe. The national grief for him was universal; and the emperor Alexander is said, with a superb and oriental acknowledgment of his services, to have displaced the largest diamond from the front of his crown, and fixed in its stead the name of Kutusoff, as the nobler jewel.

If there be an enthusiast in war, this is the time

for him. Europe has never seen such hostilities since the invasion of Attila. The allied line at this hour stretches from Dantzig to Dresden, and along the whole of this immense cordon there is war; plains are laid waste, towns burned, and human blood is poured out like water. The Russian batteries are roaring along the Vistula, at the same moment while they are roaring along the Elbe to cover the passage of their cavalry at Schandau. On the other hand, Napoleon has roused France, at all times swarming with soldiership, and shaking off the results of defeat with more rapidity than any other power of the continent. He has already raised twelve divisions, amounting to 350,000 men. A gigantic force, yet what is this to a man who actually commands, as unlimited master, 40,000,000 of Frenchmen; and as ally, mediator, or protector—all which titles but mask the king—40,000,000 more?

Nothing can be more uninteresting than the manœuvres of two hundred thousand men. The adventures of a squadron of horse, or a company of sharpshooters, would be worth all the histories of campaigns, from Blenheim downwards. But the features and fragments of battle may still be striking. One feature of the late conflict was the valour of the young Prussians, which is said to have been absolutely irrestrainable ; they charged batteries in *front*, and tore their way through every thing.   In one quarter, where they had suddenly burst in on the French, they left, within a small space, 3000 of the enemy's bodies on the ground.   The French lines were every where loaded with dead.   They were chiefly conscripts, *cochons à lait*, as the veterans called them; and when it came to the bayonet, they could not stand the strong limbs of the Prussian peasantry.

One of the charges of a column of Prussian grenadiers had nearly caught the great prize of the war.   As they came on, rushing through the heaviest fire of artillery, they reached almost the spot where Napoleon was surveying the battle.   A few hundred yards onward, and they must have taken him.

For the first time, the battle was fought *in spite* of Napoleon.   His plan of campaign was to commence at Leipsic, to which all the army-corps were on their way.   He was already mounted, and had turned his horse's head to the Leipsic road, when

he heard the first sound of the guns. He looked
much surprised, and inquired the cause; the staff
and people about him knew nothing on the subject.
He immediately sent them galloping in all directions for intelligence, and in the mean time got off
his horse, and walked about the road side in evident anxiety. A report was at length made from
Ney. " He had been attacked on his march, had
been pushed back, and was retiring to the main
body." Napoleon then mounted again, to reconnoitre, and went forward; ordering the army to
halt, and the corps in advance to return.

The firing soon became heavy; but the difficulty
was to discover where the principal attack was
made. The ground in front was a plain, but broken
and marshy, to a great extent, dotted with clumps
of trees, and with an irregular line or crescent
of small villages, and farm houses, stretching
across it. The French were drawn up, with their
rear resting on this crescent. At length the fire of
the Prussian guns, and the advance of their columns
of grenadiers, showed where they intended to break
through. Napoleon, who had again dismounted,
waiting for the reports of the staff, now threw himself

upon his horse, and galloped off in the direction of the fire. This was a period of great confusion in the French lines. They were composed chiefly of troops which had never been in fire before, and though they were brave enough, their want of discipline had made manœuvring nearly impossible. And when they were suddenly ordered to countermarch, as the Prussian fire seemed to be moving round to their rear, Napoleon was often in more danger from their balls than from the enemy's.

He exposed himself much during the day; some supposed from a wish to give determination to the troops in the first battle of the campaign; others from a feeling that his fortunes trembled on the event. He rode from battery to battery, and finally took his stand immediately in rear of the key of the position. The fire on this point was occasionally hot, and some people were struck by cannon shot near him. There was great alarm for his safety, among his staff; but nothing could induce him to move. It is not unlikely that the true reasons of this rashness were the sneers of Paris. " O Athenians," exclaimed the Macedonian in the height of his campaigns, " what trouble it costs me to be talked of by you." All heroes are alike, since the beginning of the world. Nimrod would, doubtless, not have been half the mighty hunter that he was, if there had been no makers of epigrams in Nineveh. And Napoleon this day ran the imminent hazard of being shot, that he might not be transfixed by the sting of a Parisian paragraph. The Moscow Hegira hung heavier upon his soul than he would willingly confess; and there can be no question that in this battle he exposed himself like one determined to wipe away all chance of ridicule.

Yet how absurd was it to charge a man with personal timidity, whose life had been for ten years the nucleus of the most furious of all wars; whose atmosphere had been cannon smoke, and whose rations cannon balls; who had feasted it by the week with Mars, and fandangoed it with Bellona; the *desperado* of Lodi, Marengo, and a hundred other pitfalls of the gallant nuisances of mankind. His Moscow flight was nothing: he was mad to go to Moscow, but he would have been " Midsummer mad," to stay a moment longer with the army than till he could contrive to leave it. An emperor is *not* a commandant. He had another army to

manage, a thousand miles off; more unmanageable
than all his legions, and more perilous than Kutuzoff, and his Cossacks : the unwashed and unshorn
Messieurs of the Marais, the Sansculotte warriors
of the Sections. Malets' conspiracy, too, which
had nearly extinguished his crown in a campaign
of half an hour, told him, in a style not to be misunderstood, that the true hazards of his sovereignty
lay within the circuit of the Louvre ; and, as the
statesman and the emperor, he pushed forward to face
the danger, which must have crushed him if he had
staid to play the soldier and the schoolboy. As a
tyrant he deserves all our abhorrence, and we may
well rejoice at the grape or shell which shall turn
himself and his fame into a memory. But it is no
keen encounter of the wit that can turn him into
a poltroon.

————

MAY 8th. Our conceptions of the battle are
becoming clearer. It seems to have had some
resemblance to the manœuvres of Trafalgar. The
French received the attack, resting on their line of
batteries and villages. The Prussians made the

attack in columns perpendicular to the enemy's line. There was but little *tactique* on either side, but a vast deal of furious fighting. The Prussians suffered dreadfully in their advance on the villages, from their exposure to the enemy's guns, and from their utter disdain of cover. The French, who had taken up their ground with their usual skill, suffered comparatively little for some hours. But, towards five in the afternoon, the heads of the Prussian columns got within the villages, and then the carnage of the enemy was dreadful. The whole struggle of the day was now for the villages; and some of them were taken half a dozen times at the point of the bayonet; the weight of the French guns in position in their rear rendering them generally untenable when they were stormed; or setting them in a blaze; the Prussians then retiring, until the enemy advanced beyond the villages again, when they were again stormed.

In this hideous game, evening drew on. It is the acknowledgment of the prisoners, that Napoleon's anxiety now became so great as to be remarked by every one round him; he was restless, fretful, and continually calling for fresh reports. But still

nothing could persuade him to quit his ground.
There he remained, sometimes on foot, sometimes
mounted, at the head of the old guard, constantly
sweeping the horizon with his telescope. Towards
night, the aspect of the field is described as having
been one of terrible magnificence, if men can think
of *spectacle* in such things. As far as the eye
could see, all was fire and fighting: 120,000
French, and 70,000 Germans and Russians, were,
every man, in full action; every marsh, copse, and
farm-yard, was a sheet of fire; the ground, for
miles, was covered with fugitives and wounded. The
troops on both sides fought in a whirlwind of flame,
for by this time the whole line of villages was in
a state of conflagration. On the French side a great
many officers had already fallen, and among them
Marshal Bessieres, who had been struck by a round
shot, and almost cut in two. In this emergency,
it was supposed that Napoleon was meditating a
retreat; but he was too sagacious not to feel that
a retreat, with all Germany in his rear, would
have been the signal for general insurrection, and
his ruin. He now made one desperate effort; but
it saved his army. Collecting all the guns that

were in a state to move, into one immense brigade, he ordered them to advance, cost what it might, upon the Prussian centre. It was now past seven. The heads of the Prussian columns, exhausted by so many hours' marching and fighting, in one of the hottest, too, of German summer days; were brought to a stand by this storm of fire. They were checked; but no more. The enemy could not penetrate them. They remained at the point which they had reached, and night soon falling thick, the battle closed.

Still the Prussians were not satisfied with what they had done; and after the firing had ceased on both sides for upwards of an hour, and all seemed quiet for the night; some regiments of Prussian cavalry made a rush on the enemy's lines, rode over every thing, and had nearly reached the centre of the camp, in search of Napoleon; but the whole army being immediately on the alert, and their prize evidently not attainable for that time, they turned round and galloped back, with scarcely the loss of a man.

———

Still, nothing but the battle. The allies have

taken ten guns, which they are sending off as
trophies to the Arsenal at Berlin. They boast
that the enemy have taken nothing, not even a
camp colour, nor a grenadier's cap, and that they
have already moved back some marches: great
gallantry is acknowledged to have been exhibited
on both sides. The French conscripts, though
they were mowed down like corn, continued shouting *Vive l'Empereur!* under the hottest fire.
Napoleon, on joining the army, had been heard to
say, that " He would make this campaign, not as
an emperor, but as a general," and he has kept his
word. He might have added, " As a captain of
grenadiers." But whatever may be the truth of all
those particulars, the result has immensely exalted
the good humour of the good city of Hamburg. We
are gratified, as beleaguered warriors, in the hope
of seeing our beleaguerers put to the rout without
any further trouble on our side; and as " good
Germans," we hail the good omen. The victory
would be worth something, were it gained in the
most nameless swamp from the Moskwa to the
Rhine; but Lutzen and victory! a battle fought
and won at Lutzen; on the spot where, but two

centuries ago, the great protestant Liberator broke the chains of Germany on the head of her tyrant! Lutzen! where the blood of Gustavus consecrates the ground for ever to the vindication of civil and religious liberty!—if there be virtue in the memory of mighty men and things, the battle now fought at Lutzen, for the freedom of Germany and Europe, will yet bear its fruits in the regeneration of the land.

CHAPTER XIII.

THE LITTERATEUR.

It is impossible to refuse the Germans all the praise due to good-nature, kindness of manner to strangers, and especially to general intelligence. Every one reads, almost every one writes, and altogether there is more of the active power of education visible in general society, than, perhaps, in any other country of the world. But they have two *désagrémens*, for nothing but the word can express the thing, too slight to be called vice, and too vexatious to be entitled to tolerance ; which very considerably undo the spell of German society ; and those are—smoking, and stocking knitting.

A few mornings since, I visited a man of letters. I found him in his study, entrenched up to the chin in books and papers, and surrounded with all the

printed wisdom of his country, in bindings that had
evidently known a good deal of the· " midnight
lamp."   The *nocturnâ versate manu, versate
diurnâ,* was in every thing.   In short, all was as
it ought to be in the *sacellum* of literature.   The
master of the shrine was a very intelligent person,
I believe a very learned, and certainly a very industrious one; for in a list of his daily pursuits,
which he showed to me, there was scarcely an hour
out of the twenty-four, which had not its appro-
priate study.   But the genius of tobacco-smoke
was there, writing his death-warrant, as legibly as
my learned friend ever wrote a line of high Dutch.
His pipe was in his hand; his goblet of *eau sucrè,*
its never-failing, and almost equally sickening,
companion, was beside him; and with a lack-lustre
eye, and a cheek as yellow as the yellowest page
he was poring over, was this able and valuable
man sadly smoking himself into the other world.

His chamber, his books, his clothes, every
thing about him, were tobacco ; and I left the interview in sorrow, and half suffocated.   Argument
in this distemper is but loss of time.   No logic
can pierce the integument that smoking wraps

round the brain. Nothing will ever be effectual, except a general *fusillade* of the criminals, and a *cordon* prohibitory of the entrance of this fatal gift of America for the mystification of the continental soul. The propensity too is declared by the physicians to be actually one of the most efficient causes of the German tendency to diseases of the lungs. In point of expense, its waste is enormous. In Hamburg alone, 50,000 boxes of cigars have been consumed in a year; each box costing about 3*l.* sterling: 150,000*l.* puffed into the air!

And it is to be remembered, that even this is but a part of the expense; the cigar adorning the lip only of the better order, and even among those, only of the young; the mature generally abjuring this small vanity, and blowing away with the mighty meerschaum of their ancestors. This plague, like the Egyptian plague of frogs, is felt every where, and in every thing. It poisons the streets, the clubs, and the coffee-houses; furniture, clothes, equipage, person, are redolent of the abomination. It makes even the dulness of the newspaper doubly narcotic; the napkin on the table tells instantly that native hands have been over it; every eatable and drinkable, all that can be seen, felt, heard or understood, is saturated with tobacco; the very air we breathe is but a conveyance for this poison into the lungs; and every man, woman, and child, rapidly acquires the complexion of a boiled chicken. From the hour of their waking, if nine-tenths of the population can ever be said to awake at all, to the hour of their lying down, which in innumerable instances the peasantry do in their clothes, the pipe is never out of their mouths; one mighty fumigation reigns, and human nature is smoke-dried by tens of thousands of square miles.

But if it be a crime to shorten life, or extinguish faculties, the authority of the chief German physiologists charges this custom with effecting both in a very remarkable degree. They compute, that of twenty deaths of men between eighteen and thirty-five, *ten* originate in the waste of the constitution by smoking. The universal weakness of the eyes, which makes the Germans *par excellence* a spectacled nation, is probably attributed to the same cause of general nervous debility. Tobacco burns out their blood, their teeth, their eyes, and their brains; turns their flesh into mummy, and their mind into metaphysics.

The superior part of the creation—the ladies, do not often smoke ; but then they have their scarcely less obnoxious indulgence,—eternal stocking knitting. The needles are never out of their fingers. Every hour of the day is filled up with this work, as if the whole soul of the sex were made for nothing but stockings. Some " Reformers" have attempted to reason down this infinitely peddling and graceless employment. They have argued that it ought to be left to those who can do nothing better with their faculties or fingers ; that the labour of the most industrious baroness is not worth two-pence a day; that the fabric, at the best, is abominable, and that the knitting of an archduchess would be spurned by her own footmen. But the reformers are routed by a countless majority. Through every corner of Germany, ninety-nine in a hundred of the sex, be their condition what it may, spend the chief part of their waking hours, and possibly of their sleeping ones, in making stockings. They are to be seen knitting in all times and seasons, " from dewy morn, to dusky eve," from January to December.

On they go, looping and twisting, with remorse-less industry; and if they could take their knitting-needles with them to church, they would probably consider them highly advantageous associates to their piety. Even the original, and let our sages say what they will, the justifiable, propensity of all females to look out of the window on all occasions, is vanquished by this master passion, and the most showy promenader through a German city will see whole dens full of women, machine-like, eternally twisting and looping; who no more think of glancing at his display, than if they were so many spinning-jennies.

But the more dexterous sometimes contrive to reconcile the two enjoyments, and by the help of a mirror placed outside the window, which they call an *Espion*, the fair knitter can reconnoitre the external world, luckily without deducting a single moment from the grand business and pleasure of life. When, by any accident, the stocking is laid down, they seem the most distressed of beings. As this never happens, but in compliment to the presence of some English stranger, it only increases the natural embarrassment of all parties. The fingers,

unneedled as they are, are still in a sort of instinctive manipulation.   The eye of the reluctant *de-*
souvrée is drooped upon her pendant knitting case,
as over the memorial of something ineffably dear; an
eel stripped of its skin could not be more difficult to
reconcile to the novelty of its circumstances ; and the
moment that the stranger takes his leave, the fair
sufferer eagerly uncases her implements, and is in the
full delight of looping and twisting again for the day.

MAY 9th.   War in procinct !   Within the last
twelve hours *we* have fought a battle, on our own
behalf, have gained a victory, and are now reposing
on our honours.   What we may be, or where, in
the next twelve hours is another question.   Let
no man talk of public fluctuations, who has not
lived in a country in a state of war.   If a day could
have been mentioned in which we considered ourselves in the most favourable position of security,
we should, probably, have mentioned yesterday.
The enemy had been so long inactive, and the
accounts from the allied camp were so cheering,
that Hamburg had returned to its old good-

humoured habits; and with the addition of a review of the Burgher guard for Sunday,—unfortunately the day universally chosen on the continent for all kinds of celebrations,—all the city world promised to be in gala. Our English party, too, proposed to do honour to the German May by throwing off their winter costume, and flourishing on the parades and promenades, clothed *à l'été*. But John Bull seldom quits his boots and broad-cloth with impunity. Frenchmen and French politics are sufficiently hated by the Hamburg tailors; but French fashions have fixed a grasp upon the race, that no patriotism can relax. Every thing in the shops is French, and even *Napoleon-iste*. I might have clothed myself in a sanguine silk waistcoat, the colour, "in honour of the blood shed by the French heroes;" and covered this again with a bright olive coat, worn by all the late *employés*, in "honour of the emperor's laurels;" and to those I might have added stockings embroidered *à la Napoleon;* and equipped myself like an imperial chamberlain, or any other ribboned and ordered mountebank; but against those John Bull stoutly revolts, and sunk as he must feel, fathoms deep, in

13

the opinion of the *comme il faut*, and threatened
with being broiled alive in the heavy heat of the
German summer; he in general takes the consequences, and through good and evil adheres to his
national costume.

I was one of the recusants; and resolving, like
others, wise in their generation, never to bow down
to an idol, after it was flung from its pedestal; nor
to worship the sun, after he was set; I abandoned
Napoleon and all his vanities; and tired of toiling
over pavements that seemed made only to prohibit
walking; and still more tired of experiments to
make myself understood in the most crooked and
crabbed of all languages; I returned to my chamber,
and was glad to throw myself and my cares into
bed.

The fatigue of the day, and the warmth of the
night, easily disposed me to sleep; but I was
soon disturbed by a succession of low sounds, like
the mutterings of distant thunder, or the tread of a
passing concourse. The sounds died away, and I
slept again. But in an hour or two after, I was
roused by what seemed to be distant discharges of
cannon, followed by the baying of dogs. The

cannon ceased, but the baying spread on all sides.
It was clear that the most faithful guardians of
the city were fully awake. The Roman geese had
never done their business better; all became barking
and yelling; the whole canine Burgher guard were
palpably under arms; and trusting to their watch,
and weary in every limb, I again turned to sleep.
This *insouciance* was, perhaps, too like the easy de-
portment of the Irish traveller, who, on being told
that the next house was on fire, desired "to be
awakened when it was in the next room." But I
was at length effectually roused, by a loud knocking at my chamber door, and a terrified voice crying out, "The French are coming, the French are
coming." Nothing could be a more effectual anti-
dote to slumber. It was now five in the morning of
a bright summer's day, the sun was blazing like a
fire-ball through my curtains, all was soft air and
sunshine; but the house and the city were in a
state of desolation. I had been fast asleep in the
midst of a waking world! All the household, for
the last hour, had been packing up; the street was
full of the signs of public woe, carriages and waggons
were loading with furniture, the people were hurrying

from their houses, in dread of an immediate entrance of the enemy; and the general cry was, that "the French had attacked the Russian and Hamburg troops every where in the night, had killed every thing and every body, and were at that moment advancing to the gates, to sink, burn, and destroy."

This was likely to make a grand change in the projects of the English sojourners; for too many of our unlucky countrymen are already at Verdun, to make us at all willing to swell the number of *détenus*. Yet it was unpleasant to be thus torn up by the roots. Most of us had already settled our minds for a residence in the city; at least until the interior should be so far calmed, that we could make our way through it, without being kept in chase by the French dragoons. We had gone through the first stage of foreign existence, and had arrived at the second; in other words, we had eschewed the tavern, and *table d'hôte*, and had quietly fixed ourselves in lodgings. The *table d'hôte*, to speak its highest praise, is but an amusement of a week. It is essentially foreign and vulgar: after a week the novelty, its only recommendation, wears off, and nothing remains but the noise, the hurry, and the *scrambling*. The sight of forty or fifty people all running a race of talking, snuff taking, and swallowing together, loses its charm; and, notwithstanding the classic decorations of the banquet, the plaster Venuses which bend over every corner of the saloon, or shine upon the table, smiling in the light of their own candlesticks; the Briton grows tired, and is glad to escape, and eat his cutlet alone.

By the guidance of a Hamburg friend, I had already taken a floor in a large quiet house, in an airy quarter. The family were respectable, the house was spacious, and the street, by an unusual fortune in the contrivance of a foreign town, was wide and even clean. But in taking this lodging I had another evidence of the leagues that lay between me and England. I must furnish the suite myself. But the furniture was to be hired; but then it must be hired for a *month*. I might take the apartments for but a week, or be forced to abandon them within an hour, but the Shylock of chairs and tables was steady to his month. However, this was at length got over, of course by submission on the part of the hirer; and I now had my choice of luxuries. It was my own fault if I did not sleep in a bed that might have made a tent for Agamemnon, and shave in a mirror in which the Venus Anadyomene could contemplate herself from top to toe, without stooping. The French *employés*, who, to do them justice, never lost sight of their opportunities, had brought a great deal of showy furniture with them; which, as it paid no duty, they expected to dispose of subsequently at a hundred per cent. In other instances, however, where the functionaries knew more of human nature, and their own privileges, they seized on houses, and ordered their owners to furnish them. Nothing could be more exquisite than their taste on those occasions; and the German who presumed to intrude any moveable, unclassic in the most trivial degree, was instantly ordered by his new tenant, probably the son of a cobbler, or the cobbler himself, to repair his error, by an application to some pre-eminent Parisian master of or-molu and Sevre.

This was so much a happier mode of fitting up a suite for the ruling powers, that it soon superseded the original tardy contrivance of encumbering themselves with it in the shape of baggage. And this furniture, when the functionaries felt their day going down, they, in every instance, sent to the hammer; arguing, by all the rules of military logic, that the use had given the right, and that what they had seized they might sell. They succeeded in many cases, yet not in all; the people would not always purchase their own property a second time, and the sale lagged; until the auctioneer was at last superseded by the Cossack. The owners then arrested their chairs and tables in the French waggons; and the flying functionaries were scattered through Europe, wringing their hands, and exclaiming, with tears in their eyes, against the unutterable perfidy of their Hamburg "plunderers."

Yet, there is some honey in every thorn, if we could extract it; and the Hanse-town style of fitting up apartments was certainly the better for the Frenchmen. But for their original demands, pendules and Psyches might have been another century in making their way so far towards the pole. But now, the *opima spolia* were every where; and but for my own moderation, I might have been supplied *en prince*, bathed my temples in a bowl worthy of Cleopatra and her pearl; counted the hours by a *pendule*, with as many peeping fawns and vine-wreaths round it, as would have made a throne for the " triumphant Bacchus ;" and ranged my German grammars and lexicons on shelves suspended by gilded Cupids and genii, enough to have transported my whole stock of literature on the wing to Elysium.

Yet we must now break up all our arrangements at a moment's notice. But what is the inconvenience to strangers, compared with the real miseries of the people! To all the better orders, at least, the very idea of a return of the French is full of alarm. Many a bitter recollection has taught them the nature of Napoleon's government, even in its most smiling times. But what must it be when they fall into his hands as revolters! It is only justice to say that those feelings do not interfere with their public duties. The gentlemen show the spirit of gentlemen on all occasions; and, on this day, when every thing seemed adverse, the Burgher guard crowded to their post, and not merely manned the ramparts, but gallantly volunteered into the field.

The confusion increased; every one had his report; and as it was impossible to ascertain facts of any kind, I sallied out to judge for myself, and turned towards the common centre of all news, good and evil,—the Exchange. Every street was in the same confusion: waggons packing, houses deserted, all the men running to the ramparts as soldiers or spectators, and all the women collecting their little bundles, watching from the windows, or flying about to hear the news. Among the most composed versions of the night's affair, I could collect only that Davoust had made a dash with some thousands at our posts in Wilhelmsburg, the most remote of the islands, about midnight, and after some fighting, had driven back our Hanseatics; that he was advancing, and though the Russians and all the regular troops that could be mustered, had gone out before daybreak, they seemed to be unable to stop the overpowering numbers of the enemy.

While we were listening to those details in the midst of a crowd of anxious faces, a sudden crash of musketry, which appeared close to the city, put us all on the alert. Some went to renew their packing, I, with others to the ramparts, from which there was the best chance of discovering for ourselves what was going on in the islands.

On the way we had another most distressing display of the nature of war; in the killed and wounded of the morning's engagement, who were bringing in from the field. Many of them were known to the inhabitants, and the scene, at all times startling and repulsive, was, from this circumstance, actually harrowing. Some of the dying were laid before their own doors; and it may be easily imagined with what shrieks and terrors they were received. The dead were carried through the streets in large covered baskets, or on boards; and the sight of the sheets and surtouts in which they were wrapped, and which gave many a sad proof of the mutilation within, was enough to make every one who could, get out of the way as fast as possible. The whole scene was melancholy, sickening, and frightful, in a degree not to be forgotten.

CHAPTER XIV.

THE BATTLE OF THE ISLANDS.

On the ramparts we found a greater crowd than I had expected; for, though they were beyond the point blank range of musketry, yet a chance ball might have easily done mischief, and it seemed to me that the French six-pounders might have sent their shot in among them at every discharge. A battle has been said to be, of all things, the least like a review; and certainly this engagement was as little like a display of manœuvres in Hyde Park as possible. Immediately under the rampart, was ranged below us, on a small island, a troop of Cossacks, waiting the commandant's orders, with some officers belonging to his staff. Beyond those, swept down the principal stream of the Elbe, with boats passing and repassing, as they conveyed the troops, or wounded; and more distant still, lay Wilhelmsburg, in which the struggle, after being intermitted for some hours, had now begun again.

The movements of the troops were not easy to be traced, owing to the quantity of copse and low plantation that covered the face of the ground, but they could be tolerably followed by the rising of the smoke, when any direct collision occurred.

The attack, however, was now *upon* the French, who would probably have been satisfied to remain in their position. But a combined movement, of some skill, had been concerted against them, and they were fighting only to cover their retreat. It appears that they had pushed on, rather unguardedly into the centre of the island, and thus left themselves open to a flank attack. This was now in the act of being made. The firing grew tremendously heavy, and the naked eye could soon mark the fluctuations of the fight by the lines of fire, which burst up in different quarters, sometimes at considerable distances from each other. At length the firing grew more distant, but one huge column of flame and smoke arose, for which we could not account, except by the explosion of an artillery waggon. It turned out to be the less martial catastrophe of an unlucky mill, which the French, in their usual spirit of wantonness, had destroyed in their retreat.

This was another of the features of French war; the first indication of the enemy's movements, whether in advance or retreat, being almost always a burning of some kind or other, no matter what: alike the cottage in which they had been quartered the night before, or the inn which had supplied them with food, or the fortress which had fired on them. But when they met with a mill, it became a peculiar object of destruction; possibly not so much from its use to the country people, though that consideration had its weight too in a war of revenge, as from the urchin love of a bonfire, at all risks; for which the mill, with its broad sails, and tall timbers, gave a first-rate opportunity.

Something of this malignant frolic might be expected from the composition of an army which was crowded with conscripts. But the truth, according to all German authorities, was, that the veteran took as much delight in destruction as the conscript; and that a common amusement of all, on leaving a village, was to break even the cups and plates;

and rip up the beds, for the mere indulgence of scattering the feathers into the air.

These observations are not made in any peculiar antipathy to the French, who are brave soldiers, and can be courteous ones; but woe be to the people which suffers a French army, or any other, to enter its borders, in the expectation of finding courtesy from the invader. War, under the best circumstances, is malignant enough; but what must the soldier be, after being immersed for years in the gross vices of a camp, perhaps made furious at the moment by privations and wounds, and then let loose, like a wild beast, into the midst of every thing that can indulge his appetites? What the king, or the country, that provokes war, may have to answer for to its own conscience, is beyond my calculation; but, judging from the misery produced by war, even on the limited scale round me, to pass by, altogether, the sufferings of Germany during the last ten years; there never was invented a more tremendous artifice for increasing the natural calamities, or heaping crime on the natural crimes of man.

All Germany is at this hour in a state of dread-

ful anxiety, not so much from fear of the enemy,—
for the public spirit has been wound up to a pitch
of exasperation that almost precludes personal
fear; but from bitter recollection of the excesses
that follow upon the steps of war in every shape.
Perhaps, in point of the gifts of nature,—fertility,
variety of soil and produce, noble scenery, and
fortunate position, Germany is the most favoured
country of Europe.   Its three great rivers—the
Elbe, the Danube, and the Rhine, supply an unrivalled internal navigation, and flow through some
of the loveliest spots on earth.   Yet, at this hour,
there are vast districts of this fine and fertile land
turned into little better than a howling wilderness
by the war.   Thousands, and tens of thousands of
her people, have been actually beggared; the grass
has grown in her marts; her merchants—and merchandize has seldom figured on a more princely
scale—have been broken down.   The whole productive power and healthful mind of the nation are
prostrated by the war.

Still, even the public loss was trivial to the personal injuries, the vexations of individual feeling,
the contumelies to females, the eternal scoff, shame

espionage, terror, and robbery, that ground down the people and every individual of the people. One of the most painful parts of a residence in Germany, is the being compelled perpetually to hear stories of this degradation and misery, bursting from the general lip.   At length, society had been so much dislocated, and so much in terror of personal communication, that it was not unusual to see inquiries in the newspapers, entreating " A.B. of such a province, to let his brother, or sister, know that he was alive;" the initials alone being given, through fear of bringing the eye of the French police on either of the parties.   As to the privacy, which an Englishman values, and justly, as one of the best privileges of life, it was out of the question.   The house was common property, so long as there were half a dozen French quartered within half a dozen miles.   They invited themselves, and performed their parts accordingly.   If a gentleman had asked a few of his friends to dine with him, it might happen that the captain, or the corporal, disapproved of the proceeding, and under the pretext of public vigilance forbade the meeting.   The entertainer might consider himself fortunate if the

Frenchman did not seat himself and his followers in place of the guests, or settle the matter by ordering the dinner, plate and all, to his own quarters. There have been instances, where, when the best entertainment that a nobleman's house could offer, was placed on the table; one of those military epicures has walked with his whiskered party into the room, taken a survey of the dishes, taken the master to task for their want of elegance, and finished the lecture by twisting his spur in the end of the table-cloth, and bringing the whole to the ground. Even, offensive as those insolences were, they were trifling, compared with the numberless insults and injuries committed on the feelings of husbands and fathers, during this miserable period. All laws, human and divine, were put down by the single supremacy of the bayonet. The moral of the whole is, that no sacrifice can be too great, no resistance too resolute, deadly, and desperate, that excludes an invader.

Evening. The day has passed without any further disturbance from the enemy. They seem to have withdrawn from the islands. The city, however, continues in that restless and fretted state which may be conceived, from the neighbourhood of an enemy proverbially active, and who may reach it by a hundred ways. The attack on the islands was taking the bull by the horns; if it were not rather intended to startle the citizens, by the actual sight of fighting. The Elbe may be crossed in all quarters, and a couple of hours' marching would bring a French column to the gates.

Our guns on Wilhemsburg, which the enemy had not time to carry away, are now revenging their dishonour, by firing on the French boats. The creek in which they lie is too narrow for their flotilla, and the unfortunates that remain outside have a fair chance of being battered to pieces before night.

On the ramparts I found the people, awakened at last to the possibility of capture, digging epaulements, and planting cannon. Staff-officers, couriers, and Cossacks, were galloping through the crowd; some of the burgher guard were taking their posts in the bastions; and mingled with all those matters of war, were promenaders, male and female, in their Sunday costume—the whole forming a very busy and even a very gay spectacle. A solitary bugle or trumpet was heard, as a patrole issued from the gates; but there was a perpetual lively dissonance of harps, horns, and violins, from the guinguettes, which are every where. The coffee-house harmony was in full vigour.

I grew weary of this bustle, after a while, and took a long walk into the country. But though I thus escaped the clamour of the ramparts, the sound of the cannon still pursued me. It formed a strange and vexatious contrast to the evening and the scene. All round me was sweet, soft, and pastoral; cattle returning homewards, children playing, birds on the bough; the air cool from the river, and fragrant with the breath of gardens and shrubberies; the landscape, to the horizon, flat, but full of rich, sleepy beauty; and in the midst of this luxury of quiet, came, ever and anon, the startling roar of the cannon, telling that *there* was man and mischief again.

MAY 10. The French still keep within their quarters; and from reports, of which we have a most prodigal abundance at all times, they are likely to be engaged in taking care of themselves

for the Russian hussars are again in their rear.
The enemy were undoubtedly defeated, and with
considerable loss, in their late attempt.   But the
citizens are growling terribly at their Hanseatic
legion.   There were blunders in profusion; but
what was to be expected from a corps which had
never fired a shot before, and took their first lesson
under the peppering of the French tirailleurs?
A corps, too, composed of all kinds of people:
some of their officers actually Frenchmen and
spies, who, at the first fire, made a run into the
enemy's ranks, and left their unlucky comrades to
fight out the battle as they could; all of them
totally undisciplined, and many, it is asserted, more
than half drunk. It is perfectly clear, that they were
taken by surprise.   The French embarked in front
of a battery, heavy enough to have torn their boats
into pieces.   Not a gun was fired.   They landed
in the midst of centinels.   Not a centinel challenged.   It is even said, that the whole chain were
found literally *fast asleep*.   Some of the narrators,
zealous for the national honour, attribute this un-
timely slumber to laudanum in the beer given to
them by the peasantry, in whose cottages they were

quartered; and whom, such are the pastoral virtues, the French purse has contrived to turn into very active agents; others, to the simple effects of the brandy with which they had been too patriotically celebrating the battle of Lutzen the evening before. Yet those were but partial mischiefs after all; for though the German will drink brandy when he can get it, and the Frenchman will make no serious objection to any contrivance by which he can catch his enemy asleep; yet nothing in either brandy or laudanum could have sealed all their eyes at once. The true fault lay, where it lies in every service of Germany, in the admission of foreigners into the corps. If the history of the German defeats in the late war were to be fairly written, a vast majority of their heaviest failures would be traced to this loose and pernicious habit of receiving strangers into the national armies. The roving mercenary is generally a fellow without principle, generally turned out of his own country for the want of that principle; and, as he sells his blood for money, naturally ready to make the best bargain for his blood that he can, and with whom he can. Accordingly, the desertions that occur in the course of a foreign campaign are often equivalent to the loss of a battle; plans are betrayed, attacks counteracted; and a system of treachery is so universally acknowledged, that the first account of a continental defeat almost invariably attributes it to a bribe, a spy, or the defection of some spruce knave, who had insinuated himself among the staff of his majesty the emperor, or his highness the general.

This day's work, however, has done our Hanseatics as much good as a campaign. It has fairly purified their ranks: it has given them a little field instruction too; for the French, on landing, instantly broke into detachments, and ran round our unlucky people, who, scarcely awakened, and still in midnight, found themselves fired on at once in front, flank, and rear. How they escaped at all is the true wonder. But the French have been always too fond of firing; and the broken nature of the ground enabled the Hanseatics first to cover themselves in some degree, and then to make head. The bayonet would, probably, have settled the business at once. There was now nothing for our troops to do, but to retire until reinforcements could reach them; but, by a blunder, which dishonours the national tactics, no point of retreat seems to have been marked out, and, in consequence, the fragments of the corps retired to all points of the compass. The troops which were to extricate them, were necessarily as much puzzled as themselves; and it does them all no slight credit, under such circumstances, to have been able to repulse the enemy.

MAY 11. Our battle has turned us all into heroes, and now nothing is talked of but " ambuscadoes, healths five fathom deep," making a grand attack on Monsieur Davoust, and cutting off his communications with Bremen! from which the marshal draws his supplies, and is busy stripping the unlucky town of every flitch and flask,—a mighty depredator on bacon and burgundy. Our graver heads still droop over our fate, and predict new requisitions, new battalions, and new surprises by the help of French gold and Hanoverian brandy. But those we scorn; put their sinister wisdom to the account of age, cold blood, or short-sightedness; and are determined to see nothing in the future but holidays.

There can be no doubt remaining, that the French

were as much surprised by our resistance, as we were by their attack; and that with all the advantage of the field in their favour for four hours and upwards, our people drove them in, forced them to re-cross the river in confusion, and in the course of the operation, taught them that they were not to walk over to Hamburgh without paying handsomely for their passage. They lost, probably, not much less than 400 men. Our loss was not quite half the number.

We have taken prisoners too; some of them mere boys. The conscription thinks little of chronology, and fourteen seems to be the Napoleon reading for eighteen, the lawful age of soldiership. But captivity never looked less sorrowful. The prisoners were evidently extremely glad to find themselves out of the way of further glory.

I heard one of them, a mere boy, who was asked some questions as to the number of Davoust's force that morning, answer, with boyish *naïveté*, " I cannot tell any thing about them, but thanks to our Lady, *je me trouve ici.*"

Yet it was this cruelty—and as cruelty is always folly in the end, this folly—of draining the young generation of France, to bury them in the marshes of Germany, that gave the imperial armies the extraordinary predominance, which they have exhibited in all their invasions. The Germans hold that it takes a year to make a foot soldier; two years are the established requisite for the cavalry; and, as for the cannoneer, life itself seems too short to teach him the possible perfection of ramming and sponging. But they " order those things better in France," at least, more succinctly; the greater part of the troops, amounting to nearly 200,000, which are now marching under the banner of Napoleon, have not been under arms six months, some not so many weeks; and up rise infantry, cavalry, and artillery, as if out of the ground, and not a few, as if out of the nursery, to make battle against the Russian veterans, and the hardy peasantry of Prussia. And no troops fight more gallantly than those boys. " Old officers and young soldiers," is the notorious French *beau idéal* of an army. The boys, undeterred by the hazards which experience has not taught them to dread, and inflamed by the eagerness of youth in every thing, rush into danger, often much more readily than their more practised comrades. But this is Napoleon's game of "ten thousand men a day." The conscript army, the most desperate expedient ever invented for lavishing away life, is fit for nothing from the moment when it is taken out of fire. It then perishes before the eye. It cannot endure the fatigues of the march; the dews and rains of the *bivouac*, send it by thousands to the hospital; and of all the scenes of horror and despair, that ever entered into the imagination of man, a French military hospital *en campagne*, is the most frightful. It is proverbially a sentence of death, a plunge into the grave; with nothing to palliate it, but its rapidity.

We are still talking of our battle. We have lost some officers, the French probably many more. The fire early in the day had been sharp; and from the nature of the ground, a broken surface of thickets, low fences, and narrow country lanes, the combatants were much intermingled with each other. A small volunteer corps of ours, composed of gamekeepers and marksmen, behaved with great activity, and must have inflicted formidable loss, as they were practised shots, and reserved their fire for the officers. One of the enemy's staff was thus killed, carrying orders for the advance of a battalion, and fell into the sharpshooters' hands. His pockets were stuffed with love-letters. He was on the point of marriage. Such are the bitternesses of war. An instant put an end probably to a whole family picture of happiness. It is true, that the singular elasticity of the French heart, makes misfortunes of this kind less misfortunes than in other lands; yet, without affecting any peculiar sentimentality on an occasion so much in the course of things as the death of a soldier in the field, we might regret for the moment, that the blow had not spared a bride and bridegroom. But these bustling days give no time for sorrow: perhaps, too, we may be consoled by the fact, that the tears shed in Paris, for any thing but a lap-dog, are few, and the few are soon wiped away, be the weeper of what age she will. A new *chanson*, or a new *coiffeure*, or a new opera, or a new lover, will probably be recalling the lady's smiles, before the letter of sorrow has lain another day on her *escrutoir*.

CHAPTER XV.

HAMBURGH.

HAMBURGH has recovered all her good humour.
Philosophy says, that every one is the happier for
ill-luck, as no one knows the true zest of health,
who has not felt sickness. The maxim has not
all the usual folly of philosophy. Four and twenty
hours ago, all was flight or fighting; now, all is
gayer than ever. The certainty of having beaten
the enemy, has turned " our weekdays into pleasant festival." The Alster has its freshwater
sailors again, the Cossacks are prancing in gallant
barbarism through the streets, and the general
and his Russian suite are riding about and smiling
to all the world, in the pride of new coats and
military supremacy. The Hamburger Berg has,
of course, put on a double portion of festivity,
and " true to all the pulses of the time," exhibits

a new stud of wooden Bucephaluses from Vienna, " which have been honoured by giving lessons in the noble art of equitation to all the arch-duchesses." It would be heresy to doubt the statement of their highnesses' master of the horse. In addition, we have a whole company of baboons, which " the hero of Prussia, the Konig Frederic Wilhelm himself has acknowledged to be genuine wild beasts;" conjurors who put all magic to the blush; and royal waxwork, for which the artist pledges himself, on the honour of science, that " the illustrious originals sat in *person*." Conspicuous among those is the good-humoured, though very Tartar, face of the Emperor Alexander, the *befreyer*, or liberator, a great favourite, buttoned up to the throat, and squeezed into the straitwaistcoat of a Russian uniform; with the three Graces, hand in hand, dancing round him, yet not in the startling simplicity of the antique, but all with honest German bibs and tuckers.

But the multitude themselves are much the most amusing spectacle. Our English holiday groups are all alike; but the German has still retained something of that division of orders, the costume of

caste, which made old times in all lands so picturesque. The sugar-bakers, for instance, once very
useful instruments to the city's wealth, for Hamburgh had long engrossed the sugar-refinery of the
continent, make a prodigious figure in the crowd,
with their deep blue jackets and velvet caps.
Among those, and everywhere, are to be seen
the city porters, costumed after their hereditary
fashion—a brawny body of monopolists, and as
jealous of their privileges as any knot of corpo-
rators in Europe. Then come the Vierlanders,
with their flower-baskets on their heads. Those
are a curious race, named from a district of four
parishes, or lands, a few miles up the river, on
which their progenitors, a colony of Flemings, settled some five hundred years since, and which they
cultivated with Flemish skill.

The Vierlander women supply the markets with
fruit, flowers, and vegetables, and always wear a
peculiar costume, in which it would be as impossible to reform the colour of a ribbon or the shape
of a cap, as to reform the etiquette of a German
court. They are the perfection of the northern
peasant, in clothing, colour, and corpulence. They

expend a great deal of their money on dress; and a Vierlander, young, and a belle, would sometimes be no bad subject for a sumptuary law. But all this is looked on here as a simple matter of custom, and passes off as a grace of coquetry. The bodice is a tight fabric, frequently wrought with gold and silver, in wreathings and evolutions that might raise the envy of a modern hussar. But the cap is the glory of the race; and its gala specimens are a family treasure—a *monture* of gold and silver clasps, with French lace for the younger belles, and native embroidery for their mothers. But when did female decoration know where to stop? The fair Vierlanders adopt the disfiguring principle, with the vigour of a beauty of the Chaussée d'Antin, or St. James's. The head is loaded with a straw hat of indescribable form and enormous breadth, which defeats all the toilet; and gives the whole figure the strongest resemblance to an inordinate churn headed with an inordinate cheese.

However, the women have all the beauty that nature ever intended for Flemings; they have good-humoured faces, broad, laughing mouths, and the florid complexions of the most robust health.

Health and contentment, indeed, seem to be their lot in an extraordinary degree; the secret of which probably is, that they seldom make any attempt to change the condition in which their fathers left them, and that the Vierlanders live and die gardening, cow-milking, and butter-making. They generally possess a hereditary competence; and as they desire no change, they spend their lives in the way that Epicurus did, and with honester philosophy—in their gardens. This kind of life, it is true, precludes all glory: war, statesmanship, and blue stockingism " are quite shut out;" and if it could once be universal, the wheels of the world must run down, and mankind be but a race of happy turnip gatherers. But still there is some interest in seeing little fractional parts of society like those, escaping the general curse of life, the uncertainties, heart-burnings, and rivalries, of the great world. It might even be difficult, in looking on the sallow faces and languid forms of many of the noble German ladies, and of the English too, to help drawing the comparison, between the results of a life of idleness and one of industry; between the luckless opulence which makes all effort unnecessary, and the fortunate mediocrity which makes it at once necessary and sweet; between the real miseries of high-born lassitude, and the gay and simple activity, which knows no more uneasy hours, than the bird that sings over its head, and has all its ambition fulfilled by rearing the first roses, or gathering the richest grapes of the season.

The *Kleine-madchen*, or maid-servants, in all places important ministers to society, are by no means inclined to let themselves be forgotten in the crowd; but are showing their blouzed caps, and full-moon faces, laughing and figuring every where. The Hamburghers pride themselves much on the comeliness of this race; who also wear a costume of their own, and who once rigidly preserved distinctions among themselves, worthy of the land of distinctions; the chief of which were in the form and mode of carrying the basket—an implement as essential to the German maid-servant as her tongue. In the " good old times," the basket appropriated to the cooks and house-maids, was a heavy piece of German wicker-work, carried *under* the arm, and covered with a napkin. The ladies'-maids, and *soubrettes* of the

13

toilet and chamber, as the more refined tribe,—the porcelain clay of gentle menialism,—were known by a little *corbeille à la Parisienne*, poised on the tip of the finger, and slightly enveloped in a silk hand-kerchief, or a shawl. But handsome as some of those females undoubtedly are,—for nature, un-thwarted by the absurdity of human attempts to make her better, always tends to beauty,—the *Kleine-madchen* costume is evidently chosen on the principle of the widow's cap, which, as all the world knows, but the widow herself, is constructed to frighten away all admiration; the figure ex-hibiting a dowdy degeneracy from the neatness of the Parisian demoiselle, and the face being framed in a stiff circular enclosure of frills and borders, an embrasure of inflexible starch and impregnable wire, that gives the complete idea of a linen pillory.

But the truth is, that to the eye accustomed to genuine English beauty, the foreign countenance is seldom seen to advantage. The foreign brunette is too dark; the blonde is too light; the Greek profile, grand as it is, is too inanimate; and the French favourite *nez retroussé*, seconded by the little restless brown eye, is too common-place. For the combination of dignity and tenderness, for the noblest expression of mind and heart together, the countenance of English loveliness, in its few finer instances, is altogether without an equal in the world.

But the German females have better claims than those which depend upon the exterior; they are a remarkably kind-hearted, faithful, and honest-minded generation. The German ladies, excepting where they are led away by the temptation of French manners, vindicate the character of the sex, and fairly constitute the stronghold of the national morality. Even such superficial knowledge of their domestic life as might lie open to a stranger, conveyed the impression of a mixture of gentleness and goodness, which forms perhaps the best quality for home. The ties of parent and child certainly seem to owe but little of their acknowledged closeness, in Germany, to severity on the one side, or fear on the other. The feature which strikes a stranger most, is the general prevalence of a simple familiarity, perfectly consistent with duty on both sides. The aged head of the house is looked up to with something of patriarchal respect, which he returns by something of patri-

archal affection. In England families suddenly
break off, and scatter through life, as if they were
blown up by an explosion of gunpowder: they
fly to all corners of the world, never to rejoin;
but the happier circumstances of this country frequently allow all the branches of families to settle
near each other: sons and daughters, sons-in-law
and daughters-in-law, with their children and their
children's children, come and sit under the shelter
of the family vine.   Circle spreads beyond circle;
and the ancient father, sitting in the centre of all,
like another Jacob, with the sons of Joseph at his
knee, is loved and honoured, rejoices in his grey
hairs and fulness of years, and in peace and gratitude prepares for the great change that comes
to all.

WE are all rumour still—an English reinforcement arrived at Heligoland! a general movement
of the troops in Saxony! an insurrection in Paris!
and the retreat of Davoust! Those things keep us
in a perpetual fever; and it is scarcely possible for
any one who has not been on the spot, to conceive

the fretted and anxious feeling that mixes with every transaction of public or private life, under such circumstances. But we learn, at least, the maxim of not believing any thing but our own eyes: I have just had a confirmation of its value. The report to which the most universal belief was given, was the clearance of the opposite bank,—a matter of high import to us. It was even asserted, that the French had taken to flight in such haste, that they were destroying their baggage, and selling their horses at prices which ought to tempt any Hamburgher alive to hasten over and make his fortune. To settle the question for myself, I went to a spot on the ramparts, which commanded the horizon. There it was settled at once. There was the abomination of desolation, the tricolor, flaunting to the sun, on the top of the steeple of Harburg! This was conviction; and from the flashes of steel which, even at that distance, shot out from time to time against the sky, it was further to be discovered that the flag was not there alone, but that very considerable bodies of troops were manœuvring in the adjoining fields at the moment!

I lingered till the sun went down. Often as I had indulged in the quiet beauty of the Elbe, the landscape, this evening, seemed more tranquil and lovely than ever; possibly from some undefined contrast with the scene of confusion and turmoil which it had so lately exhibited. The Elbe, a shallow and tardy stream, though sometimes a wide, and in winter a powerful one, is filled with islands; and, opposite to the city, is less a great river, than three or four canals, watering a succession of farms and pasture fields. Those islands are chiefly tenanted by peasants, who supply the city with milk and butter, and are in good circumstances, with comfortable cottages, and with no slight degree of that pastoral comfort, and hereditary opulence, which marks German peasant life. The sudden heat of the season was now giving every spot a rapid luxuriance, which, in the tangled thickets of the islands, was not unlike a diminished picture of the luxuriant Indian or African jungle. The colour of the fields, more exposed, was even already changing to a harvest hue—the ruddy brown of the ripened year. Slight glances of the different streams of the river, like the glitter of polished steel under the sun, alone showed the divisions of the islands; and the whole lay basking under a sky as bright as ever shone on Alp or Apennine.

There were a considerable number of people standing on the rampart, with the same purpose as myself, watching the movements on the opposite shore. They were gloomy, but quiet; and I scarcely heard a voice among them.

They had good reason for their gloom. " We have *no* troops," was the remark of an intelligent friend of mine. " We are left to ourselves, to fight, or fly, or be robbed, or beaten, or banished, or turned into recruits for the army of the great nation, as it may please the chapter of accidents. We know nothing of our allies, and not much more of our defenders; we know as little of Tettenborn's intentions as we do of Alexander's, and simply know, that he is a brave fellow, who will fight if he has force, and who, if he has none, which is the case at present, will, by every rule of peace or war, shift for himself, and leave us to do the same."

To my remark, that the allies had been culpable in encouraging the citizens to arm against the French, unless they meant to support them; his

answer was, " The revolt was our own, for the
French yoke was beyond all human endurance;
the city might have borne the French garrisons,
but it was blistered with their prefects, their custom-house extortioners, and a crowd of tormentors
sent hungry from France, to make us beggars,—a
rabble of blood-suckers, that spared nothing. As to
our troops, we have about 600 Cossacks with Tettenborn, which will assuredly take wing like a flight
of crows, the moment the French make a serious
demonstration ; for no Cossack will ever wait to be
caught. We have a few companies of Hanoverians,
and a battalion of the Mecklenburg guards, a few
hundreds of Hanseatics, and a burgher guard, who
will in all instances conduct themselves like men of
honour and good Germans, but who, after all, can
have no great hope of beating 20,000 French troops,
with Davoust, a rascal, but a bold and cunning one,
at their head."

I asked, whether there were any authentic news
of the campaign ?

" Yes," was the answer; " the allies have begun
their campaign too early; they want reinforcements already, and they are retreating to meet

them. Napoleon has already made up his losses, and is following them step for step. They must fight soon, and will probably be destroyed."— "Then, what is to be done here?" was the question again.—" Nothing, but to wait until it is Davoust's pleasure to come over and fix his head-quarters among us. We shall not be kept long in suspense. And I am mis-informed, if he is not at this hour making preparations for an attack. However, it is not necessary that strangers should wait for our ca-tastrophe: take my advice, and go away as far and as fast as you can; I have formed my plan."

I have formed my plan too, but I have not been able to look upon the future in so gloomy a point of view as my clever friend. 'Tis true, my bellige-rent curiosity has been more than satisfied: I have seen cottages in flames, frightened women, and ruined peasantry, men shooting and being shot, and the hideous spectacle of the dead and dying; the whole inclining me more than ever to distrust the merits of conquerors, and think more mode-rately of the goods and glories of war. Yet the interest of the scene increases; the danger is not yet come; and let it come when it may, a traveller able to walk fifty miles a day, may escape from the French chasseurs after all.

A French officer has just been brought in by some of our cavalry. He was taken pushing his way across the country; for what purpose we are not wise enough to conjecture, except as a carrier of despatches to the "Grand Army." But he has told us enough,—that "Davoust is so far from retreating, that he has received reinforcements which raise his *corps d'armée* to 25 or 30,000 men; that all preparations have been made for his advancing in force; and that the Emperor has ordered him to make himself master of Hamburgh *coute qu'il coute*." This is not cheering; but it is made still worse, by the intelligence that he is bringing Vandamme with him: of all the abhorred of Germany, the most abhorred; a military ruffian of the most reckless class, whose cruelties in his former command in the north, especially in Oldenburg, rang through the land; and of whom, Napoleon is reported to have said—"that Vandamme was a necessary evil, but, if he had two Vandammes in his army, he would hang one of them."

Our heroism has not chosen to lie hid under a

bushel, and the Correspondenten is now going the circuit of the earth with the following detail of *our* battle.

Official Account.

" On the 8th of May, Marshal Davoust having collected in a line from Harburg to the Zollenspieker about 5,500 troops, which had till then been posted along the Elbe from Luneburg to the mouth of the river, undertook, at one in the morning of the 9th, a landing on the islands of Wilhelmsburg and Ochsenwerder, leaving about 1,500 men in Harburg. We had about 1,100 men in Wilhelmsburg and 600 in Ochsenwerder.

" The enemy, profiting by the ebb-tide, embarked in force at several points at once, covered by a brisk fire from all his batteries. He drove back our advanced posts, and gradually gained ground; but as soon as the advanced posts and smaller detachments had joined the reserves in the rear, the enemy was attacked, and a brisk firing began on all sides.

" A battalion of Mecklenburgers was now sent

over to support our troops in Wilhelmsburg, while
a regiment of Hanoverians, and a battalion of Lubeckers were sent from Bergedorf and the Zollenspieker, towards Ochsenwerder on the enemy's
right flank. The enemy could not long withstand
this new attack, which was executed with great
spirit; he gradually yielded on all points, covering
his retreat by burning some houses and mills.
Our troops followed eagerly, and made some prisoners. The enemy re-embarked under the protection of his numerous batteries on the other side.
His loss consists of 300 killed, wounded, and
prisoners. Ours of about 150 killed and wounded,
among whom are thirteen officers."

CHAPTER XVI.

THE BATTLE.

TETTENBORN has suddenly removed his head-quarters to the Grasbroek, and has, by this movement, at once told us, that affairs are coming nearer to a crisis, and added to his own reputation for chivalry; for where he now is, he may be shot at any hour of the day that it may please a French rifleman to hide himself in the bushes. As there was a necessity for showing our passports in those times of trouble to the commandant, and as he was not to be found in the city government-house, I was not sorry to be compelled to look for him " in camp," this preliminary to a field of battle. After passing through a line of Cossacks dismounted, and spruce Russians, lounging about,

I found the general standing in a group of his officers at the door of his quarters, a farm-house. He is a very military looking personage, tall, strong, and erect, moustached to the full Russian regulation, which implies the concealment of three-fourths of the face; and covered with orders, as numerous as his buttons, and some of them perhaps nearly as valuable.

The multiplicity of those things in the foreign services turns them into baubles. They are given for every preposterous reason, or for none; given for having been within five miles of a battle, as much as for having been in the heart of it; given for bringing a despatch five minutes before the post waggon; for drawing pay and eating dinners in the same barrack twenty years together; for being the best dancer of a Polonaise; for being a chamberlain, a master of the ceremonies, a singer, a fiddler; for being any thing, and doing any thing. Thus the decoration becomes a mere patch, an additional flourish on the breast of a coat, a new trinket conflicting with the watch and the eye-glass—a triumph of tailorism, or a display of paste jewellery. If all the battles of the allies had been triumphs, and a battle fought every hour of every week, they could not have justified half the badges of heroism that swing and glitter on the neck of every body. However, Tettenborn has probably earned his sparkling honours more honestly than the crowd; for he has seen a good deal of service since the beginning of the war, was foremost wherever he could find any chance of distinguishing himself, and has the reputation, as he certainly has the look, of a bold Hussar.

He received our party civilly, simply glanced at our documents, which he instantly returned, asked one or two passing questions, and dismissed us with his hand to his cap. Having thus escaped the den of the devourer, we felt ourselves new nerved, and before our banquet was finished for the night, had discussed the grand question of " to go, or not to go," which some of our English friends considered to be nearly equivalent to the original, " to be, or not to be." The negative carried the question hollow. Such is the courage of circumstances and supper.

An additional infusion of intrepidity was derived from our seeing some Danish regiments march within the Hamburgh limits in the course of the day, and take up a position at our gates. They formed a very considerable body, and gave us a still better omen than their numbers, in their red coats. If the red were dingy, and the coats said little for the skill of the Danish tailors, the *colour* was British. The men were fine, tall fellows, made a good figure on parade, and had one quality which, next to the colour of their coats, made them invaluable to the Civic cause,—they *hated* the French. On the other hand, the English nation, the English cause, and the English pay, either separately or combined, have made a prodigious impression upon them; and there is probably not a man among them who, *salvâ fidelitate*, would not be rejoiced to be at this moment serving under the British ensign. The men, however, are not Danes, but chiefly Holsteiners; who are, in every sense of the word, German, and they are fully acquainted with the advantages of our " German legion," for which many recruits have gone from their own country.

———

MAY 12.   A wretched, fearful, and *bloody* day!

13

All was quiet during the night before. The air returned even no city sound; though its sweetness at this period of the season probably kept many an idler breathing it late. There was no token of the vicinity of camps, no " clang of armourers closing rivets up," nor even "the stilly hum," to tell us that we were within sight of some thousands of " warlike French." It is true, that the enemy's camp fires were seen dotting the rising grounds in rear of the little town of Harburg. But, if we could divest our recollections of the meaning of those fires, or of the hordes of military ruffians lying round them, and whom, in a few hours, we might find burning the roofs over our heads; even those fires, alternately sinking and sparkling, waning and blazing out again, like stars dimmed by passing clouds, added only to the quiet beauty of the scene. The moon alone was wanting to complete Homer's famous simile of a sleeping army. The "refulgent lamp of night" certainly spread none of her splendours over the scene. We, perhaps, too, wanted the mountain tops; for the Hanoverian hills can offer no rivalship to the glittering crags of Ida. But we had all else: the beleaguered wall, the camp of watchers round it, the river, and a broader one than either the Simois or the Scamander, the enemy beyond, the lights blazing in all quarters, and, at last, even the moon. She rose in great glory, and gradually brought to life the distant islands, and the heights beyond, until the whole horizon lay in light; as if she had spiritualized it with her silver. What a contrast to the scene which that landscape was to exhibit before she lighted it again!

About noon, as I was passing down the Jungfersteig, to spend a lazy hour over the English newspapers, I met a Cossack riding in, full gallop from the field,—to announce the enemy's approach. The fellow was here in his element, and the wild look that he gave us in passing, told instantly that some serious business was coming on. Black as his half-human visage was with squalidness and beard, there was enough left to show, what might be either fright or fury, or the habitual countenance of the Tartar, when war is in the wind. The lance pointed forward, the head stooping to the horse's mane, and the little wild horse itself shooting on, with almost the speed of an arrow, were completely in character. But the wirey and fierce countenance of the Cossack, with every feature strained by the impulse of the moment, was invaluable. I never saw any thing so incomparably savage.

The rattle of the hoofs brought a sudden rush of loungers into the streets, and newspapers and *déjeûners* were deserted on all sides. Another and another flying courier soon followed : it was evident that something formidable was at hand; and the sound of cannon shortly after began to acquaint us with the truth. The drums of the Burgher guard were beating in all quarters in a few minutes; and it was said that the enemy had attacked the whole of the islands in force. As in such cases, every new-comer had his story, and every one magnified the peril; in order to ascertain something of the fact, I made my way towards my old position on the rampart. The French were stated to be, in round numbers, from 5 to 50,000; and to this, was added the startling news, which turned out to be true, that our troops were not only entirely inferior in number to their assailants, but that they had been again out-manœuvred; that the French were " driv-

ing them head over heels" to the river side ; and
that he was lucky who could get first out of the
mêlée.

The streets were now all confusion, though the
news had not arrived ten minutes, nor had any of
those frightful sights occurred, which were so unwisely suffered to alarm public feeling in the previous engagement.   Every body was either standing in the street, or packing up and preparing
for an escape to the country.   Among this bustling
crowd, a stranger naturally found double difficulty
in hearing the truth, or making his way.   Another
obstacle was next presented, in a mob, who rushed
through the streets to compel every one whom
they met, to work upon the fortifications.   The
citizens had been so long proud of their enormous
ditch, that it seemed never to have occurred to their
tacticians, that a ditch was of no possible use while
the gates were left undefended.   And it was only
within these few days that, some Prussian general,
in passing to the allied head-quarters, having told
them, that " he could ride his horse through any
of their fortifications ; and that where the French
found the gates of a city open, they were a kind

of people who would make no scruple whatever of walking in," they had begun to fortify the Altona-gate, and haul their ship guns into the embrasures.

The enemy's attack this morning, had quickened their apprehension on the point; and, like all men awakened to sudden wisdom, the last idea drove every other out of their heads.

While the firing was going on in the islands, the singular conception was adopted, of turning the whole population into sappers and miners, and, with the aldermen for their engineers, and the lame, gouty, fat, and blind, for their operators, making their city impregnable for ever. The thought was rapidly acted upon, and without any idle respect of persons; for the *press-warrant* was given into the hands of the mob; and a rabble of half-drunken peasants, porters, and sailors, were let loose to seize upon every living soul who could, or could not, handle a spade. The proceeding soon produced the most curious and motley corps of "good-man delvers," that perhaps ever figured in the history of castrametation. Old gentlemen who had tottered out, newspaper in hand, from their coffee, to know whether they were

to be shot or sabred; young gentlemen going to
exhibit themselves on the promenades; physicians
hastening to their patients; all kinds of persons,
whose labour could not be worth sixpence a day,
and must rather be an obstruction to the real
workmen, were crowded down by their sovereign lord, the rabble, to dig ravelins and hornworks, lay culverins, and probably be laid, before
the day was over, in the work of their own hands,
by some of the French cannon-shot, which were
already beginning to find the range of the city.

A luckless acquaintance of mine, a thorough
beau, who prided himself on showing the Hamburghers the perfection of London costume, was seized
in all his glories, and ruthlessly ordered to dig for
the national good. This he did, with however
unpatriotic a spirit, for, I believe, six solid hours.
The rabble had caught him at the moment of his
emergence, "sleek as a summer serpent from his
hold."—"For what is this?" was the astonished
fashionable's question to his captors. "*Fur arbeiten,*"
(to work), was the answer from a hundred roaring
mouths. To resist, or to reason with them, was
equally useless; the mob were masters. To pro-

test against the sovereign will, was probably a waste of words; for, if his harangue were in English, it would have failed of all effect on the high Dutch ear; if he attempted his defence in French, of which he knew perhaps as much as accomplished Englishmen in general do, and which amounts to the reading of the coffee-house *carte,* or the hotel bill; this expedient would have only plunged him deeper still, for that tongue was now in the last stage of unpopularity; every speaker of a syllable of it, however guiltless of grammar, was marked as a spy; and the eloquence of a Cicero, in French, would have only increased my unlucky friend's chance of being hanged. Whether he made any additional effort for life, by a desperate dash into German, he could not be brought to confess. His fortitude yielded at last, and he dug, *malgré.* But let it be remembered in extenuation, that he was all this time in the centre of a fiery rabble, fiery with the heat of a burning day, fiery with gin, and fiery with that much more inflammatory potion—the sense of having every thing their own way. Those fellows might have flung him to feed the fishes of the Elbe, if they pleased; or have ground him in one of their own sugar-mills; or roasted him in one of their furnaces, and blown his dust to increase the arable lands of Hanover; and all with perfect impunity at the time. He wisely embraced the gentler alternative of the spade; and delving with an indignant heart, had the short-lived glory of contributing to the defence of Hamburgh. But the day's experience inoculated him with wisdom for the rest of his life, and, whatever he might be, he was a worshipper of his majesty, the mob, no more.

The battle was still going on. For a while the firing had lulled, and hopes were entertained that the enemy were in retreat; but it soon appeared that they had been merely attempting either to draw the Hamburgh troops forward, or to march round them, and cut off their escape. The firing suddenly opened again, and from its increasing loudness it was evident that the French were rapidly gaining ground. The agitation in the city was now excessive; the hurried scenes of leave-taking, and flight to the Danish territory were renewed, and the women and children were sent off in crowds.

War is at best but a gloomy business; but he who desires to fill his mind with its gloomiest aspect, should not look for it in the operations of the regular armies. Let him look in the peril of the opulent and tranquil city, in the peril of the peaceful people, in the father, brother, and husband plucked at a moment from the pursuits of domestic life, and flung, with strange weapons in their hands, into the midst of deadly struggle ; the man, in this half-hour surrounded by his family, and looking forward to a long and undisturbed life; and in the next, seeing the whole prospect broken up, hurrying away every human being belonging to him, with probably but faint hopes of ever seeing them again; and then snatching up his musket and hastening anxiously, or desperately, to the field.

The multitude now surrounded another of my friends, and would probably have had his services, reluctant as they would have been ; but for their having already grown weary of pursuit, or their being satiated with capture, or their seeing a trio or quartett of old gentlemen flying from a coffee-house; a prey too tantalizing to be missed, and after whom they soon set off at a speed which left little doubt of their success.

As I passed again through the Jungfersteig, I

found it deserted by all its usual haunters. But the signs of the times were there. A huge ammunition-waggon, covered all over with the ducal Mecklenburg coronet and inscription, had just arrived; and a party of the Mecklenburg guard were lounging about it, and listening to the fire. In another corner, the alarm post of the Burgher cavalry, were standing a troop of this fine corps, gloomy enough. Not a syllable was to be heard among them. The whole Jungfersteig, which, on other days, was a perpetual promenade, was now utterly silent; or the only sound was the occasional explosion of musketry, or the clang of some horseman galloping up to fall into the ranks. It is impossible to doubt that those gentlemen would have exhibited the spirit of soldiers in the field; but they must have also felt the formidable stake for which they were playing, and that not merely their own existence, but the interest of every thing dear to them was in the game at that moment. A soldier's funeral is proverbially one of the most melancholy of all displays; but here was the still more melancholy one, of the quiet people of a great city, of its men of commerce, literature, and all the various pursuits of rational and meritorious life, on the point of being sacrificed; for all might be over in the next five minutes.

The action had now continued for some time, and the firing was becoming constantly heavier: it was at length one unbroken thunder. As the confusion of immediate flight passed away, and the females of the principal families were gone, the streets were deserted by all but a straggling Cossack, an express riding full speed, or a few of the common people standing mournfully at the corners. The multitude had withdrawn into their houses; where they remained, probably waiting to see for what new master they should be compelled to huzza before the day was over. But a change was at hand; a long sheet of steel, the bayonets of a column of gallant Holsteiners, began to glitter down one of the streets leading from the Altona gate. Nothing could be more opportune. The people rushed down from their houses, and crowded the streets instantly. The Danes were received with wild exultation; and one old fellow electrified a gentleman of my acquaintance with his snuff and his joy, as he danced about him with Gallic grimace, exclaiming, "*Nous sommes sauves! Les Danois sont ici!*"

We followed the column. The windows were crowded with people eager to have a view of the Holsteiners; and all was shouting, clapping of hands, and waving of handkerchiefs. The troops came up in high spirits, in the expectation of being let loose at the French, for whom they had the instinctive German hatred. A corps of sharp-shooters headed the column; and they rather swept, than marched, along towards the scene of action, singing in chorus a pretty opera air! which formed an extraordinary contrast with the perpetual peal of the musketry. It was impossible for soldiers to approach the spot of blood and death with a more gallant bearing.

But their march was too late; the French were already masters of the islands, and continued driving their defenders before them. They were now near the river side. Our force had been altogether too small; not above a thousand men, and those chiefly volunteers and recruits, against four or five thousand regulars, drilled by Napoleon's sergeants and corporals!

From the ramparts all the movements were visible, painfully visible; for the French were evidently forcing our unfortunate soldiers before them in all directions. Still a fire was kept up, which must have cost the enemy a considerable loss. But retreat was inevitable, and the great anxiety now was to cover the retreat. The Holsteiners had arrived only in time to see this unlucky catastrophe, and they were now drawn up on the *Grasbroek*, one or two companies only having been sent across the river. Every boat that could be procured was rowing as fast as it could across, to re-embark the troops. The whole affair would be called a skirmish, compared with the great scale of continental battle; but a battle of 100,000 men might not have been fuller of eager interest than this struggle of a few corps. While one portion of our troops got into the boats, an attempt was made to form a rear-guard, by groupes, which continued firing on the enemy as they began to show themselves through 'the thickets, and along the edges of the river. But this was soon at an end: the whole French force threw themselves forward, and rushed on at once, like a mob, firing as thick

as hail, and shouting. The French are a remarkably mob-like race in action; for the Frenchman's
first preparative for an engagement is to pack up
his coat, which he reserves for parade; and to cover
himself with his grey surtout, which, thus under-
going the wear and tear of the field, as well as the
other drudgeries of service, soon becomes ragged.
Nothing but the tufts in their caps, and their
musquets, could prevent these fellows from being
taken for a crowd of clowns in full riot at a fair.

Our troops at length got over, still heavily fired
on during the whole crossing by the enemy, who
seemed to enjoy the mischief, like boys let loose
to play; if we were to judge from their antics and
huzzaing. When they had reached the water's
edge, they could come no farther, and the firing,
of course, died away.

I was now beginning to have my share, slight as
it was, in the public calamities: for the family in
whose house I lodged, had taken wing, and I was
left to manage for myself; though the house was not
altogether a solitude, for a company of Mecklenburg grenadiers were billeted in the lower rooms,
and they contrived to make them vocal enough.

The *tables d'hôte*, too, such as they were, were on the point of breaking up ; and, for a stranger, there was no alternative, but trying what could be done in Altona.

To Altona, then, a party of us went, and found the strongest imaginable contrast to all that we had left behind : handsome saloons, gay crowds, and an immense *table d'hôte*, whose hilarity seemed not at all affected by the presence of war within a quarter of a mile. On this day the town was unusually crowded ; for many of the Hamburgh families had come in, preparatory to their moving into the interior of Holstein. The conversation naturally turned on the events in Hamburgh ; and the opinions were as various as the speakers, until a young Danish officer of dragoons, a genuine Scandinavian, with Albino eyes, and a head as scarlet as his own coat, coming in to take his *chasse caffé*, astounded his hearers by the intelligence, that the results of the day would be, to place the French in a situation to bombard the city whenever they pleased ; the last island which they had captured being within a few hundred yards of the ramparts ; and it wholly resting in the bosom of that man of mercy, Davoust, whether he was to starve Hamburgh, to take it by storm, or to burn it, houses, warehouses, batteries, and burghers, together.

But other and better news, soon after announced, that the Danish troops having been actually engaged, and his Danish Majesty having a " paternal regard for Hamburgh," he had determined to protect it with his last regiment and his last rix dollar; that henceforth we might sleep in safety; and that we had nothing to do, but after having finished our wine, walk down to the water's edge and see there on parade half a dozen of the finest regiments that ever baffled the tricolor.

The evidence was not too far off, for even the most epicurean contemner of this world's affairs. We left the table, and walking down the gardens, saw the showy phenomenon of what seemed the whole host of Denmark drawn up between us and the setting sun; 4 or 5,000 soldiers manœuvring under the canopy of one of the most magnificent of summer skies: all was bayonets, plumes, and banners, thundering drum and sounding trumpet. The citizens were crowding out from the gates of Ham-

burgh, to enjoy the sight; with as little appearance
of care, as if they were 500 miles, instead of simply
500 yards, from their persecutors. The French had
disappeared, and seemed to have sunk into the earth;
for, gaze as we might along the islands, and many a
telescope swept them; not a vestige of an enemy
was to be seen, nor even a vestige of the action,
except a solitary farm-house, which had been set
on fire during the struggle, and which smouldered
still. All this was promising; and we were all delighted, and all seeing perpetual victories, and perpetual summer; when a sudden blast of cold wind,
descending, to every body's wonder, from a sky that
looked painted from the zenith to the nadir with
roses and violets, the very pavilion of sunshine and
serenity, and where the sun himself, giving " golden
promise of a bright to-morrow," lay pillowing his
chin, not upon " an orient wave," but upon an occi-
dental cushion of crimson, richer than all the velvets
of the sophi; startled us with the menace of a tempest; a menace which was duly executed, and which
soon and furiously broke up the gaieties of the
evening, sent the citizens flying home in hundreds,
and drove the unlucky Holsteiners to their *bivouac*,

which was, for this night, at least, in the open
Hamburgher-berg with no better bed than straw,
and no more satisfactory shelter than what they
could find in the lee of a showman's booth, or the
burrow of a sand hill.

CHAPTER XVII.

THE ENVIRONS.

THE Germans are habitually a brave people, and the Hamburghers remember the French government too well, to give up any struggle that can keep them out of the hands of Napoleon. They are still determined to fight it out, if they can find any help in Europe; and the Emperor Alexander's promise is still looked upon as a pledge of the advance of a Russian army. This is the popular view of the case; but the graver counsellors shake their curled fronts, and say; that while emperors themselves are not always to be depended upon, and Tettenborn cannot be everywhere at once, Cossack as he is; the French are in sight, and are even carrying on negociations with our friends the Danes; as is evident to any one who will but walk as far as the water side, and see the French staff crossing from the governor of Altona's house to the islands, a dozen times a day.

My especial counsellor has again advised me to put my valise in marching order, mount the best horse that I can get in the stables of the hotel, and leave the city and its ill-fortune as far behind as my charger can carry me in a day's journey. One piece of intelligence which strongly reinforces this wise advice is, that the waggons with the wounded in the late engagements, have been sent this morning at day-break into the country; a measure which shows that the authorities themselves are not very sanguine in their hopes of resistance.

But it is proverbially hard to "convince a man against his will." The crisis is not yet come; the people are still in good spirits. What is war but chance? The perpetual variety even of the hazards has some interest; the allies are still masters of the field; and we may still see the good ship, "City of Hamburgh" run down the pirate "*Le grand Napoleon.*" Besides all this, there is an actual interest in a national attempt to throw off chains, a natural sympathy with the uprising of a people against the proud and the oppressor, superior to all others. Heroes and armies are but triflers and trifles in comparison.

This view of the case is not universal; for some of the strangers in Hamburgh are taking occasion to wind up their affairs, embarking in my old abomination, the Blankenese boats, and making the best of their way to Heligoland; others less involved in mercantile objects remain.

But Hamburgh is becoming an inconvenient residence, in more points than its hazards. The chief families have already left it for the interior; and society is totally at an end. The club, and the coffee-house share the same fate, and are now little more than gloomy coteries of individuals depressed by the circumstances of the times; or places of actual danger, from the number of spies which the French employ to watch the popular proceedings, and which the Russians in turn employ to watch the French partisans. An Englishman's openness of speech, is a formidable disqualification for living in quiet in such times. All the pleasant intercourses of the day are thus cut off; and the stranger is to all intents and purposes alone.

Another source of inconvenience is, the inevitable difficulty of leaving the city, in case of any serious advance of the enemy.

The teazing propensity to gates and passports is among the hundred evidences of the foolery that passes for wisdom on the continent. The passport system is intolerable ; it has all the demerit of being a nuisance to the honest traveller, while it never excluded a knave. All that can be pleaded for it, vexatious and wasteful as it is, is that it provides a little contemptible patronage for the little court ; and a little meagre subsistence for the lank, liver-coloured, half-beggars and half-thieves, who contrive to starve upon it at their desks from year to year. Its impediments to national intercourse, its annoyances to the traveller, and its demoralization of the miserable officials, who pilfer both traveller and revenue, never enter into the heads of the military personages who exercise sovereignty on the continent. But the gate propensity has not even this beggarly patronage to plead ; and yet nothing is more frequent than to find a town, which could not resist an army of Friezland hens ; a sort of cemetery above ground, whose whole population is divided between cripples and old women; shutting its gates daily with as much scrupulosity as if a hundred thousand Tartars were roving the land, and threatening to make a bonfire of every pauper of this decaying workhouse. So it goes on, frontier or interior, war or peace, alike; the crazy gates must be kept close, until the commandant has ascertained that the coming post-chaise is not a Trojan horse, with an invasion in its belly; and that a yawning Englishman and his valet may be admitted without danger of blowing up the empty magazine.

In Hamburgh, the same absurdity is practised, with even more vexatious punctilio. For the last hundred years it has been out of the case of strongholds; it could have no hope of being shot at, starved, slaughtered, and burned, for six weeks together; glory was excluded in all quarters, for the whole affair would have been ended in as many hours by the advanced guard of any of the armies that have flooded the fields of the continent with their prodigal and profligate blood during the hundred years. The city had but a ditch and a rampart; yet its gates must be opened and shut with as much precision as if *Louis le Grand*, or Alaric the Goth, were waving torch and banner over the Hamburgher-berg. Unlucky was the jovial culprit, even in the most piping times of peace, who prolonged his Christmas banquet in the environs till *five* in the afternoon, for the gates were remorselessly shut at half-past four. Unlucky was the citizen, who wiping the dust of his counting-house from his soul, roved the evening fields in the merry month of June; for unless he could speed back by half-past nine, in the fields he must make his *bivouac*. And the vexation was made still more vexatious by the perpetual change of the hour: for, once every fortnight certain minutes were added or taken away; and the citizen-errant must keep an almanac in his pocket, and regulate his coffee by the town clock, or sleep in a ditch. Even the mail-bag could not be suffered to pass, when once the gates were shut; from the obvious hazard that an enemy might be franked in, as it went out; take the postman by storm, and advance from the capture of the bag to the spoliation of the city. And all this solemn vigilance had been transacting in times when the rivalry of sovereigns was concentred in their opera boxes; when the black eagles of Hapsburgh and Brandenburgh were domestic fowls; when the Napoleon eagle was in the shell, and the world was on half pay.

The only expedient for sending the post-bag, was, literally, dragging it by a rope over the rampart, and then dropping it down to be ferried over the *fosse*.

But in this gravest of grave cities, from time immemorial every thing has depended on the mystery of locks and keys, as much as the capitol ever depended upon its geese. Pending all the deliberations of the burghers, be the subject what it might, war, politics, or the price of beer; the preliminary act of national wisdom was, to close all the gates, and set strong guards upon the padlocks. The second act was to lock the doors of the stadthouse; and the keys being formally delivered to the president, and the secrets of the council thus precluded from evaporating, the debate was in a situation to begin.

The gates were kept shut on Sundays during Divine service; a well-meant precaution, but which succeeded only in making the people hostile alike to the restraint and its cause. But upon all occasions, whether " domestic treason or foreign levy," the primary expedient was to bolt and bar; to the infinite annoyance of all persons unaccustomed to find their movements bound up with the blunders of the most solemn council of burghers underneath the moon.

Those precautions had, of course, always been found utterly useless for any better purpose than stopping a post-chaise, or imprisoning a mother and her young ones, longing for fairings and fresh air. Every enemy which had taken the trouble to advance to the gates during the last century, had found them, like the Homeric valves, opening by instinct. The Danish army had always walked in, when they had occasion; and a more burgher-like army was not upon the earth. On their last warlike approach, in 1801, five thousand of those sedate soldiers gently moved to the edge of the ditch at night fall, where they made no more disturbance than its own ducks. All Hamburgh, too, was in a state of equal tranquillity. The senate slept, the people slept; among a population of a hundred and fifty thousand, there was not a waking eye, nor a distrustful bosom. The gates had been locked, and the keys laid under the official pillow; and having thus performed the last duty of civic precaution, the commonwealth had lain down on its flock-bed, secure against fire, flood, and the arts of man.

The Danes, in the same spirit, piled their muskets on the glacis, wrapped their cloaks round them, and quietly committed themselves to slumber. Nothing could be more profound; not a shot was fired, not a centinel challenged; not even the postman, the Charon of the ditch, and the only human being on his legs at that hour, was impeded in ferrying over his bag. Day dawned, but it dawned on none of the ferocities of civilized war. Neither shot nor shell exploded in the ears of this easy community; there was neither scaling of ramparts, nor storming of barriers; but the Danish general, prince Charles of Hesse, got on his horse, waited till the usual hour of unlocking the gates, and then, while one half of the citizens were in their beds, and the other half inhaling the morning air at their shop-doors, and poisoning it with their pipes; he marched his army through, took possession without resistance, and remained master of the city until some months after; when, for reasons of state, which, of course, no man could comprehend; it was his pleasure to withdraw.

But the Hamburghers were to have another lesson, of a more pungent kind. In 1803, the French, under Mortier, invaded Hanover. Of all the instances of national panic, this was the most remarkable, and the most ridiculous. Hanover could have annihilated the army that the French marshal led in, to frighten it out of its life, domineer over it, and eat it up. It was a conscript army! in other words, a mob of boys, utterly in rags, shoeless, musketless, half-starved, and almost wholly undisciplined. The Hanoverian army, on the other hand, mustered 20,000 men, in the highest state of discipline and equipment; brave, and even an acknowledged model to the other services of the continent.

But absurdity was the continental order of the day. Napoleon was " Lucifer *à cheval.*" Half a dozen German blockheads, with their old brows loaded with hereditary titles, and their heartless breasts frosted over with stars and embroidery, voted that resistance was an impossibility; submitted to the fashion of the time, and gave up army, government, and country to the men without powder, ball, or breeches. The English cabinet were all astonishment; the old king, George the Third, a true Englishman, who would have died in the last ditch of Hanover, before he would have signed the national disgrace; was all indignation. The Duke of Cambridge was sent flying over, to stop this singular proceeding; but the affair had been expeditiously settled; he found every thing ruined, and had not time to carry anything away, but himself and the cream-coloured horses. The Hanoverian troops were outrageous at the surrender; but to fight without arms was hopeless. They did all that was left to them to do; they refused the French temptations to take service, made their way in crowds over the frontier, and finally enlisted in the English levies, and formed that very gallant and distinguished corps, the German Legion.

But this leads only to the Hamburgh moral. A French army, 500 miles off, is a dangerous *neighbour;* but Hamburgh had scarcely so many yards between her and the Napoleon dragoons. She was huge, helpless, and rich; while Mortier was a

bold beggar, without a franc in his military chest;
and had been sent, for the simple purpose of clothing and feeding an army of vagrants in the north,
until they should be fit to " serve their sovereign
in the south." An aide-de-camp was accordingly
despatched to the burghers, with the formidable
message that " the Marshal wanted money." The
senate met, and replied, that they had none. The
aide-de-camp replied, that in that case, the Marshal must take the trouble of finding it for himself, sack their city, and send the whole corporation
to French dungeons, or to the shades of their fore-
fathers.

The conferences were tremblingly renewed; but
the sum demanded was enough to shake the state
from its propriety,—it was no less than 4,000,000
marks[1]. The burghers remonstrated; the demand
impinged too deep into the national soul, to pass
without many a bitter deliberation; but the Frenchman was impracticable. Mortier had but one plea,
necessity; and but one argument, free-quarters.
There is no reasoning with a logician who answers

---

[1] The mark is about 16d. sterling.

a syllogism by cutting off the head. The sabre argument settled the case; and the city, with many a pang, at last paid the money.

The environs of Hamburgh abound in villas, several of them large and handsome, but not handsome on the English scale. They are chiefly long, low buildings, with a profusion of windows, which shows that our tax on light and air, of all taxes the most obnoxious, has not yet reached the burghers. Those villas generally have large gardens, and are airy and cheerful; French furniture has been making its way into them within these few years, but the natural German taste is for huge presses and tall cupboards, solid piles of mahogany, and the heavy utilities of an English parlour a hundred and fifty years ago; a time on which, probably, England herself has not much improved since. The gardens are full of produce, for the soil is fertile, the air pure, and the people are remarkably fond of fruits, flowers, and all that belongs to country life. The native German manners, too, are amiable, the people simple and

pastoral, and there is a look of quiet comfort in
their households that greatly attracts a stranger.
In England, our villas are *fac similes* of London
houses, transported *en masse.* The house to which
I have been at last induced to transfer my quarters,
might be a mansion in an American forest.

It is a genuine German country residence. Spacious, irregular, but convenient, hollowed into bed-
rooms, numberless, and of all shapes and sizes, with
a garden that looks like a new recovery from the
wild, rich, intricate, and diversified with all kinds
of flowers and floridness; and not a few oddities of
antediluvian ornament,—arbours and box-trees,
carved into an architecture worthy of the primitive
ages. Yet some parts of this little wilderness have
evidently been tamed by a more delicate hand. It
has under its shades a small marble fountain, pouring a feeble thread of bright waters in honour of a
sleeping nymph, " Venus, or grace, or dryad of the
wood;" a little half-weedy lake, reflecting the remnant of what may have been an orangery; and, in a
secluded corner, thick with woodbines and willows, a
sepulchral urn, to the memory of a fair one, whose
loss is described as having left the world without

13

her parallel. The Germans are nothing without sentimentality; and in all times and places they are sentimental; though even Germany is not yet guilty of a *Père la Chaise.* The French are still their masters in the art of tears shed for the public, deliberate distress, and anguish in artificial flowers.

Whether the urn should be reckoned among the decorations of the place, may be questioned, but it has one ornament which precludes all controversy: this is a nightingale, the queen of all its tribe, an absolute Catalani on the wing, which fixes its "procreant cradle" here, and trills for hours all sweet melodies ever sung by nightingale. Altogether the spot is a delightful exchange for the heavy temperature, stagnant air, intolerable pavement, and perpetual, superfluous bustle of a foreign city. Here the traveller may linger, like a Sybarite, if not sleeping on rose leaves, at least treading on them in every path, hearing innumerable traits and tales of the French, Spanish, and Italian lords of the soil under Napoleon; and, with the peace of a cosmopolite, watching the distant ways of this belligerent, and very idle, world.

CHAPTER XVIII.

THE SPANISH SKIRMISH.

THE man to whom every day dawns, with the chance of his being shot or starved before its sun goes down, may well be forgiven for living the life of Master Barnardine—

" Master Barnardine, you must rise, and be hanged,"

and caring little about the romance of things; which may account for the few histories of adventure from the pens of soldiers. But this is the land, and this would be the time, to collect, perhaps, as curious a variety of anecdotes of men and things, of odd developments of character, and of striking and touching adventure, as modern warfare could supply. Napoleon's policy or restlessness was perpetually moving his troops of all nations from garrison to garrison, and Hamburgh has seen a crowd of strangers pinning her stubborn neck down by the bayonet, from every corner of Europe. It is singular enough that she found the Spaniards the most intelligent and civil, and the Italians the most boorish and insolent. But there were, of course, exceptions to this anti-Ausonian spirit; and among the viceroy's troops, if we are to judge from the slight narrative given here, there were some who could feel with due abhorrence the unprincipled nature of even their great countryman's ambition.

A skirmish on the Seville Road.

" We were lying in camp at Bayonne, when the news of the British entry into Madrid put us all on the alert. I belonged to the third chasseurs of the Milanese division, and we were ordered to escort stores to the army of the south. Our convoy was strong, through fear of the guerillas, who were beginning to be troublesome again, and who seldom let any of our waggons pass, without exacting a very heavy toll. But, to keep up our spirits, we were informed that this kind of fighting, which vexed like a swarm of gnats, was at an end by the time we got rid of the mountains on the fron-

tier. At all events, we were chasseurs; the plunder
of a guerilla's pack was sometimes worth a little
trouble; and even a brush with them now and then
would serve to vary the dulness of the road.   All
turned out as we expected, but the face of the
country: we had heard of the frontier as all that
was luxuriant; we found it all barren, league on
league of grey-stone, burned earth, and melancholy
valleys, the very spot for a hermit.   But the guerillas gave us but little time for thinking of the
landscape; they were on us every where. We however suffered little loss; as our convoy was a complete
battalion of infantry of the line, two squadrons of
good cavalry, and my three companies of chasseurs.
The whole affair was generally the most animated
thing possible.   Whenever we heard a musket
shot, the whole column closed up and halted, until
we found on what quarter the attack was coming.
We no sooner saw the hats of the Spaniards, than
we threw off like a pack of hounds.   My chasseurs
were up the hills in a moment; a brisk firing began;
the cavalry rode round the base of the hills to lie in
wait for the fugitives; a few were shot, a few taken,
the enemy disappeared like ghosts; and we moved

on again.   In this way we passed along, until we
reached the Sierra Morena.   There the badness
of the roads, which had been neglected from the
commencement of the war, broke down a considerable number of our waggons; and as we had now
reached a country completely in the power of our
troops, the officer in command thought it better to
go forward with the main body, than linger for
their repair.   Some hundred men were left behind
to escort them accordingly, with orders to follow to
a town three marches off, which was to be the head-
quarters of the convoy.

"I had been taken ill, and remained with the
waggons: the delay, however, was trifling; and in
twenty-four hours they were on the road again. Unluckily the commandant of our escort, in order to
make up for lost time, took it into his head to
move by a narrow forest-road; instead of that
through the open country, which made a circuit of
some extent.   I observed to him the hazard of
this route; he gave me civilly to understand, that
I was not then at the head of my regiment; I said
no more, and into the forest we plunged.   For
some time all went on well; but the forest grew

thicker, the road narrower and more broken, and at last a grove of oaks brought us almost to a stop. We here found our advanced dragoons, who waited for the column, that they might not be entangled alone in the grove. We had scarcely worked ourselves a dozen yards among the trunks and copse, when an advanced marksman fired, and in a moment after we saw people with muskets in their hands running round us. Their numbers increased rapidly, and we soon had them in every direction —front, flanks, and rear. Our commandant had now found out his mistake, and had nothing to do but to get out of it as well as he could. The column, of course, formed at once. The infantry were posted at the head and in rear of the waggons; my chasseurs formed line on each side from front to rear; and the dragoons were pushed into the wood, on both sides of the road, at twenty paces off, to act as skirmishers.

" The fire had already begun, and the enemy had all the advantage—he might single us out as he pleased, while we might take our revenge by firing at the trees. We saw some of our dragoons tumbled from their horses, while others galloped back to us wounded. Platoons of infantry were advanced to support them, and they soon also began to feel the effects of the fire. Our next experiment was to send thirty dragoons to cut down every thing before them. They charged gallantly, but they could not cut down oaks and elms of a hundred years' growth; and in a few minutes we saw about one-half of the troop gallop back again, followed by a shout and a shower of balls.

"We were now situated awkwardly enough, and in fact, had nothing for it but fighting. The commandant was a good officer, though he had entered the wood; and the soldiers fired at a desperate rate. We made our way, losing men continually; still we got on, until we came to an *abattis* of trees, in the very heart of the forest. Here the business was for life and death: the enemy, though only peasants, were bold and capital shots; and it was not till after an hour of despair and carnage that we broke through the barrier, wound our way through the forest, and again saw the light of heaven. This cost us nearly all our waggons, two-thirds of our escort, the commandant a severe wound in the knee, and me a ball in the shoulder.

" This was an unlucky affair, and it left us all in
ill humour. We moved on, determined to try no
more short cuts; and about half a league further
saw another grove. We all shrank at the sight;
but, above the trees we saw, at a turning of the
road, the chimneys of a château. This, of course,
would afford quarters for the officers, a hospital
for the wounded, and plunder for the rest. I now
remonstrated on the necessity of losing no more
time ; but the commandant's wound had made him
outrageous, and the sight of Spanish property was
not easily resisted among our troops at that period.
So, it was determined to try what was in the inside
of the chateau.

" We left the few carriages that remained to us
in the road, and sent our sharpshooters up the grand
avenue—a stately range of oaks. There was not a
soul to be seen in the house: the windows were
closed; and, but that the dogs barked fiercely, we
should have thought that the whole had been
visited by the plague. The soldiers hammered the
great door with the butt-ends of their musquets,
flung stones at the windows, and at last began to
fire at the shutters. All was useless. At length

as we were beginning to lay faggots against the
door, a small window was opened, and a man's
voice inquired—'what we wanted?'

"One of our officers, who had already served in
Spain, answered, that we wanted to get in, and have
some refreshment and rest. The voice replied, and
bade us go to a farm house in sight, where we should
find provisions. 'No,' said the officer, 'that is
not enough; open the door, or we shall get in in
spite of you.'

"'You shall not get in,' said the voice. 'We
have force enough to defend ourselves; retire at
your peril.'

"This defiance put the troops in a rage. They
looked on it as an insolent challenge; and while
some of them prepared to scale the windows, others
ran off to bring up our guns, to burst open the door.
The commandant, however, would not allow them
be used, through fear of bringing the guerillas
upon him again. At length they broke open the
door with the levers of the guns. As it fell in, a
line of fifty men drawn up in the court within fired
a volley, that knocked down one half of our people
in front. The rest fell back for a moment; but the

whole corps now rushed on, and filled the court before the Spaniards had time to reload. A few were killed on the spot; but the greater part made good their retreat into the château, and from that into the grounds; where our soldiers, as soon as they saw the rich furniture of the rooms, did not think it worth their while to follow them.

" I was extremely grieved at the whole affair; and indignant and vexed as I was at so much unnecessary mischief, I was led, partly by curiosity and partly by a wish to be of what service I could to the unfortunate people of the house, to enter the court, and see what was going forward. At this time the first attack was over, and the soldiers had gained possession of the apartments above; but there was still a scene going on that I shall never forget. Some of the Spaniards had either been unable, or disdained, to retreat; and at the further end of the court, against the wall of a chapel, stood six or seven men who seemed determined to die. They had made a little breast-work of some loose wood, and from behind this they kept up a regular discharge.

" I remarked among them a very noble-looking

man, in an embroidered cloak, who appeared to be
their master, and beside him a boy of fifteen or
sixteen, who cried out continually, " Kill, kill the
French!" This lasted a few minutes, and we lost
some men at every discharge, till, at last, our
soldiers infuriated at this defence by a handful of
servants, rushed forward; seven or eight took aim
together at the master, and fired. I saw the boy
fall at the moment: the master staggered a few
paces back, and then advancing, flung himself beside the body. The servants at this sight lost
courage, threw away their arms, and, springing
upon the pieces of wood, climbed over the wall,
and made their escape through the gardens; our
soldiers offering them no interruption, as the resistance was fairly at an end, and they were anxious
only to share the plunder with their comrades in
the château.

"My servant and I were now the only persons in
the court; and I was so much shocked and disgusted with the whole scene of rapine and cruelty,
that I did not know whether to advance or retire.
I saw the court covered with dead, and felt the
natural shudder of every man, not altogether har-

dened, at beholding death in such a shape, while the ear was filled with the shoutings and riot of plunder above. But as I gave a last look to the spot where those gallant and unfortunate Spaniards had made their stand, I thought that I saw a hand waved from among the corpses. I immediately went up to them. The first face that I saw was the boy's. It was turned upwards; and pale as it was, I think I never saw one so handsome. It still retained a slight expression of disdain, which gave a kind of loftiness to its extreme beauty, and reminded me, even in that moment, of the Belvedere Apollo. But he was totally dead. It was natural to feel something at such a sight. I continued almost involuntarily gazing on the face, till I was roused by seeing the figure at his side raise itself slowly from the ground, and sitting up, look me in the face, saying in a low tone, ' Barbarians, is not this enough?' I almost felt as if an apparition had risen before me. The hollow voice, the large eyes nearly glazed, and yet haughty and threatening, absolutely checked my breath. However, I made some steps towards the wounded man, in the idea of offering him assistance. He evidently misconceived me; and turning himself round with pain, clasped his arms round the boy, kissed his lips two or three times, and then looking up at me, seemed to await the mortal blow.

"I was doubly shocked at this, and I believe a tear stole into my eye. I told him in Spanish, that he was wrong in taking me for one of his murderers; that I was deeply grieved at all I saw; and that if I could not help those round him, I might be of some service to, at least, himself.

"He fixed his eyes on me, and said, 'You are a Frenchman, and yet can feel!' It was no time to enter into explanations; I merely replied, 'I wished to take him from that place, and desired to know where my servant and I should carry him to shelter.'

"'It is too late,' said he. 'I am dying. If it were otherwise, I should not'—and he looked at his son's corpse—'at this moment be so calm.'

"I still entreated him. 'Well, then,' said he, 'if you will do me this last kindness, have me carried into the chapel, where my place has been long prepared.'

"I raised him by the knees, my servant put his

hands under his head; and in this way we carried him gently towards the chapel. It was then that I first saw that he was mortally wounded.

"The door of the chapel was open, and there we laid down our melancholy burthen. Under all the depression of the moment, I could not help being struck with admiration as I glanced round. The altar, columns, steps, were all of the finest marble, and the most exquisite sculpture. But the most striking object was a monument of Carrara marble in the centre. It was a dome on four pillars, under which was a female figure lying on its side, with the head resting on the arm, as if in deep sleep: the face and form were of exquisite loveliness. At the four corners of the monument were four large wax tapers burning; and a large black velvet pall, which appeared to have been covering the figure, lay beside it on the ground.

"The wounded gentleman was evidently exhausted by his last effort. I spoke to him, but he was unable to answer. As his countenance gradually assumed the calmness of death, I never saw any thing nobler. He could not be more than between forty and fifty. The large black eye, the arched brow, the cheek slightly tinged with emotion, the mouth, moved with a faint smile which seemed to say that all human efforts were hopeless, and that yet he thanked me; all made up such a face as we see in the pictures of Titian or Da Vinci. It was the Spanish countenance in all its grandeur and all its melancholy.

" I gave him some wine and water from my servant's canteen, and, after an effort, he said, in a dying tone,

" ' Sir, I had once a wife, an admirable creature! Heaven took her from me in the most unfortunate and painful manner. She was worthy of heaven. She died five years ago; I built this tomb for us both: lay me beside her.'

" I could not speak. He pressed my hand, and said again, ' Sir, I thank you for your feelings. If you will let me make one more request, it shall be my last. Bring the body of my boy, that I may look upon him once more, and die with him beside me.'

" I shrank at this. The place was now entirely silent. The soldiers had either gone away or were busy in the remote parts of the château. There was nothing round me but graves and death. I felt an involuntary horror at going into the court, where I should see but bleeding bodies. I will own that I felt a dimness come over my eyes, and shook like a woman.

"The noble Spaniard would urge me no further; he sat up, lifted his clasped hands, and fixed his eyes on heaven, and after a struggle obviously of inward prayer, sank back on the ground with a sigh which made me think that all was over. This awoke me; I went out, and with my servant, whom I found at the door, brought in the body of the boy, and placed it by his father's side.

"While I was gazing on them as they lay together in their sad beauty, I saw the curtain of the altar rise slowly, and from under it peep an old man, who looked round him in great terror. I called to him to come forward, and promised him safety. He was an old servant of the family: and on seeing the bodies, he was in an agony of grief, flung himself on them, tore his white hair, and cursed, as well he might, their murderers. As he clasped his master's hand I saw the eyes open; they were turned upon the boy's countenance, then on me. I heard the lips whisper, 'God bless the hand that brought us together!' then laying his arm round the boy's neck, and pressing his lips to his cheek, the spirit departed with a deep sigh.

"The old servant and I knelt beside them, and, I believe, wept together.

"After a while, as we heard the soldiers returning, we rose and covered the bodies with the pall from the tomb. The chapel was now nearly dark, and the soldiers came in with lighted torches. They asked what was under the pall; and on being told, turned away with looks and gestures of genuine regret. They did not even look at the servant, who stood close to me, expecting to be put to death, notwithstanding my assurances of his safety.

"The drums now beat, the plunder was gathered into the court, cars and waggons from the stables were loaded with the rich moveables of the mansion; I waited until all were on the march, then giving some money to the old man, and bidding him call the fugitive domestics to do the last honours to his masters, I walked, with a melancholy heart, through the deserted court, and followed the convoy.

" From the first rising ground I looked back upon the château—the moon was touching its towers; and when I thought of what was below, I wished, for the first time, and from my heart, that I had never been a soldier."

CHAPTER XIX.

THE BERLIN DECREE.

In the depth of the winter of 1806, the city authorities were roused, I believe, from their beds, to receive a tired French aide-de-camp, who had galloped all the way from Paris to announce to Hamburgh that her four millions of marks were thrown away; that she was no longer mistress of a shilling of her own; that an imperial order had been issued, declaring that the city must be taken into French hands; and that Marshal Mortier, with the promptitude of an imperial general, would be within her walls before breakfast. The announcement naturally threw the inhabitants into dire dismay: all was instant flight, burying of money, hurrying off goods to Altona, which, as a Danish town, might be presumed safe for a while; and that bitterest feature of public distress, the parting of fathers, brothers, and sons, from their families, through fear of being made the immediate objects of French vindictiveness, shot, seized as hostages, or sent off for the conscription. The English factory, composed of the chief merchants, and with whose credit that of almost every house in Hamburgh was concerned, felt that they would be marked out as the first objects of vengeance. They were not mistaken. On the day after the arrival of the aide-de-camp, on the 19th of November 1806, the French troops entered; and almost immediately after, an order appeared, for the seizure of all English subjects, as prisoners of war.

One of the characteristics of the French measures of violence was, that they were always turned into means of extortion. The French functionaries were hungry after gain in all instances, and, like their armies, were chiefly sent to make up for the deficiencies of pay at home. Bourrienne, the French prefect, was said to have been actually told by Napoleon, in so many words, " Go, and make your fortune." And this commutation of plunder for penalties, which may seem the more merciful part of the system, was in fact one of its heaviest aggravations. An intelligent merchant, with whom I had some occasional intercourse, mentioned this shape of the grievance as utterly intolerable.

" If those rascals," said he, for he had the true German hatred of the French, " when they came here first, had had but the honesty to say, we have come to rob you of your last ducat, all would have been understood. Even, if they had told us, we mean to burn every yard of cloth in your warehouses, and make you beggars for life, we should have been better pleased; for the suspense, at least, would have been saved. But, on their first appearance in the city, all was smiling and bowing, and every *gens-d'arme*, or *douanier* of them all, was full of ' regret' at being compelled to look into our warehouses, or take the inventory of our goods; but, for every smile and bow, we had to pay upon the spot. Next day the visit was repeated, some trifles were taken away, merely, as they declared, to show that they were doing their duty; with a hint given, that if they overlooked some of our bags of coffee, or bales of broad-cloth, all was a matter of personal civility. For this civility, we had to pay again; so it went on. Every day a new visit, followed by a new civility,

which of course required a new payment, until at
last we all grew sulky, and drew our purse-strings.
For a week we had no more visits; and some of my
friends congratulated themselves on their resolution.   I acknowledge that the calm frightened me,
and, as it happened, with good reason. The thunder-clap came in the shape of an ' imperial decree,' for the instant seizure of ' all English
goods,' no matter whether already bought with
German money or not; and for the imprisonment
of every man suspected of dealings with England,
dealings in which every man in Hamburgh was
more or less concerned. We now quietly resigned
ourselves to ruin, and, to save trouble, I sent the
keys of my warehouses to the next functionary,
a very polite personage, who had robbed me so
often that I wished to see his face no more. Nothing could be more gracious than his answer; he
returned the keys instantly, saying, that he fully
relied on my *honour*. We were fools enough to
bite at the hook for the tenth time. We met,
bargained with our robbers, and after an infinity
of begging and bartering, saved our goods at the
expense of nearly seven hundred thousand pounds

sterling—a sum, more than their original cost, and which wrung us to the very dregs; but which we paid, merely that we might have some material for carrying on the little home trade left to us. Foreign trade, of course, was all stopped; and we, undoubtedly, had the full pleasure of seeing our goods in our warehouses, for there they were instantly locked up, a new order having prohibited our selling any of them in Germany; and there they remained for the various purposes of rotting, being eaten by the rats, and being mulcted at pleasure by our bowing friends."

At length, the merchants were exhausted, no more money was to be forced from them by either hope or fear, and Napoleon's decrees for burning " all English goods," began to be regularly put in force. The unfortunate merchant who had paid originally for the goods, and had since paid as much more for their protection, saw the business settled by a bonfire. The word English now served as a pretext for all kinds of private as well as public plunder. If the searching officers took a liking to a pianoforte, or a service of plate, a picture, a carpet, a China bowl, any thing; no matter from what part of the globe it came; it was instantly discovered to be of the enemy's manufacture, convicted accordingly of hostility to Napoleon, and transferred to the officer's private keeping. If an Italian violin, a Nuremberg telescope, a set of Frankfort drinking glasses, a Vienna mirror, or even a Paris *pendule*, caught his taste, it was found guilty on the same count; the name of English convicted it, and the traitorous article was transferred to that durance from which it never saw the light until it appeared at some stall in the Boulevarde des Italiens, or the Rue du Temple.

In the mass of those oppressions too there were some which insulted and vexed the citizens in a peculiar degree. It may not be known that the savings' banks were an old German invention, and that an excellent one had been long established in Hamburgh. The people deposited there the smallest sums, and received the regular interest. In some instances those deposits had gradually risen to a considerable magnitude, constituting a means of setting up in trade, a marriage portion for a daughter, or a resource against change of circumstances, disease, or old age; yet on this almost sacred fund the French authorities cast an eye. A pretext was soon found for its seizure; it was construed into a deposit of foreign money; and this sole dependence of a crowd of unfortunate beings was mercilessly confiscated.

Commerce is charitable, and it has in general, from its habits, the advantage of distributing its charity in the most useful and ingenious manner. Many of our presumed inventions relative to the maintenance and education of the lower orders, have been the old practice of the Dutch and German traders; and one of the best arranged poorhouses in Europe was in Hamburgh, liberally supported, and a great object of pride and interest to the citizens. But the French found out that they wanted an additional barrack for their recruits, and some additional thousand francs a year for their own pockets. An order was issued accordingly, seizing the funds, converting the schools and dormitories into lodgings for the soldiers, and turning the whole establishment adrift without ceremony. Those, and a hundred details like them, are in the recollection of every one acquainted with the state of this oppressed city, from the fall

13

of Germany, in the battle of Jena in 1806, to its recovery in the immortal Moscow campaign, a dreary period of six years, in which the continent drained to the dregs the bitterest of all cups,—the cup of slavery.

But, God in his mercy forbid, that such things should go on for ever! a change was at hand. The Russian war began, and even in the first rumour of that war, there was something like a prophetic consciousness that better times were coming at last. It is scarcely superstitious to say, that there is an impulse which often forewarns men, or, at least, nations, of remarkable changes of good or ill. Nothing can be more unquestionable than the sudden hope which was felt throughout Europe on the commencement of hostilities in 1812.

Yet there could be as little comparison between the vast, active resources of France, and the sluggish and unsystematic strength of Russia, as between the practised skill, brilliant renown, and disciplined courage of the French, and the inexperienced bravery of their opponents. The name too of Napoleon alone seemed decisive of the contest. Among all the able leaders of even the French

and German armies, he had never found one who
approached to his own extraordinary talent for war.
But the Russian officers were hitherto almost unknown. Their emperor had seen battles, and had
brought to the field manliness, and an honest determination to do his best; but he was wholly without
experience as a leader. Still, with a full sense of
all those difficulties, there was an undefined feeling,
an impression, that Napoleon had seen his proudest
day, that he must sink, and that Fortune, or a
higher hand than Fortune, was about to exact a
severe vengeance for his long period of triumphant
crime. But, in the intermediate period, all Germany
was sinking into pauperism; her higher orders were
driven to despair by perpetual insult and robbery;
her lower compelled to criminal courses by the
mere pressure of hunger. The system of smuggling
had become the only resource of trade, and a more
pernicious and demoralizing system never was offered to tempt the natural evil of man. Fraud on a
greater or lesser scale was rapidly infecting all commercial transactions: every thing bore a fictitious
name in the invoice; coffee passed the customs as
horse-beans, sugar as starch, and pepper was alter-

nately pease, rape-seed, and a hundred other things.
The quantity of oaths, forgeries, and bribery, that
made this traffic pass down the consciences of the
douaniers, may be imagined. All was mystification, which yet mystified no one; hungry artifice
openly arrayed against bloated plunder.

Yet some of those contrivances were amusing
from their ingenuity. The short distance between
Altona and the gates was a strong inducement to
smuggling; for the Danes had made their town a
complete West-India warehouse, chiefly stored by
the Hamburgers, and the contest was now between
the activity of the French customs and the Hamburgh trader. A kind of insurance was, at length, effected on the art of stealing pepper, coffee, and sugar
(for those were the favourite commodities), through
the gates, and the rival wits of tyranny and slavery
were never more completely tried. A fellow one
day came to the gate, offering a barrow full of sand
for sale; the centinels laughed at his making a
market of this species of commodity, which was obviously in more than sufficient abundance at their
feet. He however begged of them to let him try
his fortune in the streets. He passed in, cried his

commodity until he was out of hearing of the
French, then threw out his layer of sand, and discovered a cargo of sugar below.

One evening, when the populace were returning
through the Altona gate, they were caught by the
antics of an old fiddler, apparently half mad, or half
drunk, who was dancing and playing in the midst of
a circle of children. Among the other oddities of
his figure, he wore a wig of the old German style,
a monstrous pile of horsehair, most prodigally
curled. The populace laughed, the centinels
laughed, and the guard having nothing else to do,
came out, mingled with the crowd, and laughed
too. In the midst of this general festivity, the
old fiddler, in one of his *pirouettes*, trod on some
one's toe. A quarrel arose, and the French, always
sensitive on those occasions, ran back to the guard-
house for their muskets. The fiddler, in great
terror, ran back along with them, and claimed their
protection. The guard sallied out, and the populace instantly dispersed. In the mean time the
fiddler had walked quietly away. It was ascertained, a few days after, that the whole was a
smuggling *ruse*. The fiddler was contraband all

over, his rags were filled with packets, and the packets filled with pepper, sugar, and tobacco. Even his wig was a conspirator against the law; for in every curl was fastened a nutmeg, a spice against which, for whatever reason, the terrors of the French police were peculiarly inveterate. The dispute was a part of the plan; the fiddler's taking refuge among the Frenchmen disarmed their vigilance; and while they sallied forth to extinguish rebellion outside the gate, he walked in, with a cargo of West-Indian produce, that would have made the fortunes of the whole guard.

The system of search began at length to be but a cover for insult. The garrison were aware of the popular abhorrence, and they exhibited their sentiments on the subject by stripping men, women, and children of shoes, coats, hats, bonnets, and every part of their dress in which there could be a possibility of concealing contraband goods. The increasing irritation of the people was retaliated by the increasing brutality of the searchers. The most respectable families of the citizens were soon obliged to undergo the same insolence; and uniformly, on passing the gates, see their carriages opened and searched in every corner; while the ladies were ordered into the guard-house, and there, in the midst of soldiers, peevish and embittered by the knowledge of the public hatred, were compelled to undergo the most offensive examination.

The passport system too, which, if the object were to discover at once the most vexatious and the most trifling contrivance for keeping the peace of the community, would deserve the palm; was screwed to the highest pitch in this harassed city. A passport was required for every thing. If a family left town for their villa, though but a mile off, and but for a week; a passport must first be procured for themselves, and for every moveable that they took with them, a bed, a chair, a table; the delinquent furniture that stirred without a passport being forfeited to the law. A paper must actually be sent to the *douane*, stating the number of pounds of feathers in the beds, the number of changes of linen, &c. down to a pocket handkerchief. All must go to the *douane*, there to be weighed, registered, and all this registering and official impertinence to be duly paid for. Further security, too, must be found by the proprietor, for the return of his chairs and tables within eight months; or he must pay the same duty as for newly imported goods. If a family carried as much tea or coffee out of the town as would make their breakfast, the penalty was almost as heavy as if they had smuggled it in; and the first insolent *gens-d'arme* whom they met had a right to overhaul the whole party, a right which he generally exercised with the loyal activity of the sword.

As for the popular luxuries of wine, brandy, and tobacco, which by long habit had become necessaries; the difficulties attendant on their use were nearly equivalent to a direct prohibition. More than three bottles of wine, which once was as much in common use as beer, could not be sent to the next door without a regular passport; and half a dozen would have drawn down the whole vigour and rigour of the offended *douane*. A present of a cask of ale often involved as much delicate negociation with the police, as if it had been an affair of life and death; and the steps were so intricate in the transfer of the merest trifles from house to house, that the matter often ended in confiscation, if not in fine. But troublesome as it

was, to be thus compelled to apply to the public
offices on every occasion, the annoyance was still
increased by that well-understood official vexation,
delay. The clerks of the custom-house, chiefly
imported in the train of the army, all assumed the
air of masters. The citizens were the conquered,
the *serfs* of those barons of the inkstand. For, one
of the misfortunes of a Frenchman is his national
habit of looking down upon the people of all other
countries; the honour of being *né François* settling
the question of superiority, and he being generally
content to take no further trouble in the establishment of his claim. It would, of course, be unfair
to take those fellows as specimens of the French
character; they were the off-scouring of France, the
rabble who naturally follow in the train of an army,
at all times a wretched school; and in this instance
rendered worse, by its being a requisition army, a
hungry multitude, who had been sent, to fill themselves up with plunder from a country which it was
the policy of their master to impoverish. They had
been flung out of French life to scramble for a subsistence among the beggaries of Germany; they now
felt that their time was short, and they were only

the more active in their rapacity.   The passports
gave those people a perpetual means of insult and
exaction.   A man hurrying into the country to see
a dying relative, to seize a flying swindler, or to save
a friend or a fortune from instant ruin, must first
undergo the official caprices of those gentlemen,
who might withhold his passport for days or weeks
together; and all who know the vexation and offence
of waiting the pleasure of the minor masters of office
even under the best *régime*, may imagine how the
misery was envenomed where the parties were the
beaten, the plundered, and almost the prisoners,
on the one side; and a whole host of *petits maitres*,
half military, half *garçon de boutique*, all coxcomb,
and all swelled to the skies with personal and
national vanity, on the other.

But the storm was brewing; men would not be
men, or not deserve the name, if they could rest
under such perpetual degradation.   The curses, at
first not loud but deep, soon became both deep
and loud.   Even among the multitude, the miserable
money which they still could earn in their trade of
smuggling, was converted to the purchase of ammunition and arms.   The populace grew visibly

more sullen, and the French garrison found itself compelled to be more on the alert. The forced civilities of the leading families declined; and though the enemy, with that adroitness which every where characterizes them, tried to keep up their own spirits, and those of their adherents, by giving frequent balls, and making it a point that the members of those families should attend them,—a refusal being notoriously construed into disaffection,—yet their balls fell off, their gaiety became visibly more constrained, and it was evident for some time before the explosion, that the garrison of Hamburgh felt themselves to be in the midst of a hostile population.

CHAPTER XX.

THE INSURRECTION.

FOR the last ten years no head has slept on an easy pillow on the continent. Even in France, triumphant, haughty, and all-contemptuous France, the nation has added but another example to the old moral, that all is vanity. Her conquests have only increased her burthens; she feels that she has been fighting the world only to make herself the more abhorred, and a slave; that she has been breaking down the thrones of other countries, only to compel their people to fabricate from their ruins weapons against herself; and that she has at last succeeded in nothing but the erection of a wild and unnatural influence over Europe, for which she pays a no more trivial price than perpetual torrents of blood, and her last hopes of liberty. The miseries of an incessant conscription, and the iron weight of a despotism unrivalled for malignity, are even now bowing down her crowned and helmeted head. Her power is still tremendous; but it is all straining and convulsion. This cannot last. I see the iron legs already mixed with the clay. She will fall, and her empire will be remembered only for a furious ambition, a more than infidel scorn of the obligations of kingdoms to God and man, and a most bitter, subtle, and merciless disdain of every feeling that could impede its seizure of the general tyranny of mankind.

But Germany, as the victim, has naturally felt the working of this evil principle, under more direct and undisguised sufferings. Here it is war in procinct, the soldier and his sword, fear and flight at the coming of the enemy, a hideous crush and sacrifice of life in the collision, and the battle followed by a long course of plunder, insult, and heart-breaking oppression, worse than the worst evils of the field. But, as suspense is often more anxious than actual infliction, perhaps no spot of the continent can be fixed on as the seat of keener anxiety than a huge open city, lying in the very current of the war, and supposed to be inexhaustibly rich. Perhaps as much of the fever of life as ever disturbed the heart of man has been felt within the walls of Hamburgh since the beginning of the war. It was here no English perplexity, reading its gazette over a breakfast-table, and pondering what the enemy might be thinking of at the other side of an impassable channel. Here every wind blew with tidings of actual hazard; and who could tell how immediate that hazard might be? The rumour might be realized with a dreadful celerity, which left no time for escape from the most fearful visitation of public misfortune; the newspaper conjecture of the morning might be authenticated before night, by the appearance of twenty or thirty thousand military robbers and murderers at the gates, hot from some massacre of their countrymen, and threatening to turn house and householder into dust and flame.

This extremity of suffering is still fortunately averted from this great and intelligent city; but its past miseries ought not to be forgotten, where men are to be roused to the last resistance against an invader. The conduct of Napoleon's troops and officials, from the period of their entrance, has been already adverted to, and it was singularly vexatious; but from the arrival of the Moscow news, it became altogether intolerable. Whether from mere vindictiveness, or the feeling that their reign was to be short, the system became hourly more capricious, insolent, and severe.

The phrase of " free quarters" is proverbial for all the worst kinds of military spoliation; but in Germany at this period the word " garrison" was almost equivalent to free quarters. The people were robbed indiscriminately; they were trampled into the very mire of slavery. If the soldier was lodged among the poorer families, he was in every sense master; he forced them to sell their furniture, their clothes, every thing that was saleable, for his subsistence. He insisted on having his meals dressed in his own style; and on finding any deficiency in either the material or the style, grew outrageous, broke the furniture, laid the flat of his sabre upon the family, and threw the plates and dishes out of the window. The officers, many of whom had been raised from the ranks, were scarcely more manageable than the soldiers; not only a regular entertainment was required for them at the expense of the house, but they insisted on having the

choice of whatever rooms, furniture, or provisions
it might please them to require; in some instances
they chose the whole house, and every thing in it,
which it was a matter of too much *delicacy* to
refuse; and the family were consequently obliged
either to divide themselves among their friends, or
find another roof.

The wastefulness of this style of living, kept up
for months, and sometimes for years, was enormous;
for the garrison was seldom less than from ten to
twenty thousand troops, sent apparently for no
other purpose than to be fed and clothed until they
were fit for service, and then marched away to be
followed by another swarm of boys equally raw,
ragged, and mischievous. The public purse was
hourly declining by the constant restrictions on
trade; and still it was only the more wrung by un-
ceasing demands for the subsistence, arming and
clothing of conscripts; until the whole population
was on the verge of mendicancy.

The insolence which accompanied the extortion
made it yet more grievous. The governors, the
generals, the aides-de-camp, the *employés*, down to
the valets of those important personages, exer-

cised a regular trade of plunder, under the name of "compliments" for official favours. The general going out of command, demanded a *compliment*, sometimes to the value of 4 or 5000*l*. The general coming into command, expected to be welcomed with a *compliment* not less by a livre. Every creature connected with him made his predatory rounds; and the grand process of threat and exaction went on, until there was nothing more left to exact. Industry was at an end, the people were pauperized, and another year of the same system must have seen the city deserted by every one who could leave it behind him.

But a crisis was ripening. The French troops and partizans had uniformly ridiculed the idea of defeat at Moscow; and woe to the blabbing politician who dared to hint that the emperor was not already sitting on the throne of the Czars. Men may talk themselves into any thing; and the French had talked so long and loftily of the physical impossibility of the "grand army's" being beaten by anything earthly, or, perhaps heavenly; that they succeeded in vapouring themselves, from the general to the drummer, into the most amusing and most hazardous state of security. But the truth grew, and like all truth, prevailed. The Russians *were* advancing to the frontier of Germany; they passed the frontier, they entered Berlin; their hussars were riding over Saxony; the Cossacks were in Mecklenburg, in Saxony, in Hanover; the allied lance and sabre were glittering round a circle of a day's journey from the city: still the garrison continued to scoff at the idea of danger; when an adjutant, " bloody with spurring, hot with fiery speed," galloped in from Magdeburg, with orders for the immediate flight of the whole force.

The populace had long and well known the state of affairs. The mere confusion that in all cases attends the sudden movement of an entire garrison, now gathered them from all quarters; and they determined that they would have some revenge before they parted with their old friends.

The quarrel began with the *Krahnleute*, or city porters, a body of old establishment, with peculiar privileges, and very tenacious of them, but in general a remarkably well conducted and trustworthy race. Some arrangements were probably made among those people during the night; for early in the morning they assembled in great numbers on the city quay, where it was supposed that the enemy would embark their baggage. The sight there was not calculated to soothe them. The French *douaniers* had already taken possession of a number of barges, and were proceeding to load them with goods brought from their *dépôts*. The history of those goods was well known; and the whole process excited such palpable ill-will, that the porters employed in loading the vessels soon refused to work any more. Soldiers were ordered down to compel them; they worked for a while with the bayonet at their backs, but stopped again. A strong reinforcement of troops now came to complete the embarkation. But the public wrath was only the more inflamed. The populace shouted for every fresh repugnant. The bargemen joined the porters, and both resolved that neither goods nor soldiers should go on board. The heads of the *douane* now interposed; but where every *douanier* was personally known, and marked by personal abhorrence, this but rendered the tumult furious. Showers of stones and missiles of all kinds suddenly rained upon *douaniers* and soldiers alike. The tumult rapidly spread in all directions, and wherever a custom-house *employé* was seen, he was hooted down, pelted, and insulted in every possible way.

The Baumhaus, so called from its being near the booms which closed the port, had been the original scene of the insurrection; but in the course of a few hours, it had run through every part of the city, where a remnant of the detested *douane* was to be found. Every toll-gate, guard-house, and store, the whole apparatus of the *régie*, name abhorred of German ears, and not too popular under any of the hundred titles of excise, in any land; was demolished in the face of day. Down went the signs from the shops, which had once thought themselves only too much honoured by being permitted to exhibit the imperial eagle, or the picture of Napoleon in his glory. The billiard-rooms, " *à l'Empereur*," the *cafés* with their French gilding and *affiches*, all followed the example; and, before night fell on the labours of the new regenerators, Hamburgh was gallantly purified from every vestige of its Parisian loyalty.

One injury which the honest Germans peculiarly felt, had been the confiscation of the *Eimbeckshe-*

Haus, or public cellar.   This was an establishment
of the fourteenth century; for, as the native wits
say, the first fact in the history of every German
city is, that in it has been drunk beer.   The original
purpose of the building was for the public stowage,
and sale of the Eimbeck and Brunswick brewing.
But, as all the pleasures of the old German life
were in some way or other connected with beer,
round this central indulgence had grown a young
generation; and the *Eimbeckshe-Haus* at length
contained apartments for dancing, concerts, and
suppers.   Business, which makes a part of the
national pleasures, made its way too; and there
were apartments for the sale of goods by auction.
One thing more was alone necessary to complete
the circle of human affairs; and the *Eimbeckshe*
contained a room for the reception of the dead by
accident in the streets or river, probably no uncom-
mon result of its symposia; and thus the *Haus* became an epitome of the world—a German microcosm,
a cycle of mortality.   Among the odd traditional
customs connected with this building, was, that in
one of its rooms, the public executioner was privileged to have ingress and egress without taking off

his hat, or being questioned on his business. Thus life, death, and the giver of death, had their share. The hangman himself had here " a local habitation and a name ;" and, though at no time likely to be a popular personage, he possessed in this spot a consciousness that he had a public stake as well as any of the solemn burgomasters carousing within ; though abhorred of men, he was yet a citizen in this stronghold of beer.

But the vaults of the Haus had the higher reputation of containing some of the best wines of the German vintage. Its Rhenish of every kind was celebrated ; and though their antiquity might be exceeded by the stock of some of the cellars on the Rhine itself, it could exhibit binns that had not been opened for half a century. The *Raths-keller*, or city wine store, was one of the boasts of the Hamburgher.

But this famous establishment, thus dear to every bibulous prejudice of nature and nations, the French had seized, almost at the moment of their entrance. There might have been some allowance for so tempting a capture by an army coming in hot and thirsty from a march over the Hanoverian sands ;

and the people would probably not have felt the circumstance as more than that " *fortune de la guerre*," which prepares a foreigner for every thing. But the wine was said to have been not drunk, but sold; and the price to have been put to neither the public account, nor even that of the French requisitions, but into the private pocket; and, while the citizens were called on to supply the garrison with wine, and to give the French officers the keys of their domestic cellars, the public wine and the public money vanished together.

On this day the memory of the plundered *Rathskeller* was strong; and many a French customhouse officer, flogged in front of it, as an expiation to the manes of the Hockheimer and Johannisberg, might have wished that the binns had never felt the grasp of war.

The conduct of the garrison, during this furious period, exhibited the extreme uncertainty of depending on a military force in a popular insurrection. There is no ground that so soon slips away from under the foot of power as a regular army. The garrison might have driven the mob into the Elbe, yet they were panic-struck; they heard themselves execrated; they saw their barriers torn down before their faces, and their guard-houses burned over their heads; their antagonists were a mere rabble, many of them women and boys, yet they scarcely dared to fire a shot. The people ran from one object of destruction to another, and exercised their rude justice, without any impedi-' ment, except from their own precipitation.

One act of vengeance pleased every body. A French fellow in the police, who, by his peculiar insolence and extortion, had attracted the favour of his employers sufficiently to be made a commissioner, was early marked out for especial retribution. As it was presumed that the garrison, however torpid during the morning, might at length make some resistance, the people prepared for this exploit with rather more than the usual form. After gathering their force in some of the by-streets, and sending out a few women to reconnoitre the state of the commissioner's defences, which amounted to nothing but closing his shutters, the whole multitude made a grand attack upon his castle. Never was manœuvre more expeditious, or more successful; the whole house was instantly in possession.

13

The ladies were peculiarly heroic; they led the column of attack, and were seen in another moment at the windows in the full glory of patriotism and pillage. The commissioner had been a man of many callings; for, to his political character, he had added that of a trader in sugar and coffee, prizes which now peculiarly stimulated the public zeal. The women returned into the streets with their caps and aprons loaded with spoil. When his stores were completely gutted, those heroines gave up the honours of the day to the men; the *Arbeitens-leute* rushed in, tore down the furniture, flung a part of it out of the windows, conveyed the rest into carts, and, in the course of the day, completely cleared the house. The walls remained, and it was nothing but the scorn, or the weariness of the multitude, that spared even the walls. The police despot was completely stripped, unfeathered, plucked to the bone; never was public functionary more thoroughly taught the value of the *vox populi*.

The French troops remained passive during the whole course of this proceeding; but the burghers, naturally alarmed for the results of an experiment, which they justly conceived might soon

spread beyond the houses of the culprit commis-
sioners; at length assembled, and armed some of
the old city guard. In the afternoon a troop of
Danish cavalry were sent for, and the city was
comparatively tranquillized.

But the blow had been struck; the French *employés* perceived clearly that their villain occupation was over; and during the night the greater
part of them took their way out of the gates, and
fled wherever they could fly to a French garrison.

The injury done to the French individually,
after the first effervescence, was but trifling; though
some of this forbearance was owing to their own
dexterity. A striking instance of the effect of discipline occurred in the day. In the height of the
tumult the populace had attacked a toll-house, in
which there were but three soldiers. The little garrison speedily felt the untenable nature of their post,
and sallied forth, to make their escape to the main
guard. The populace gave way before their presented muskets for the moment; but on seeing
them turn, pressed upon them, throwing stones,
and threatening them with instant destruction.
Fortunately for the Frenchmen, their pursuers had

not fire-arms; otherwise their tale would have been soon told. They still retreated; whenever the crowd came too close, the three presented, while but one fired; in the check of the pursuit, they gained a few steps; and thus they went on from street to street, firing, one at a time, and deterring the crowd by the two in reserve. If the three had fired together, they must have been overwhelmed. But those dexterous fellows still baffled the multitude; who at length, wearied by their firmness, suffered them to rejoin their comrades without further molestation.

The runaways from the city were less fortunate. The peasantry had long arrears of bitterness to settle with the douaniers. They had been too often forced to submit to the insolence of the guard-house, and see the plunder of their eggs and poultry, to throw away their opportunities of retaliation. The first news of the flight roused them from all their thickets; they posted themselves at the bridges over the Elbe, seized the officers, flagellated them, stripped them of their money, which the peasants not untruly declared to have been robbed from themselves; in some instances stripped them of their clothes, and in all turned them back to Hamburgh. The sabre blows, kicks, and *sacrés* of other days, were fully remembered, and poetical justice was seldom more handsomely done.

But the French were still too powerful in Germany; and an express sent to the general commanding in Lower Saxony, brought back a furious answer. The principal citizens felt that the disturbance would be visited on them in robbery. There was no allied force sufficiently nigh to be of any use; the Danes would not resist any *open* declaration of French authority, and the French had 30,000 men at Magdeburgh! The *fusillade* and the *mitraillade* were the natural expectation of the populace.

In this crisis was seen the want of a leader. If but one man of popularity or rank had started up, the foot of a Frenchman would never have repassed the threshold of Hamburgh. With the villages in its immediate vicinity, and its population of 150,000, it could have raised a garrison of 50,000 as muscular and stubborn bodies and minds as any in Germany. Its ramparts were unfit for a scientific defence; but with the porters and bargemen of

Hamburgh behind them, they might have cost an army. The whole city is intersected by canals, whose number may be conceived from there being no less than ninety bridges over them; and, if those bridges are chiefly of wood, they were but the more easily convertible into the means of cutting off an enemy's communications. The streets long, narrow, and winding, the houses solid and lofty, and the river at once forming a barrier, and opening an intercourse with the country and the ocean, supplied all the features essential to defence; and Hamburgh might have become only a more successful Saragossa.

But the leader was not to be found. The French came back; the senate shrank before the menaces of Lauriston; military execution was suffered without resistance by a city and populace, which but a few days before had manfully, if not defeated the garrison, at least reduced it to inaction; and the result of this deficiency was the mulct of the public purse in sums of money, and the harassing of the population by personal injuries, tenfold the probable sufferings of the most daring resistance.

A military commission was established on the

arrival of Lauriston's orders; and, as a commencement, six of the people, of whom a considerable
number had been arrested on the arrival of the additional troops, were handed over to the tribunal.

The conduct of this tribunal was tyrannical and
infamous in the highest degree. The French military law appoints a counsel for every prisoner. But,
in this instance, the counsel appointed was a French
corporal. The sentence was read in French, which
the poor fellows so little understood, that when
they were conveyed from the court, they were
ignorant that they were to be put to death. They
were taken outside the gate to the open ground,
between the city and Altona, and there first found,
to their astonishment and horror, that they were
to be shot. Even this cruel murder was made
more cruel by the manner of executing it. The
duty was entrusted to a platoon of conscripts, who
had, probably, never fired a musket before in their
lives. The first volley failed to kill *any one* of the
prisoners; it was, of course, to be repeated, and
thus those unfortunate men were made to undergo
the repeated bitterness of death; until, after successive discharges, all were slain! The whole pro-

ceeding, too, was atrociously expeditious. From
the entrance of those unfortunate people into court,
to their being laid corpses on the Hamburger-berg,
the time was but three hours.

This murder excited universal indignation; and
the populace required but a word to have risen.
The higher citizens, in dread of the bloodshed and
ruin that must have followed from their collision
with the garrison, increased as it now was, and
ready to repel the slightest symptom of revolt, immediately applied to the prefect, declaring that
they would not be answerable for the result.
This demonstration produced its effect: twelve prisoners who had been ordered for trial next morning, were withdrawn; and the violences on both
sides, excepting a few personal rencontres, were at
an end.

From this period, the people and the soldiery
kept at a cautious distance from each other. The
people hated them, and, probably, would have exhibited their hatred in the most summary manner,
but for the expectation that the Russians were at
hand, to inflict a more sweeping vengeance. There
was also a small ingenuity about the French which

they never suffered to lie idle; but which, like all
petty dexterity, soon deceived no one.   Every day
had its report, propagated by the police, and believed, under pain of disloyalty to the fortunes of
Napoleon.   On one day, " the allies were defeated
with prodigious slaughter ;" on the next, a new army
was coming headlong from the Rhine; and on the
third, when scepticism had grown stubborn, all
doubts were to be silenced by an *affiche* posted on
the *prefect's* house, ordering the citizens to prepare
for " His Imperial Majesty's reception." At length,
a more formal programme announced Napoleon's
immediate approach.   This seemed sufficiently
authentic ; and the unhappy city was preparing to
rejoice with a sorrowful heart, when the sound of
drum and trumpet was suddenly heard. The first
impression was that the emperor was come; the
next was mutiny or massacre.   At all events, the
troops were in motion.   They had started up from
their dinners, and fallen in on parade with their
artillery.   Some new violence was naturally looked
for, and for a while there was considerable alarm
in the city; but the French took their way to the
gate.   The populace gradually crowded after them,

15

to be assured that they were about to get rid of their plunderers. The French still moved on, and the multitude followed, still in silence and wonder. The troops gave no molestation, and they received none. They passed the gate; the rampart was at length between the parties; the enemy had actually fled; the Steinthor was no longer dishonoured by a French patrole; and to the infinite public joy, Hamburgh was once more FREE!

END OF VOLUME I.

GILBERT and RIVINGTON, Printers, St. John's Square, London.

THE

YEAR OF LIBERATION:

A

JOURNAL

OF THE

DEFENCE OF HAMBURGH

AGAINST THE

FRENCH ARMY UNDER MARSHAL DAVOUST,

IN 1813,

WITH

SKETCHES OF THE BATTLES OF LUTZEN, BAUTZEN,

&c. &c.

IN TWO VOLUMES.

VOL. II.

LONDON:

JAMES DUNCAN, 37, PATERNOSTER ROW.

MDCCCXXXII.

LONDON:
GILBERT & RIVINGTON, PRINTERS,
ST. JOHN'S SQUARE.

CONTENTS.

VOL. II.

iv   CONTENTS.

CHAPTER XXI.

───────

THE COSSACKS.

THE first consciousness that a man could eat, drink, or sleep, without being called to account for it by a French policeman, was one of universal and acknowledged delight. That a citizen could sit in his own shop, walk in his own garden, or cross the next street, without a passport for the use of his limbs, were discoveries that diffused their proportionate exultation. The people rushed out of the gates, to feel that they were not followed by a dozen French bayonets at their backs; and roamed through the fields without the fear, for once in ten long and wretched years, of the *gend'arme* and the flat of his sabre, before their eyes.

Let none either doubt or ridicule those feelings,

who have not known what it is to be under a
foreign yoke. If there be one infliction which
beyond all others breaks the heart of a people, it is
the infliction of a hostile power fixed in a country;
not merely flooding it with war or the horrors of
war, for those have some compensation in the rapidity of their havoc, in the hot-blooded resistance
that they rouse in the brave, and in the gallant
despair that will not live to be shamed and scorned;
the true calamity is in the *chain*, the long course
of small but universal irritations, the perpetual petty
robbery, the sleepless insult, the unwearied invention of new stings for the slave ; the iron, rusty as
it is, that enters into the soul, and that enters it
rust and all. Heaven defend England from ever
seeing the foot of an enemy ; but if it should come,
let her wipe out the traces, though it were in
her heart's blood; for it is happier to shed that
whole generous tide at once, than to have it soured
in all its fountains, and, though it be drop by drop,
not the less utterly drained.

But while the multitude were in jubilee, their
superiors were in perplexity. None had seen the
Russians, though every one affirmed that they

were on the road. If the French recovered from their fright, and returned before the Russians came, the burghers well knew the formidable price that a French army exacts for the recovery of its senses. The result of the deliberation was, to send messengers to look for the allies, wherever there was a hope of finding them, and hurry them on to the defence of the city. One of those messengers at last found Tettenborn at the head of his Cossacks, but still three days' journey from the ramparts.

But a new difficulty arose. The object of the allies was to make Hamburgh the centre of a northern insurrection. To do this the old forms of government must be first renewed. Tettenborn insisted that the change should be *spontaneous*, to please the allies. The citizens supplicated that it should be *forced*, for fear of displeasing the French; a matter of sufficient peril in case of a change of fortune. Tettenborn, in return, declared that his ear was not made for the sound of mayors and municipalities, when he came to meet burghers and senators; and that if he was to enter Hamburgh as an auxiliary, he must enter it as a German city;

concluding by the intelligible sentence, that if he found it a French city, he must treat it as a French one. There is no hope of arguing with a reasoner who is at the same time a Cossack. The city became German without delay, the functionaries laid down their tri-colored titles, and the transaction was curiously concluded by a saving manifesto, of all screens the feeblest against the thunderbolts of Napoleon. This half-treaty, half-protest, was as follows:

" All the French authorities, civil as well as military, having quitted the city, and the Russian commander, Baron Tettenborn, having declared that he acknowledged no authority in Hamburgh except the ancient government of the senate and citizens, and that he would receive no deputies except from them; the members of the ancient senate have thought it their duty to provide for the interest of the city, and have accordingly resumed their functions."

But the city had to remain nearly a week longer in suspense; for no Russians appeared. The French partizans were on the alert again, and in defect of arms, fought with reports; they asserted that the

Russians had gone off in fifty other directions, leaving the citizens to the vengeance of Napoleon; and that there was a strong French force moving down from Pomerania, and ordered to do military execution upon the revolters.

The mingled uneasiness and curiosity of the people, led multitudes out for successive days on all the roads by which the Russians might be supposed to come. But no tidings were brought back; and some of the people who had gone the farthest did not return at all. The French patroles were known to be along the Elbe. Positive intelligence at length came that their troops from Pomerania were within a day's march; they were at length actually seen by the peasantry, and their numbers, as usual, magnified by alarm, were computed at 10,000 men; the Russians were gone to the moon! The mixture of fear, indignation, and surprise, in the city during this period, was indescribable. But, towards nightfall, on the 17th of March, accounts were brought that a corps of cavalry was seen advancing. It was soon ascertained, to the great delight of the people, that they were Russians: all was now congratulation, " Hamburgh was saved." By degrees a little knot of Cossacks were discovered from the ramparts; they made their way, with some difficulty, through the crowd, waving their lances, and answering the general salutations with good-humoured laughter and grimaces: they were received with huzzas; lamps were placed in the windows, and the Cossacks enjoyed, if not a triumph, at least an ovation.

But the next day was the grand exhibition. The old fatality, by which public shows so generally select rainy days, was broken for once. The sun rose on a sky as blue as ever Claude painted, a premature May in March; and between dress, delight, enthusiasm, and curiosity, the whole city was in gala. The ramparts, under any circumstances, a beautiful object, were crowded early with all the handsome women of the city. The guilds and trade companies had put on their ancient costumes, which, like all those of the feudal time, are striking and picturesque. A deputation of the senate, with the keys, took their stand on the glacis at some distance from the gate; but a more attractive display was a group of the prettiest maidens of Hamburgh at the gate itself, all clothed

in virgin white, and loaded with garlands to be
presented to the victorious baron and his bold
riders. All the Gallicism of this famous old city
had vanished like the vapour of its own fosse, and
Hamburgh was herself again: with her furred burgomaster, furbelowed senators, gallant train-band,
and sharp-shooters, all in Tyrolese feathers and
green, a celebrated corps in the establishment of
every German free city. The morning flew; proces-
sions, shouts, expresses in full gallop, popular songs,
and the full chorus of all the coffee-house minstrels, breathing, fiddling, and harping loyalty in
the loudest strains, passed the time. At length
there came signs of other entertainment: and distant
guns, the rush of the populace, then the glitter of
the volunteer cavalry, and, finally, the moving of
a grey forest of pikes, told that the Cossacks were
at hand. Tettenborn rode on at their head, as
gravely as he could: but he must have thought
his new friends mad. His Cossacks palpably did
so, and their barbarian visages were all wonder,
laughter, and burlesque. They were brown as
baboons, and not unlike them. The Calmuck
visage had probably not laughed so much since

it swallowed ginseng in the shadow of the wall of China.

This was triumph, and but a part of the long triumph of the Cossacks, the longest ever enjoyed by soldier or general : for it was a continued march of shoutings and celebrations from Moscow. Such are the eccentricities of fortune. How would it have shaken the ghost of the great Macedonian in his grave, to think that a Scythian namesake, one of those savages, whom he would have scarcely recognized, but as a more untameable ourang-outang, should have enjoyed, at the head of savages, even more polar than himself, a course of honours to which the entry into Babylon was but an exhibition of gilt gingerbread, fleeting as a lord mayor's show, the promise of a young politician, or any other of the habitual emblems of things made to pass away.

But description breaks down under me, and the rest of the task must be left to the Correspondenten, which, seldom liable as it was to ardours of any kind, next day fluttered all its poetic plumage, and was fairly on the wing.

" On the colonel's arrival at the gate, and the

presentation of the flowers, the rejoicing rose into an enthusiasm that seized on all, ' Long live the Emperor Alexander! our deliverer! our preserver! —Long live Wittgenstein;' and again, ' Hurrah!' exclaimed thousands of voices incessantly; innumerable handkerchiefs waved from all the windows and carriages; the companies of the different trades waved their gay colours; hats adorned with green boughs were seen carried on long poles, or on the points of swords, or thrown with loud huzzas into the air. All the church-bells rang, everywhere were heard the firing of muskets and pistols, and the cheering of innumerable spectators. On all sides the people pressed forward, and adorned the horses of the officers who rode forward with green boughs; the ladies threw flowers and garlands on them. Many were seen to weep for joy; friends and strangers embraced, and congratulated each other on having lived to see this day. In every street were busts of the emperor Alexander, crowned with laurel. Colonel Tettenborn stopped a moment before each bust, and gave a huzza, which was repeated by the people with enthusiasm. Again we say it, never since the building of Hamburgh was such a transport of joy seen in it, thanks to the *mildness* of the French government!

" In the evening the whole city was illuminated, and in the theatre ' God save the King' was chorused by all the audience. When Colonel Tettenborn left the theatre, the people took the horses from his carriage, and drew him home, when they lifted him out of the carriage in triumph on their shoulders. The illumination lasted till morning, and during the whole time music and acclamations successively followed without a moment's pause."

Those demonstrations were extravagant, but there was nothing fictitious in their raptures. The people were actually filled with delight at their escape from the intolerable insults and exactions of the enemy. Nor was there any revolutionary bitterness in their joy ; they asked for nothing more than to be allowed to return to their old habits, to follow their natural pursuits, and to get their bread without the eternal clang of the bayonet, or the bitter voice of some military ruffian alternately sneering and cursing at them. The exultation of the people was the outcry of nature.

13

But the Cossacks were still the great object; and a multitude of tales were told of their humour, sagacity, courage, and pre-eminent faculties for eating and drinking. Many of them had brought an additional horse, for which the populace seriously accounted by the belief that a Cossack, pushed for provisions, carried the horse with him as livestock. It was said that the whole French municipality of one of the German towns, having been suddenly missed, the truth turned up, only on an examination of the Cossack wallets—the Frenchmen had gone the way of the horses! One of the stories, in particular, which always preceded the march of the Cossacks, and always found its *locale* in the last city which they entered, was gravely domiciliated in Hamburgh; *un peu embellie*, I presume.

A party of those wild warriors had sallied from their bivouac in the market-place, to take a view of the city; and peculiarly attracted by the coloured bottles in a French chemist's window, which they conceived to be various kinds of the choicest wine, they ordered the chemist to indulge them with a trial of his vintage. The man, utterly surprised, and in great alarm, endeavoured to make them acquainted with

the facts of the case ; but as he knew nothing of
the dialect of the Donski, he got no other answer
than an incredulous shaking of heads, which soon
proceeded to a half-drawing of sabres. The argument was at an end in a moment; and the chemist
bringing down all the goblets in his house, with fear
and trembling, poured out his red, green, and blue
stock of acids and alkalies, expecting to see the
first taste returned by a blow of the sabre. However he was " *quitte pour la peur.*" The bottles
were emptied with great expedition, a handful of
francs were thrown to him, the party retired, and
the little Frenchman breathed again.

But one steadier fellow than the rest, lingered
behind, and continued to acquaint his host that he
wished to have something stronger; and, suiting
the action to the word, seized upon a bottle of
aqua fortis! The little Frenchman, naturally calculating to see him drop dead on the spot, and to
be hanged for his murder, threw himself on his
knees, and in an agony of gesticulation, implored
him to abandon this formidable luxury. But the
Cossack had fought all the way from the Don to
the Elbe, and had seen too many Frenchmen throw

themselves on their knees, to be susceptible of this species of appeal. The chemist's wringing of hands, and tearing of hair, only convinced him that he had hit upon the true treasure at last. He swallowed the contents of the bottle at a draught, and then walked coolly away. The chemist, satisfied that his next visitation would be from a file of Russian musketeers, to put him to death for having poisoned a whole troop of his imperial majesty's cavalry, and especially burnt one of them alive; instantly packed up his few valuables, sent for a passport under some pretence, and prepared for flight to any part of the world where there were neither czars nor Cossacks. But, before the delays of office could be got over, and while the unfortunate Frenchman counted the minutes till the arrival of the passport, he heard shouts round his house. The whole pulk were in the street; a party rushed into his shop; he prepared to be torn limb from limb without mercy; but, to his utter astonishment, at the head of the party was the aqua fortis drinker, who, seizing him by the hair of the head, and brandishing his sabre over him, pointed to the place where stood the empty bottle,—and demanded more! One of the troop now came forward, and explained, that the liquor had received so high a character from their comrade, that the whole corps desired to have a trial. The Cossacks were rich; francs and French crowns were showered on the counter; the chemist's cellar produced its last bottle of the favourite dram; the Cossacks drank its last drop, and the little Frenchman made his fortune.

The qualities of the Cossacks as " field troops," have been extravagantly exaggerated; for a regiment of well-appointed English cavalry, or even of French, or German, would ride through ten thousand of them. But it is no part of their *tactique* to meet such troops. They even seem timid in the field; and a dozen smart Frenchmen, in a block-house with a six-pounder, would keep a horde of them at bay. Yet, they are individually brave, and often adventurous to an extraordinary degree. In Germany, there have been instances of single Cossacks riding twenty or thirty miles a head or in flank of the army, and, of course, in perpetual hazard. But their vigilance and patient attention, where they have any particular duty assigned to them, are admirable. It is the Russian custom, to assign two or three Cossacks as a personal guard in the field, to the general officers, and sometimes to the commanders of regiments; and from this simple precaution, there is no continental service, in which so few instances occur of officers of rank being taken prisoners in the field. An instance of capture by surprise, probably, never occurs. The Cossack is perpetually on the watch, and precedes or follows the officer wherever he moves. As a guide, too, through a new country, he seems to have a peculiar faculty for discovering the right road; like the directing organ of a bird, or a blood-hound, the Cossack makes his way by a kind of instinct, and is a much safer guide than nine out of ten of the maps. He has also an admirable eye for ground; and where the object is to take up a position, either to await an enemy, or make the most of a small force, the commonest Cossack might often give a lesson to the quarter-master-general.

Some of those qualities are perhaps quickened by his living in vast plains, and his being thus compelled, like the American Indian, to make every journey something like a voyage of discovery.

But there is no clearer fact, than that different nations have an original distinction of faculties, probably intended with reference to their circumstances. If the Englishman, placed in a locality unrivalled for its natural means of trade, possesses beyond all other men the natural diligence, vigour, and sobriety of mind, essential to turn those means to their highest value; or if the Greek, seated in a country which from its natural divisions and intersections implies a division of governments, and their consequent struggle, was, by nature, the most subtle, active, and eloquent of men, the only *native* politician in the world; or if, enjoying the most picturesque and most brilliant of all countries and climates, he was gifted by nature, with the finest powers to take advantage of its unrivalled beauty ; this was little more than the course of nature. We see it in all the inferior creation ; there every living thing is *placed* according to its faculties ; the strong-winged eagle is *made* for the summit of the mountain; the lion is *made* for the desert, as much as the desert is made for the lion; the butterfly is *made* for the honey-suckle and the rose.

From the butterfly to the Cossack is a long stride; but the vigilance and keenness of the inhabitants of the Steppe, are nature, however heightened by practice. The surprise of a Cossack patrole, is among the rarest occurrences of war; from the moment of his being fixed on an outpost, he is indefatigable in ascertaining all the features of the country.

One evening, as a friend of mine was passing over some fields at a considerable distance from the city, he was hailed by a Cossack. He went towards him, conceiving that his object was to make the wanderer give an account of his movements at the suspicious hour of twilight. This was soon settled; for, few as the Cossack opportunities may have been of meeting with Englishmen, and knowing not a syllable of the language, they all readily recognize the accent. But the young Cossack, for he was a mere boy, had another object. On the horizon was a thicket, which in the shade of evening, might favour the advance of an enemy's party, and from its ridgy line was not unlike a party itself. The boy could not stir from the spot where he was fixed by his officer; and there he stood with

his eyes exploring the thicket. My friend gave
him such answers on the subject as he could. The
dialogue in broken French, " tesselated" with still
more broken German, was not likely to be very
instructive. But the Cossack contrived to make it
answer his purpose; and there he was left, lance in
hand, standing by his little horse, and still turning
his quick Indian-looking eyes to every point of the
champaign.

With all the exterior of the north, the Cossack
sometimes exhibited the taste of the south for
splendour. No coxcomb in the French or German armies could be fonder of an embroidered
cloak, a pelisse of sables, or any ornament, gold,
silver, or steel; forms that seemed to claim kindred
with the bear, exhibited, with palpable enjoyment,
upon their shoulders the epaulettes torn from
some prostrate general officer, or frost-nipt chamberlain of the " grand empire;" and their little
horses, rough as wolves, were frequently festooned
with coloured decorations and tinsel chains, and
looked as proud of them as their masters. The
horses of some of the superior officers, however,
were remarkably beautiful creatures, finely formed,

and as full of animation as the Arab; they were
chiefly bony and thin, from the length of their
march, but they bounded along like antelopes,
taking evident delight in the sound of the trumpet,
the perpetual clang and glitter of their caparison,
and the bustle and tumult of the wild men round
them.

The conduct of the Cossack himself was by no
means the counterpart of his physiognomy. The
Tartar had either been libelled, or he had submitted to civilization with marvellous rapidity.
We heard of no excesses on their march, though
many of the German châteaux contained nobles
stained by French partizanship; and the troops
had been frequently exposed to severe privations.
In Hamburgh they conducted themselves with
perfect harmlessness, and merely rambled about
the streets gazing at every thing with the natural
wonder of novelty, and most amused of all with
the gaze of the multitude. Their wrath was reserved for the French; upon them the whole Tartar
talent of evil speaking was lavished in the most
unmeasured manner. When the name of Paris
was mentioned, they tore their yellow moustaches

with indignation; they swept the palm of one hand with the other, to express how completely they would clear the earth of every thing French: and " Paris must be destroyed," was often the whole extent of their European vocabulary.

CHAPTER XXII.

THE TAVERN.

May 18. Intelligence has arrived from Bernadotte *at last.* Never was Napoleon, in the height of his fame, more in the public lips than this crown prince of Sweden during the last month. And never was there a cheaper purchase of fame : for it was achieved by the sole act of doing nothing. "*Il ménage bien ses troupes,*" was the spirit of public opinion; and he was sentenced to the fate of the *faineans* and *far nientes* of all past and future obscurity. However, he has moved at last, though our politicians are more profound than ever in their perplexity as to his motives. With some, a threat from the "grand head-quarters general of the grand army of the allies,"—for such is the amplitude of the established title—has awakened his fears ; with others, it is the discovery that Napoleon, (who was undoubtedly

very much chagrined at his election, though to get
rid of him for the time, he permitted his canvass;)
has *another* crown prince in reserve.   But with the
wiser in the ways of men, the stimulant is said to
be those English guineas which are so longed for
by the thirsty finances of Sweden, and which the
English envoy is understood to have the power of
refusing, on the slightest appearance of tardiness
in the Swedish army.   If so, the guineas, the most
powerful galvanizers on record, have rapidly put
new life into the prince's councils; and regiments, pontoons, waggons, and a corps of French
cooks, have already taken up a position on the sands
of Pomerania.

My last view of the Danish auxiliaries was under
a burst of rain.   The burst continued for a fortnight.   We had, during that time, every possible
change of weather, except calm or sunshine: blasts
that seemed to rush direct from the pole; dim,
suffocating, slate-coloured mist; torrents of wild
rain; dull, thick, dreary heat; dismal, persevering
droppings, that might have made us confound the

air with the mire under our feet, and fairly drenched the soul. And it is in a foreign city alone that this state of things can be enjoyed in perfection. The unflagged streets, the gloomy houses, the large uncarpeted rooms, the sullen stoves, the wild doors and windows, that seem made for every purpose but to shut, and which succeed only in gathering and concentrating every wind of heaven on the unfortunate tenant of these sepulchral chambers, make a rainy day a peculiar continental misery; and, according to the philosophic traveller's adage, " almost justify an Englishman in hanging himself, and a German in enduring the conversation of his countrymen."

But this succession of tornadoes had an effect which made them almost welcome. They flooded the river, and the river flooded the islands. Thus, the French could not stir, unless they sailed or swam to parade. They had begun to throw up some works for bombarding the city; but the Elbe forbade the proceedings, washed the works away, and perhaps washed the cannoneers along with them, for our telescopes could see nothing as far as the horizon, but water, marsh, and floating stubble : the enemy

had disappeared. We now looked forward again
to nothing less than the demolition of Davoust's
corps, and the complete deliverance of the territory.
But our little history still continued a checquered
one. The summer sun suddenly beamed, the sky
brightened up, a blast of the north wind for a day
swept away the floods, dried up the morasses, and
we saw the French at their work once more : troops
were evidently crowding into the islands; and a
battery was beginning to rise within an easy range
of our most combustible quarter. Another startling circumstance was the announcement, that the
negociations between England and Denmark had
been broken off (if they ever existed); and that
the Danish battalions were instantly to return
within their own territory.

It is curious to observe how often fame is the
child of circumstances. Before the arrival of the
Danes, the Hamburgh public opinion was certainly
not zealous in its praise of Denmark. Nothing
could be less liable to the charge of courtiership,
when the name of the king happened to occur in
conversation; and the act of unquestionable manliness and promptitude by which the Danish king-

dom was saved from France and ruin, by the
British conquest of its fleet and capital, was lauded
as it deserved. But when we saw 5000 troops,
bold, well-looking, and well-appointed, march in,
and take part in the defence of the city, the change
was prodigious. The forgotten merits of the national character were not more speedily drawn from
their oblivion, than the princely virtues of the
sovereign ; and, for the fortnight during which the
Danes were our sword and shield, the popular sentiment never flagged. But the Danish drums beat
the march, the commandant of our burgher guard
announced that the troops were about to retire, and
from that moment angry history resumed her rights
again. Denmark, which is as honest a little kingdom as any hiding-place of royalty upon earth, was
now pronounced to be a mere province of France.
Her king, who is probably a better man than
a battalion of such potentates as his ancestors,
was declared a tool of Napoleon; the Danish
cabinet was given over to a fate, which shall be
mentioned in no pages of mine; and the whole
transaction, which was possibly one of bitter necessity, was affirmed to be one of the blackest in-

stances of state swindling, the least plausible
Machiavelism, and the most unjustifiable *Gallicism*,
in the annals of war, peace, and perfidy, since the
deluge.

The Danes expressed great regret at leaving us,
without having had, at least, one grapple with the
French, whom they mortally hated. But they
marched. We followed their bands and banners to
the verge of Altona, saw the last flutter of their
plumes, listened to the final flourish of their tam-
bours, and then turned back to ponder on the results of fighting 25,000 French and their field-
marshal, with 800 Cossacks, a few half-drilled battalions of city volunteers, and our city field-marshal,
Von Hess, an excellent solicitor, and by no means
a bad pamphleteer. The phraseology of this condition of things may be light, but the feeling is of
a different order; for the result may be the cutting
of all our throats, and that too within a week, a
day, or an hour. The enemy have been always
within bugle call. They had burrowed themselves
from the rain; but they have now started from
their holes again, fresh as vipers in the sunshine;
and many an anxious eye lingers this evening on

the roofs and little heights round the city, watching the twinkling of their bayonets in the sun.

We were all in bad spirits, Danes, burghers, travellers, and Cossacks. The Danes have got nothing by their campaign, but, in the first instance, a three days' bivouac under the naked sky, bathing them in a perpetual gush from the clouds, that might have soaked the courage out of a Cœur-de-Lion. And even when they were at last transferred to quarters at the gate facing the enemy's position, the enjoyments of the Hamburgh stables and outhouses were scarcely preferable to the weeping skies themselves. They took their departure, dirty, dejected, and sick of us, our stables, and soldiership. If they had kept their own secret, they might have given out with impunity that they had returned from Siberia.

DINED at Altona, and saw, with *my own eyes*, (a matter essential to all knowledge in times like these,)—the French officers ferried backwards and forwards from the islands to the Danish governor's house; negociating, of course. These fellows play us like trout.

The public room where I dined opened on the river; and the sloping garden, the gay crowd promenading it, the garden air, and the sheets of water glancing among the islands, made the prospect gentle and pleasing. But all was soured by the French epaulettes. Those emissaries have come, under the pretext of arranging something about the return of a body of Danish sailors from France; but there can be no doubt that they are much more solicitous about seizing the boats that may be sent for them, and which they will inevitably use for throwing troops upon our city.

I was called off from those contemplations, by the laughter of some Englishmen near me. They were gazing at the performances of a solitary German at his little table. Foreigners charge us, nationally, with a supreme devotion to the pleasures of eating and drinking. But, they do themselves great injustice; they have the most incontestible superiority in diligence, steadiness, variety, and quantity of devouring. I have always seen the Briton put to flight, and the foreigner left fairly in possession of the field. A Frenchman, let loose in a tavern, is the most sweeping devastator that ever united velocity with vigour. He is a locust of the largest size, and leaves the soil bare to an atom. Even his *pain à discrétion* is but another name for a feat of swallowing, that would do honour to a pelican.

The German at dinner, rivals him in havoc, though he may fall short of him in rapidity. The Gaul is the wolf; the Goth is the vulture, and goes calmly, but completely, through his work. He throws into it the inexorable perseverance that distinguishes his nature in all things; drudges like a steam-engine, and bores his way through the most difficult deglutition. The man to whom my attention was drawn, was a squat, obese figure, but still young; with a calm grey eye, and a physiognomy profoundly fixed on the dish before him,—palpably a German. He had already out-dined all the English; and was now proceeding in his banquet without the chance of a competitor. It became first a matter of amusement, to calculate the number of dishes which he contrived to clear; then a matter of fear, lest he should drop off his seat, and out of the world together, in a fit of apoplexy; then, a matter of actual wonder, to see how thoroughly he mastered all the terrors of his task, and yet preserved his appetite, his equilibrium, and his senses.

The German cookery is bad, but the German dinner is prodigal; and the dishes seemed to be endless. The only symptom that we could discover of human failure in this indefatigable feeder, was the occasional letting out of a button, between the courses, and gradually an increased stiffness of figure, as repletion took its slow effect. Still he sat, and fed, sipping merely a liqueur from time to time, in the interval of removing the dishes. We left him disappearing in the twilight of his corner, still engaged, with the steadiness of a philosopher deep in some mighty problem; giving up to his plate every faculty of his body and soul, never interrupting the process by a syllable to any human being, but when he called for a fresh dish or liqueur; and evidently thinking that a Cleopatra of Dantzic jelly, or Westphalia ham, was worth all the " black-browed queens of Egypt" in the world.

We have just had a visit from a soldier of chi-
valric renown ; the duke of Brunswick. He is the
beau idéal of the hussar, sits his horse like an
Arab, strikes off a head at full speed, bears fatigue
as if he were of iron, sleeps on straw, or stone, in
gallant preference to the embroidered canopy and
eider down, and has sworn never to take off his black
helmet until he dyes its feathers red in the blood
of the last Frenchman on the banks of the Rhine.
The determination is somewhat barbarian ; but we
are to recollect that those Frenchmen have already
stripped him of his dominions, and hunted him like
a wild beast, from parallel to parallel of Germany ;
that he bears the blood of Arminius in his veins ;
and, above all, that this is the day of war, when
savagery is the peculiar honour of our ridiculous
human nature.

The duke rode through the city, reviewed our
burgher-guard, which he complimented in high and
handsome terms; gave a glance at our fortifications,
at which he laughed; and then galloped off, to join
the allied sovereigns, negociate a little for the recovery of his dukedom, and probably, in his first
battle, change the colour of his feathers in his own

heroic blood, and be trampled by the charger of
some proud field-marshal, who but a few years before would have been proud to wipe the dust from
his shoes.

———

THIS evening as I was walking on a rather lonely
quarter of the rampart, I was met by a little, odd-
looking man, who immediately began a conversation with me.   He was meagre and ill-clothed,
but whatever of hat remained to him was on one
side, and he wore his clothes with an air that seemed
fully to disregard their patches.   I was, at first,
doubtful whether I had encountered a mendicant
or a footpad; but I was mistaken.   He was a politician; a character, which, I admit, might be occasionally compatible with either.

His object was, to inquire " the last news from
England—he was afraid that things there were not
going on quite so well as could be wished." I was
unfortunately barren of all news. He next observed,
that " the English government were apt to be remarkably in the clouds upon all continental affairs." I
was not qualified to deny it. He then gave it as " his
candid opinion, that the ministry was not strong."

I was thinking of giving him a shilling, to mend the constitution of his coat and breeches; but I was now deterred by the fiery look of the little settler of nations. The place was dusky, the time was late, his hand too was busy in his pocket, from which he might have produced something of a very different nature from my reluctant shilling; the politician might have evolved itself into the financier, and I might have been the payer of a forced loan. I suddenly wished him good night, saved my shilling, and left him to arrange the world and his purse with the first twilight burgher that fortune might throw in his way.

CHAPTER XXIII.

THE BOMBARDMENT.

20TH. Last night was a foretaste of the kind of entertainment which Davoust is preparing for us. I have for some time slept at the villa, and after spending the afternoon of yesterday in Hamburgh, turning over the German gazettes, which are all fear and trembling; and listening to reports, of which one half regularly contradicted the other; I took my solitary way through the fields. Whether the highest disregard of danger proceed from apathy, idiotism, or courage, has been an old question; but few things seem more extraordinary than the little change which the presence of the enemy produces upon German life. In the cities there may be fear and flight enough; but, in the open country, where a company of chasseurs, or a troop of horse, may, at any hour of the day or night, burn every house in the village over its tenants' heads, and send the tenants themselves to the other world, all goes on with the tranquillity of a conclave of philosophers.

What the feelings of the people of London would be, with twenty thousand " warlike French," encamped at Battersea, and a range of nightly fires showing their outposts from Shooter's Hill to Richmond, will I hope never be more than matter of conjecture. But here is the solid German, digging and delving, ploughing and sowing, enjoying his beer at his inn-door, and corrupting the atmosphere with his pipe, and doing all, as much at his ease, as if every musket of France were rusting at the bottom of the Elbe, and the world had learned common sense, and abjured murder for even the best pay and promotion under the sun. It may be strongly questioned, whether a meal the less has been eaten, or a pipe the less has been smoked, from North to South of Germany, during the war; except where they have been confiscated to the use of some sweeping French commissary, a race who certainly leave but few luxuries to vitiate the popular tastes.

Every thing here is contrast. The French had been all day throwing up batteries in the islands. Their workmen were seen plainly with the naked eye; and though those batteries seemed to us mere rude mounds of earth, and altogether different from the shapely faces and angles that figure in the books; the enemy know their business well, and it is but a rough rampart that will not let a howitzer lie behind it.

The evening was lovely; one of those blendings of spring and summer, when we have the freshness and animation of the one mingled with the richness of the other; the country people were in their fields, making the most of the light; every tree was in full green; the thrush singing in every brake; the sun going down, like an old potentate, after his day's war or wisdom, sinking in huge cloudy curtains of indescribable vermilion; the evening star, silvery and soft, as poet or painter could desire, watching, like an Eastern slave over his couch;—and in the midst of all, came the roar of a gun! The enemy were trying the range of their batteries.

The recording angel must have been dissolved

away long since, if he has shed but a single tear over every exclamation that resembled my uncle Toby's. Yet, if mine added nothing to his task, it was not for love of the disturbers. The cannon spoiled all the scene at once; there was guilt and misery in the sound; and I never remember to have looked upon the bounties of earth or heaven with a stronger impression of the follies and the crimes of man.

About midnight I was suddenly roused by one of the servants knocking at my door, and crying out that " the city was on fire." I rose, of course, and found all the household hurried out of their beds, and gathered in great alarm. The report, in the day, was, that the French had sent an officer to demand the surrender of the city, on pain of its being burnt to the ground. I now went up to a turret, which commanded an extensive view, and saw that they were throwing shells from their battery on the nearest island.

The very idea of a bombardment implies hazard; but I was soon comforted for the fate of Hamburgh, by seeing the singularly ineffectual nature of the enemy's fire. They threw a good number of

shells, but at least three out of every four burst
in the air. There was no visible burning in the
city; and, except a variety of lights which now and
then hovered about the roofs or ramparts, there
was even no appearance of any movement. It was
evident that this bombardment could do no serious
injury; and I now stood gazing at it as a fine
fire-work. In this sense, nothing could be better
worth seeing. The long trains of red flame from
the fuzes described all kinds of serpentines and
curves, through a sky as blue as lapis lazuli; and
the bursting of the bombs, which generally occurred
at the height of their course, was magnificent—an
orb of perfectly white light blazed and spread
broadly upon the eye, suddenly showing the vanes
of the steeples and turrets below. The cannon too
from the ramparts now began to answer, and the
horizon was covered with sheets of brightness, like
perpetual flashes of summer lightning. I watched
a while, but day-break soon began to show itself;
the shells became invisible, and the bombardment
at length died away.

In the morning I found that my anticipations
were correct: the shells had done but little harm.

3

A few people, who had imprudently exposed themselves, were wounded. Some houses had been set on fire, but the flames were soon extinguished, and the chief loss was in the breaking of windows, which must be laid to the charge more of our own batteries than those of the enemy, for at every explosion the large panes flew out of the casements. The bombardment, in fact, had only the effect of prompting the people to take precautions against a second experiment. We find it difficult to know, whether the feebleness of the enemy's fire arose from their want of means, or from their wishing merely to frighten the citizens into submission. It is said, that they have not above half a dozen guns with their whole force. Yet, how Napoleon, the cannon-lover, would suffer a whole army-corps to take the field so unprovided, is not easily to be accounted for. But they seem to be in extraordinary want of ammunition; for they have employed a singular species of commissariat in the purchase,—the fat and handsome milk-women of Wilhelmsburg. Those flourishing peasants have, by either fear or force, become their notorious agents in Hamburgh; bringing their letters in their stomachers, and their francs in their pockets. In return, they carry back gunpowder in their shoes; thus adding another material to the explosive temperament of the sex.

All business is necessarily at an end. For who can give his hours to bills and barter, when those hours may be numbered, and he may be awoke in his first sleep, if he have the philosophy to sleep at all, by finding a nine-inch shell gamboling about his bed-chamber.

An officer arrived this morning from Harburg, and had been closeted with the governor, or the senate, or both. The rumour is, that he came to demand our immediate submission. But we scorn to be frightened in day-light, and have sent him back with the indignation of a city of Bayards. *La Gloire, ou la Mort!*

For our heroism we shall be bombarded again to-night. But we have got a lesson, and are making preparations: they are not of a very high-sounding order, wet blankets, cow-hides, straw pounded with mire, and clay compost, but all excellent things for their purpose; which is to cover our tow magazines, hemp stores, and other matters of a combustible nature, which, lying along the river side, are most exposed to be shelled.

The bombardment failed; but we must give the French credit for its principle. It is, in war to try every thing; for the simplest attempt sometimes does wonders. Many an army has been on the point of giving way, if but an additional troop of horse were hounded at them. Many a town has hung out the white flag to the puppy impudence that attacked it, without a second cartridge for its pistols. War is at best but a showy bravado; and the more showy braggadocio is the conqueror.

But the Frenchman took back with him something more expressive than a senatorial speech,— this was the wrath and execration of the populace, who brought before him, and *forced* him to look at, the body of one of the Hanseatics, which had been found grossly and inhumanly mangled on the field.

The French correspondence here is kept up by a whole host of spies. The Russians attempt to thin their numbers, from time to time, by seizing, and sending them off, we presume, to Siberia; they have not put any to death: but the French

prisoners still seem to have perfect knowledge of
all that is going on. I passed their prison in the
market-place this evening; the windows were
crowded with exulting ruffians, half naked, half
frantic looking Fauxbourg fellows, thrusting their
hands between the bars, shaking them at the
people, and shouting.

But whose is the fault? Every nation is eager
to speak French, to look French, to be lessoned,
laughed at, and plundered *à la Française*. The
nobles of Europe cannot swallow their meals unless a Frenchman has had the presidency over their
soup, cannot draw on their boots without a French
valet, nor wear their own heads with any degree of
satisfaction, unless a French hair-dresser has done
them the honour to take them into his hands. Our
daughters *must* all read Telemaque, the perfection
of high-flown tediousness; or Voltaire, the perfection of impudent wickedness; or they are cy-
phers, the Graces fly from them, and nothing but
Paris, and an elopement with their own dancing-
master, can restore them to the level of human beings. Our soldiers *must* wear French caps, sword-
knots, pelisses and moustachios, or they must lose

the faculty of fighting, be fit for nothing but to mount guard on ball-rooms, or marry squires' daughters, and, most insufferable of disgraces, be taken for Englishmen, and nothing but Englishmen, after all.

This professorship of taste marks the Frenchman throughout the globe; for, like the seeds of the thistle, he floats on every wind, and sticks and thrives every where. But on the Continent he is *par excellence* the coffee-house keeper. He is occasionally found trafficking in every necessity of man; but the supreme employ of his genius is in the *Café.* From the Arctic to the Antarctic, and from Cape Horn to Constantinople, he is found eternally boiling, burning, macerating, and money-making at six sous a-head. He cooks by circles of longitude and latitude. But it is coffee-pot in hand that he levies his supreme and universal poll-tax upon the children of men.

But this trade gives him a formidable opportunity of doing the business of Napoleon. All, here and every where else on the Continent, is espionage; and as every man spends at least half his time in the coffee-house, and every idler all his time; as every coffee-house is a species of 'Change for the morning, and a species of club for the night; and, as through it pass the whole smoking and sipping multitude of a Continental city, it may well be imagined what advantages must occur to the memory of the smart waiter who trips from groupe to groupe of those portly personages, once bemused in politics and their third bottle. The handsome *dame* who sits enthroned in her bar, in the glory of rouge, perennial ringlets, and *embonpoint* increasing every day; has but to lend an ear, to receive the opinions of the whole community, rising round her like incense; and *M. le Mari*, who has no more to do than the gods of Epicurus, may amuse his leisure in the little grim closet, where he sits like a caged Sultan, or a chained tiger; with transmitting the family recollections to Fouché by the night's post.

Of course this is stated as no national imputation; for there are probably thousands and tens of thousands of French who would disdain this infamy. But, whatever France may become, under a purer government, there can be no question that Napoleon's system is carried on, to an extraordinary degree, by espionage, and that the multitude of French valets, lower *artistes* of every kind, and coffee-house keepers in Germany, are the readiest instruments of the all-inquisitive and all-corrupting police of Imperial France.

There was a sort of sportive malice in the shells which fell last night in the streets. If the by-stander stood still, they stopped with all gravity, till they burst and took him off along with them; but if he ran away, they followed, coursed him from street to street, and were to be distanced only as a grey-hound might be by a hare, by doubling. One fugitive was mentioned, who, returning late, probably from the billiard-table, found one of those perilous associates suddenly blazing on the pavement before him. He started off immediately, and the shell was not behind-hand, but continued bounding and burning at his heels, for a considerable distance. At last, he luckily saw an open door, rushed in, and had but just time to close it, when his pursuer made a bound after him, struck the door, and exploded; fortunately without injury, but, as it may be presumed, not without a warning against keeping late hours in bombarded towns in future.

CHAPTER XXIV.

=====

THE GUARD SHIP.

MAY 21. Last night the Swedes arrived. We had waited in a good deal of anxiety for the coming of those heroes of the north star; and towards evening I made one of the crowd which went to the gates to see them make their entry. They were but two weak battalions; but we were comforted by being told that they had been sent forward by forced marches merely to man the ramparts for the night, and that the sun should rise on a whole army. The men were stout, strong-limbed fellows, but with the sheepish physiognomy, which white eye-brows and eye-lashes inevitably give, added to white moustachios, which they wore in profusion, and which transform the countenance into that of a German boar. Their uniform was blue, with yellow facings. They marched loungingly to the sound of a little band of flutes and clarionets; harsher music would have better suited their rough Baltic visages.

On the whole, they had a good deal the look of a militia regiment in its first days of training: but what foreign soldiery have not that look? After having seen, by one accident or other, almost every soldiery of Europe, I must acknowledge, that I have never seen any troops which equalled the military air of our own. There may be some corps of pet cavalry, or now and then a guard regiment, which, by the favour of the court, makes a showy figure on the foreign parade; but a British regiment in line, in movement, or passing the commanding officer, fairly extinguishes them all. The foreigner always seems to lounge under arms. He steps heavily, looks dejectedly, and exercises clumsily. We may talk of John Bull's gravity as we will; and off parade, he certainly lets his limbs carry him without much regard to the Graces; but under arms, he exhibits an alertness, a smartness of air, and an alacrity of movement, that it is not easy to find in the grenadier guards of any palace on the Continent. He is a spruce, erect, and neat-looking soldier, compared with the Austrian, the Prussian, or the Frenchman. He is unquestionably the only one who has the look of being proud of his profession.

However, rough and yellow-whiskered as our Swedes were, we were very well pleased with their arrival, and made up our minds for being left in peace for the night. Our batteries had been firing at intervals all day, but ceased towards sun-set, and I strolled down to the river side to see what our six-and-thirty pounders had done. To my un-military vision, nothing could have more ef-fectually relieved us from future bombardments. The enemy's batteries had disappeared, or left no other evidence of themselves than mounds of clay, torn and bulged in all directions by our heavy balls. The enemy had withdrawn their guns at day-light, and left their works to be battered about by us, without resistance. They now re-sembled the ruins of a cluster of mud cottages, and not a Frenchman was visible. The farm-house smokes were rising as regularly as if all the world was at its ease again. Little groupes of people were lingering on the rampart, with their eyes fixed on Harburg. The citizens were coming out to promenade again. The voices of the sailors, working their vessels in and out of the harbour, added their cheerful sounds to the hum of the city. All was tranquillity, and the promise of tranquillity. The occasional sparkle of a musket in the setting sun, which is sometimes seen at a remarkable distance, was the only drawback on this hope; for it showed where a French patrol was posted.

However, there was not much in the Frenchmen to startle us. The burgher guard mustered strong, and were in good spirits, though grievously wearied out with the perpetual duty;—constantly on the ground in the bad weather, exposed on the marsh at the foot of the ramparts, in itself a serious trial of health and strength; and, of course, withdrawn from all their customary business, and turned into mere soldiers : still we were not beaten yet. The Hamburgh paper, too, did its best to keep up this state of the public feeling, by putting every thing in the most favourable point of view; and we had the following version of the late occurrences.

" Hamburgh, May 20. This afternoon, Friday, we saw two battalions of excellent Swedish troops enter the city, the Danish troops, who had at first undertaken our defence, having left us two days ago, and retired into their own territory. The enemy, undoubtedly informed of this circumstance, attempted, on the night of the 19th, to cannonade the city from the islands.of the Fidel and Wilhelmsburg, of which he has been for some time in possession, and on which he has thrown up intrenchments, and erected batteries.

" But, as he could perceive no effect resulting from this trial, and he was so warmly answered, that his batteries were much damaged, he was obliged to give up his fruitless attempts. Now, that, in addition to the great talents and unremitting zeal of our honoured fellow-citizen, his Excellency General Tettenborn, we have to rejoice in the aid of the brave Swedish troops, we have no reason to fear the attempts of the enemy. His Excellency received the brave Scandinavians before the Stein-Thor, where they entered the city with military music and loud huzzaings, between a double line of our burgher guard under arms. Waggons having been sent to meet them from Lunenburg and Mecklenburg, they have come from Pomerania in a short time, and they immediately took their post on the Gros-bröeck. More Swedes are expected, which are already on their march to Hamburg and the Elbe."

The spirits of all people are buoyant in proportion to their having been exposed to calamity. The chance relaxations of the pressure are welcomed with a vividness that can be learned only from experience: as the Siberian enjoys his short summer; or as a man recovering from a fit of the gout enjoys the first feeling of being able to put his foot to the ground. The Northerns are not by nature peculiarly festive, but the prospect of relief from the intolerable vexations of the French government had, a month before, made them gay, and their present chance of escape was welcomed as a triumph. If we could but have *secured* their absence for a week, Hamburgh would have flourished in festinos and fancy-balls. News from the grand army too had come to exhilarate us all. Napoleon was either " sure to be beaten, or was going to negociate, or was going to be undone." I met, in the morning, some German gentlemen, who were so perfectly satisfied of the immediate retreat

of Davoust and his myrmidons, that they were
making arrangements for going to the islands in the
course of the day to purchase horses, those being
a constant article of sale among the peasants on
the breaking up of an army,—a period when the
robbed naturally make reprisals on the robbers.
The Cossacks, too, had got into the French rear,
and with the famous hussars of Nostitz, were
" picking up French patroles and aides-de-camp
without number." Fatigued with walking, talking,
and triumph, I went to bed, and fell into a sleep
which might be envied by many an emperor.

From this " heavy, honey-dew of slumber," I was
roused, in utter darkness, by a frightened voice at
my door, in which I could distinguish nothing more
than " *feu de peloton*," and " *Levez-vous, Monsieur!*" but this was enough to have roused a
regiment, in such times; I rose, dressed, and, on
going into the hall, found all the world awake
before me. The people of the house were busy
packing up trunks for a race into the depths of
Holstein; messengers had been dispatched for
horses, the women were in terror and tears, the
servants running about blundering, and wringing

their hands, and all that I could learn from those
bewildered people was, that the French had crossed
the river in front of the city; had stormed gate,
rampart, battery, every thing; were sweeping all
before them, and would be in the very hall where
we stood, before the half-hour was over. Strange
as all this sounded, it yet seemed to have some
probability, from the previous conjectures of many
of our military men, that the enemy would make
a dash on Hamburgh, whether to plunder, burn,
or convert it into a place of arms.

One of the messengers had by this time returned, with the double ill-news, that there were *no*
horses to be found, the owners having driven them
all away for fear of their being seized by either
friends or enemies; and that the Swedes, Hanseatics, and burgher guard were beaten to a man
by an overwhelming force, and flying in all quarters. To confirm his words, a very heavy fire of
musketry, which had paused for a short time,
recommenced; and actually, whether from the
change in the wind, or our more eager attention,
it seemed to be rapidly approaching. This, I took
for granted, was the time appointed by the fates

of war for my retreat, as I had no intention of falling into French hands. After listening awhile in the midst of a crowd of tremblers to the " platoon fire," which was now a perpetual roar of musketry, mingled with the discharge of a battery now and then; I determined to follow general example, and returning to my chamber, packed up my principal chattels in a portable shape, put a case of English pistols in my pocket, and with a travelling cloak thrown over my shoulder, deemed myself a match for any chance by flood or field. I was sufficiently active, and felt, that once out of gun-shot, a regiment of light infantry would have found it not easy to make prize of me.

However, as I knew that half the absurdities of human conduct are born of hurry, I felt also that it would be wise, before I took wing, to ascertain for myself the real state of affairs. I sallied out accordingly, and took the road in the direction of the firing; expecting to find some returning soldier or peasant from whom I might glean something nearer the truth, than was possible from the puzzled brains of our staring and breathless messenger. I met neither; but, as I passed along, saw all the cottagers wide awake, and in great terror; the men and women listening at their doors, not a word exchanged among them, but every ear fixed on the firing, and every eye turned upon the heavens, which sparkled with the keen and incessant flashes of the musketry. At length, as I went slowly on, ignorant of my way, in the dark, and guided only by the ear, I found the discharges sensibly slackening; and, on inquiring from some people who were hastening back to their cottages, learned, that whatever the affair was, the enemy had got the worst of it, and were retreating. This being evidently confirmed by the state of the fire, I recollected the terrors of the fair whom I had left behind in agonies at the expectation of a French visit; and postponing my curiosity to the natural wish to relieve some of their anxieties, I returned to the villa, communicated my good news, was thanked in half a dozen dialects of the Elbe, and then, having with some difficulty escaped from this effusion of national gratitude, returned full speed to the scene of action.

But all was now nearly quiet; dawn was begin-

ning to glimmer over the spires of Altona; and,
by the time of my reaching the river side, the sun
was in the horizon, and every object was ruddy
and visible.

The whole affair had been a brief but bitter
skirmish, in which the enemy were defeated; but
it had effectually roused our city; all the troops
were out; the Swedish regiments were now scattered along the high bank, some lying down,
some cleaning their arms after the night's work,
and some getting ready their breakfasts. Where
I stood, a couple of field-guns, which had done good
service in the fray, were still pointed towards the
enemy; some military carriages, with their drivers,
and a caissoon were in their rear; on different
points of the shore, small groupes of the burgher
guard, and Hanseatics, were talking over the
night's occurrences, or lying down and watching
the movements in the islands; the country people,
who were now coming to market with their little
waggons and cattle, were crowding round the soldiery to learn the news; and, between the cattle,
the guns, the scattered troops, and the gazing
peasantry, the whole was perfectly like one of the

Flemish pictures of "an army reposing." The landscape, rich, flat, and verdurous, with the quiet Elbe shining along, might have delighted Hobbima, but the figures were for Wouvermans. Not a Frenchman was to be seen; and it would have been difficult to conceive, in this scenery, the site of such late and angry struggle; but one memorial was there still—the guard ship, which I had seen anchored in the middle of the stream for some weeks, gallantly displaying the Hamburgh flag; she was now lying close under the bank, almost a wreck, totally dismantled, and with her hull and sails riddled with balls.

The truth of the affair was this. The French, who had found the guard ship an impediment to their proceedings, determined to make themselves masters of her, and collecting a force in the nearest island, embarked under cover of night, one hundred and seventy men on board of some river boats, and made an attack on the vessel. In this instance, as usual, they appear to have trusted as much to their arts as their arms; for the centinels on board were said to have been found *asleep*. There were about thirty of the Hanseatic Legion in the vessel, and it is certain that they suffered her to be surprised. However, the French, whose element is certainly not the sea, contrived to perplex themselves, and between the current and the cables, were so tardy in getting up the ship's sides, that the Hanseatics had time to recover their senses, and commence a dropping fire. The enemy, now conscious that they had no time to lose, made new efforts, and though they took the space of half an hour to accomplish what half a dozen British sailors would have done in five minutes; they at last reached the deck, drove down the soldiers, and cutting the cable, attempted to steer their prize towards their own quarters. But here their sailorship failed; and after puzzling themselves to make the vessel obey the helm, and hoisting every sail to catch the breeze, they found that she would move but one way, and that way directly under the Hamburgh batteries. The firing on board had already produced its effect in alarming the shore, and the sensations of the captors must have been nervous enough, when they felt themselves inevitably drifting under our guns. They were not disappointed. The troops had by this time been alarmed, and were drawn up along the high bank. Even in the dark the white sails of the vessel had been partially visible; and the moment that she came in front of the line, the whole, guns and musketry, poured a general storm of balls into her. The enemy were so astounded at this weight of fire, that they lost all presence of mind, never returned a shot, let the vessel drift, and, in a few minutes, she ran aground. The fire continued, as heavy as ever, and no Frenchman could peep over the side without being instantly shot. Their only object now, was to make their escape in the best way that they could; they had kept the boats at hand, and all who were able to get into them, began ferrying away to the shore; many tried to swim, and were drowned; some remained on board. The fire now turned on the boats, of which several were sunk with their fugitives. As day broke, boats from the Hamburgh side were sent with troops; who took possession of the ship, liberated the Hanseatics, and brought in the remaining Frenchmen prisoners.

This was an unlucky enterprise for the enemy; out of the hundred and seventy they had thirty killed, and a hundred and two wounded; those, with the drowned and the prisoners, accounted for almost the entire party. The loss of the Hanseatics was fifteen men, who had fallen in the attack on the vessel.

We were still lingering on the bank, when something came moving from behind a sandy mound on the opposite island; the people gathered to ascertain the phenomenon; and, at last, as it came nearer, and began to make signs, we made out the monster to be a man, but completely naked; whom we took for granted to be one of the enemy wishing to desert, but afraid to swim the river. The strong sunshine on his skin made him exactly of the colour of scarlet; he looked like an enormous unskinned salmon. A boat was on the point of being launched to bring him over, when an older head among us recommended a little more caution on the subject; and probably having had some French experience himself, said that the deserter might be merely a decoy duck to bring our people under fire from the copse at the landing-place. As the copse was certainly there, and thick enough to hide a French patrole; and as the trick was perfectly in their style, the boatmen drew back, the spirit of adventure cooled, and the Frenchman was left to make his way back to his clothes and his quarters, which I presume he did; for, shortly after, he either hid himself in the copse, or swam the little branch of the stream between the island and Wilhelmsburg; at all events, he disappeared. The failure of the night's attempt has raised our anticipations once more; and wagers, the usual mode in which hope extravagates in a place of trade, are offered that Davoust will be gone, or a prisoner, before the week is over.

As this field-marshal is become a bug-bear to us, anecdotes of him abound. A singular story is told of his marriage. When Napoleon wished to get rid of an obnoxious officer, regiment, or army, he sent them to look for glory forthwith. Moreau's army were no favourites of his; and he notoriously constructed the expedition to St. Domingo for their express use. He either despised or disliked Leclerc, his sister's husband, but who had probably presumed too much on their relationship, a crime never forgiven by the great man; and he appointed him to the head of this forlorn hope. Leclerc had made up

his mind to repose on his laurels, and enjoy Paris
and the palace for the rest of his days; he was
thunder-struck at the news, and strove to escape
the honour in all possible ways. " What was he
to do with his family concerns, how leave his fair
wife all unguarded in the midst of Paris?"—" You
must take her with you," was the reply. " But
she will refuse," said the husband.—" Impossible!
when it is my order," said the Dictator.—" But I
have a sister, too young to take, too young to
leave, too sensitive to be left to poverty, and too
poor to find a husband," said the general.—" Set
your mind at ease upon that point," replied the
Dictator; " she shall have a husband, and by this
time to-morrow. In the mean time, go and order
your horses for the expedition." Leclerc found
that eloquence was in vain, that his master's sensi-
bilities were not to be touched, and that his epaulettes might tremble, upon any further indecision.
He made his bow.

Napoleon rang the bell. " Send up General
Davoust!" The general duly appeared. " Davoust,"
said Napoleon, " you are not married; you ought
to be; I have found a wife for you; you shall be

married to-morrow." The bridegroom elect was all astonishment at this rapid accumulation of happiness. His countenance caught Napoleon's eye—"Ha! you have made a choice for yourself, General. That is wrong; I have settled the whole matter: you must marry Mademoiselle Leclerc. Here is her address; you will find her at the boarding-school; go, and lose no time." Davoust had now recovered breath; and he stated that if he were to marry, another lady was entitled to his devoirs. Napoleon rang the bell again. " If General Leclerc is in the palace, send him here." The general came. " Gentlemen, go together to this address," said Napoleon, " and bring back the young lady mentioned in it. Leclerc, you will make Davoust known to her; she must come to the palace without delay, and be married, that you may be satisfied of my word, before you set out for the coast. Let me see no more of either of you, till the affair is settled."

The generals set out, in what temper may be conceived; found the young lady, who was alternately indignant, tearful, and astonished, but finally submitted; and, before the sun went down, Da-

voust was a happy man; and Leclerc, booted
and spurred, set off for St. Domingo, in which he
rapidly laid the bones of his thirty thousand *braves*,
and his own!

CHAPTER XXV.

―――

THE BOMBARDMENT.

MAY 23. We are still to have the old chequering of good and evil. There are rumours that our Swedish battalions have come without the permission of their prince; that General Lyon, the English officer, who bears the whole burthen of British war and diplomacy in the north, has been the only cause of their arrival; and that his object being the preservation of a large depôt of English arms, forwarded for the use of the northern peasantry, an object about which, of course, no foreign prince cares; the consequence of all those *contre temps* is, that the complying Swedish officer is to be disgraced, the Swedish force withdrawn, and Hamburgh abandoned, for the third time!

From Altona we can see the French officers again passing daily to the Danish governor's house, and all appearances strengthen the report, that a quiet sale of the city is going on. Our volunteers are still staunch, but they look dreadfully jaded; the constant harassing by night and day must soon wear out men unaccustomed to service; and the business must end in either a fierce popular explosion, or an unconditional surrender, the work of disgust, weariness, and despair.

We have had another night's bombardment. Its effects have been trifling, so far as the actual damage was concerned; but it renders the populace more restless and insubordinate; they are busy all day in carrying their furniture to every spot which they consider to be a place of comparative safety; and great numbers are sending their furniture and every thing portable to Altona. The merchants are unloading their barges, and emptying their warehouses; all this produces waste, hazard in the exposure of their goods, and heavy expense in the mere carriage. Altona is within a quarter of an hour's walk of the gates, and yet the carters find their trade so valuable, that there are instances where they charge to the amount of four or five pounds English, for a single trip: the beggars are the only lucky in the midst of all this human bustle and misery; while the streets and every thing in them are assuming the look of a wilderness, the Savoyards and barrel-organ men go on grimacing and grinding as provokingly as ever; it is harder to find fault with the innocent chimes of the cathedral: but their regularity of jangling, gay or grave, is actually vexatious; there they go on, hour by hour, ringing their waltzes, while the ears of all below are untuned.

The French had sent in another officer during the day, to warn the city that it *must be burned!* in case of non-compliance. As twilight fell, I followed the crowd to one of the rising grounds outside the gate of Altona. The people round me were chiefly Hamburghers, who had come to the Danish territory for the security of their families and property. The sun was scarcely down, when a sound of cannon turned every eye on Hamburgh. A bomb was rising in the air, from the French batteries, and rushing with a long train of light above the roofs, like an enormous shooting star; the guns of the city soon returned the fire, and the air was rent with the perpetual roar.

To have a more distinct view of the batteries, some of us went to an hotel, which commanded an extensive view of the islands; but the windows were already crowded with the guests and people of the house; and I should have had the *misfortune* of merely hearing the cannonade, but for the politesse of a French lady, who probably conceiving Monsieur l'Anglois to be an amateur in matters of war, was resolved that my tastes should not be disappointed, and insisted on making room for the stranger.

The night was remarkably fine; and Nature, who carries on her operations without much regarding the performances of man, was sending up her breath of fruits and flowers, lighting her stars, and colouring her hills and dales with moonlight, as if the work of wickedness were not going on at the moment. The moon was serenity itself, and lay undulating on the water like a burnished argosie, or pearl balloon, at anchor. From our casement the fire was completely visible, and we could see the whole sweep of the shell from its leaving the mortar to its explosion. But while I was gazing on the bombardment, my French friend pointed

silently to the river below, where a large dark body
was stealing up under cover of the bank. It soon,
however, came into the moonlight, and was conjectured to be an armed vessel. In another moment,
we had the proof, for she began firing from a
heavy gun in her prow into the thickets on the
opposite island, where it was supposed that a
French patrol had been established. The fire was
not returned, and if the enemy were there, they
contrived to hide themselves completely; for no
fugitives were seen along the face of the island,
which was now fully visible. The armed vessel
still continued to throw grape into the thickets;
to which we were so near, that we could hear the
rattling of the shot on the trunks of the trees, and
against the walls of a farm-house, which peeped out
as romantically as possible from the shade of this
little grove. My French companion seemed as ten-
derly interested by the sight, as she might have
been at a scene in an opera. She exclaimed, on seeing
a discharge which might have blown away thicket,
farm-house, and all, " *Ah, mon ami, quelle jolie
nuit pour une canonade.*" Whether this meant
surprise at the contrast of the serenity above with

the formidable business below, or the native delight of her country in every thing in the shape of a spectacle, must be left to the curious in French and female nature to decide.

The gun-boat continued firing on from time to time, as if to perplex the enemy in his other quarters, for here not a shot was returned. But the dew was beginning to fall, 'and Madame made the sudden discovery that her ringlets were drooping beyond the line of beauty; she started up in alarm worthy of the occasion, and wrapping her shawl round her arm, sprang away like a frightened fawn.

———————

Germany is now filled with national songs, and they are all of war. The sufferings of Prussia, her gallant rising, her glory and her revenge, are the chief topics, but Alexander the *Befreyer*, and his Russians, come in for their share; and even the Cossacks have found bards, for the first time, in history. The majority of those effusions are, of course, the very lees of poetry; some of them do not soar even to the affectation of metre, but are printed straight forward, like the prose, for which they might be very fairly mistaken. The established poets shake their heads over those degenerate specimens of the German Parnassus; but, doggrel and desperate as they are, they are popular, and produce a powerful effect upon the public spirit.

This is the true solution of the old problem,— why does poetry perpetually rise and fall in national influence? Why is it at one time like a national beacon, shooting out its brightness over every quarter of the land, and at another utterly rayless? Because its true use and power are, like those of the beacon, in the national night and storm; it is extinguished in the sunshine. The graces of poetry are undoubtedly capable of being appreciated in the piping times of the world; but its true vocation is in the sterner periods, when public hazard and personal anxiety sharpen every sense, excite every faculty, and give a new sensibility and electric vividness to every organ of the mind. Even the severe and engrossing topics that are the direct creation of war and popular suffering, give an appetite for lofty contemplations and

vigorous thoughts. Throughout the millions of
Germany at this hour, there is, perhaps, scarcely
a man whose mind is not absorbed and agitated
with thoughts of battle or flight; of triumph, or
the precariousness of life and all human things;
with hopes and fears turning on the weightiest
concerns of our being;—the mental eye, filled with
the brilliancy of military achievement, or the terrors of unsparing defeat and massacre; the mental
ear filled with the crash of falling empires, or the
roar of nations rising, like the ocean, to sweep
away the traces of overthrow, and clear the land
of stain and ruin together. All is exciting, ap-
palling, overwhelming, magnificent. The true
Muse should be pictured, not as the figurante of a
capricious and luxurious public taste, nor as the
delicate and rose-crowned minstrel of nobles and
kings; her instrument should be neither flute nor
lyre, but the trumpet, bound with night-shade and
laurel, or whatever wilder emblem gives the combined images of anguish and glory.

And this too solves the problem of the singular
influence of poetry in the remoter times of nations. They were all times of trouble: not that

troubled times instinctively produce the higher genius, but that the popular susceptibility is more prepared for its impression. It is unquestionable, that the same process seems to take place in the whole range of the human faculties. In times when nations are thrown off their balance, their efforts to recover it, their very reelings and tossings to reinstate themselves, often develope a vigour altogether unknown before. Sudden hardihood, quick invention, dazzling enterprise, throw a lustre over the nation which the world had consigned to obscurity for ever. Holland, in her insurrection against Philip II., exhibited a heroism which might have rivalled a nation of Rolands and knights of Malta; not simply the fortitude of brave men, bravely resisting a cruel oppression, but the brilliant intrepidity, the restless and romantic enterprise, of a land of cavaliers; not simply the weight of the sword, but the flash of the sword.

And this keen excitement may be among the uses of war; a permitted plague, but converted to at least a partial good. The national faculties are cleared of their sluggishness; their lazy superfluities are frightened, starved, or scourged away; the sinews and muscles start out; the national form is exercised into a more active, vigorous, and noble shape. Healthier tastes and manlier objects become familiar; a new fount of life seems let loose in the veins; old things are past away, all things become new; and a reign of intellectual vividness and generous ambition dates its origin from calamities which threatened to overthrow, and ultimately to extinguish the national mind.

That this change *does* take place, is beyond all question. Every people recurs to *its* time of public struggle as the birth of its mental distinctions. Its sea has grown phosphoric during the storm; the barren has brought forth, and its offspring has been ushered into light in providential throes; the stagnation of its atmosphere has been shaken and purified even by the tempest; it has obtained the mastery of a new soil, thrown up, like one of the volcanic islands, only by the struggle which threatened to strike the land into dust and ashes.

Yet, the decay of this superabundant energy and susceptibility is almost as much a matter of common observation as its rise. Prosperous times come, adversity exercises the nation no more, and with it the public vividness fades. The generation of heroism, and genius, seems to sink visibly into the grave, and to be succeeded by a tamer and more feebly proportioned race of mankind. The intellectual armour has been laid aside, and we cannot recognise in the costume of common life, the forms that we once saw towering in light, and nodding with the victorious crest and plumage. All the public elevation has subsided; an age of mediocrity has levelled and buried all: orator, and hero, philosopher, and poet, have passed away from sight together, like retiring visions; the people refuse to discover beauty and power, where once every sound was enchantment, and every touch creation; and genius is declared to be no more!

Yet the Muse still lives—but without the popular susceptibility she is without an audience and an instrument; her harp is unstrung, she is nothing. With it she is every thing: even her rudest efforts work little short of miracles; the most triumphant changes have been wrought by songs in which we can now discover nothing but the infancy or the barbarism of poetry. Armies have been raised by a ballad, tyrannies subverted by a

ballad; dynasties, that seemed as firm as the earth,
have been scattered into utter dismemberment and
exile by a ballad; which in cooler times astonishes
nothing but criticism. We see but the rudeness
of the block, where other generations worship-
ped the idol; the old spirit of the worshipper is vanished, and with it the power of the divinity. What
can be more unpoetic than the Marseillois hymn,
a mere cento of rabble phrases, the *maximum* of
feeble inflation : yet the Marseillois hymn worked
wonders while the minds of men were hot and
ductile with revolution. It shot invincible courage
into the rabble that composed the early soldiery
of France; as if it had turned the lightning from
heaven into their bosoms. It disciplined the idlest,
most fickle, and most insubordinate race on earth,
the populace of Paris and the French towns, into
armies of veterans. That single song did more
for French triumph in the field, than all the honours of the ancient monarchy, or even all the
terrors of the republic. It unhappily too gave a
vigour to the republican principle, which enabled
the successive atrocious governments of France in
its day to domineer over Europe, France, and hu-

man nature: in the mouth of the multitude it was an answer to every thing.

It now seems, what it is, a trivial and commonplace production; but those alone can conceive its influence, who have heard it sung by the republican mobs in Paris, or by the republican armies in the field. If the troops were hungry, they sang the hymn; if they were worn out with the long marches through the Flemish swamps, or the sands and forests along the Rhine, they sang the hymn; if they fought from morning till night, and finished the day, famishing, broken down, and half-naked, the chorus of the Marseillois put new life into them. At Fleurus, at the Lines of Weissembourg, in the desperate struggles along the Sambre and the Meuse, in all the murderous battles of the early revolutionary war, the hymn was to them courage and victory. If this tinsel performance were to be produced now in France, it would perish in its birth, like a hundred other efforts of much superior poetry. But it was the cause, the time, the public preparation, that made all its magic. France was filled with the dæmon; and every nerve was irritated into fierce delight by the sounds that not, like the harp of David, exorcised the evil spirit, but seemed the echo of his own bitterness, and wildly predicted the fall and bereavement of diadems and nations.

CHAPTER XXVI.

___

THE HANSEATIC LEAGUE.

THE reign of Charlemagne was the foundation of the political system of modern Europe. It was a continued period of forty-three years of war and legislation: the battle of mind against barbarism. The northern invasions had done their work: they had hewn down the decaying establishments of the Roman empire, like trees of the forest. Then came Charlemagne; a man of unrivalled sagacity, military boldness, and political vigour; to clear away the ruins which were already turning the soil into a morass; to cover the land once more with health and fertility, and direct the revival of man. No prince of his age was so distinctly made for empire: a self-taught warrior, legislator, and states-man, he first reduced, combined, or civilized the whole circle of the martial tribes of southern Europe.

Then turning to the north, he carried on a war of thirty-six years with the tribes of the Baltic; and died, only after having exhibited the highest faculties for government, seconded by the highest success of polity and arms, the first of European monarchs, lord of the widest extent of empire since the days of Rome; and without a superior, since his day, in authority over men, in kingly qualities, in unbroken triumphs, and in permanent benefactions to mankind.

Even to the north, where his triumphs were won by fire and sword, he was a signal benefactor. War is the severe school of nations. The vigour and activity necessary against a monarch and a warrior who carried the whole south and west of Europe in his train, brought out the latent powers of the barbarous tribes; and partially weakened as the nations round the Baltic were by this incessant warfare, they had acquired habits of industry, self-dependence, and political union, which, at the death of Charlemagne, placed them in a position to become conquerors in their turn.

The vices which finally extinguished the dynasty of Charlemagne, relieved the north of the only rival which it had to dread; and the nature of the country—watered by large rivers, indented by bays, and, above all, containing in its bosom the Baltic, soon turned the popular mind to commerce. But a still more powerful influence civilized the people. Charlemagne had planted Christianity among them; and rude as was the Christianity of Charlemagne, and suspicious as all religion must be which is planted by the sword, its better spirit gradually made way among their institutions. Its first result was in reconciling those half-savage tribes to each other. The missionary passing through the camps of the wild sons of violence and plunder, offered to them the sight of a being whose principles and life were regulated on grounds totally distinct from their own, and who forced their respect without the hazardous and sanguinary distinctions of war. Where the monastery rose among them, they saw a building nobler than any of their castles, tenanted with a crowd of blameless men, living together in quiet piety; opulent by their superior intelligence and industry; surrounded with lands whose cultivation and beauty shamed the neglected and barren state of their own; masters of a rank of

knowledge to which the barbarian, in all ages, bows
down with wonder and reverence, if not with superstitious fear; and this whole splendid communion
sustained by a declared adherence to the precepts of
peace. The worship of the sword was thus rapidly
approaching its close. Men discovered that all the
best advantages of life might be more rapidly obtained, more fully enjoyed, and more securely held.
by abandoning the old career of rapine; and from
that hour the spell of barbarism was broken. The
peasantry flocked round the walls of the brotherhood,
where they received not only spiritual wisdom, but
assistance in their difficulties, medicine, food, and
clothing, education in their ignorance, and protection against the outrages of their lords. They next
built their village round the monastery. The village
grew to a town; its opulence, or the funds of the
monastery, purchased the right of self-government
from the feudal sovereign; and a little republic
was thus formed, guided by a wisdom which was
not to be found in the councils of idle and brute
barons; and urged on to opulence by that resist-
less animation, invariably belonging to a state of
society where every man is free to follow the bent

of his genius, and every man is secure in the fruits of his labour.

Before the end of the thirteenth century, Europe was studded with those privileged cities. They were to be found along the shores of every sea, on the banks of every great river, in every spot where the productive industry of man could be expended to the highest advantage. They were to be found flourishing alike on the Danube, the Rhine, the Elbe, and the Vistula; on the borders of the Baltic and the Mediterranean. While the rest of Europe lay, reduced almost to its primitive barbarism, under a race of dissolute or impoverished princes, those were the arteries which gathered and sent life through the frame. Even war owed its science and its laws to those cities of peace. Forced to raise troops for their defence against the rapine of the sovereigns, their chief citizens officered their armies, and, transferring the sense of justice and civilization, even to the camp, they gradually constructed that code of arms which, rendering due honour to the virtues, even of an enemy, has eminently tended, at once, to ennoble the principles, and mitigate the horrors of war.

But, as the intelligence of the privileged cities increased, they discovered that another important step remained to be taken for their security against the sovereigns. The deposition of the emperor, Frederic II., had thrown Germany into confusion. Some of the commercial towns on the Rhine were surprised and plundered by the vagrant soldiery. The other Rhenish towns, indignant at the outrage, adopted the cause of their brethren. An alliance was instantly proposed; and, in 1255, the first confederacy, an " alliance for ever," of no less than sixty Rhenish towns, was published to Europe[1].

Hamburgh is said to have been founded in the ninth century by Charlemagne, who placed in it a garrison to watch the more than doubtful fidelity of his Saxon subjects; but its situation on the Elbe soon gave it a higher rank, and it shared largely in all the commercial opulence of the time. Lubeck and Bremen, founded probably in the following century, alike distinguished themselves by the daring spirit with which their mariners ventured

[1] Mallet, Histoire de la Ligue Hanseatique.

on the *long* voyage to Norway; the skill with which they navigated the Sound, then a scene of fabulous perils; and the wealth and the wonders which they contrived to bring back from the Russian provinces, then the peculiar seat of witch-craft, and all the terrors of a superstition, mingled of the wildest tales of Europe and Asia.

But it was that grand stimulant of nations, the Crusades, that showered gold on the north. The German chieftains, summoned by their emperor, and retaining the hereditary love of war, had more than vied with the enthusiasm of the south, in embracing the sacred cause. But they were poor, and the money and the ships of the commercial cities were essential to their enterprise. The greater part of those gallant champions left their remains in Palestine. The ships alone returned, and they brought back the precious cargoes of the East, the knowledge of the Mediterranean naviga-tion, the passion for luxuries hitherto unknown, and the determination to share this brilliant traffic with its masters, the Venetians and Genoese. The success of the Crusades had thus far aided the northern towns. Their failure was the next thing necessary to the success of commerce. And the event soon occurred. The Saracens and their climate, the expense of the armaments, and the jealousies of the princes, broke down the passion of the Crusaders for triumphs in Asia. But their valour must be employed. A simpler crusade lay before their eyes. Saxony, Denmark, Prussia, almost the whole coast of the Baltic, were still heathen. The Knights of the Cross were let loose among them: their cabins were burnt, their harvests seized, their warriors put to the sword. The cause was finally victorious; but the land was a wilderness once more. It must be filled. Colonies of civilized Germans were now marched into the fields which had been tenanted by the fallen tribes; walls and towns were built; ships and harbours followed; and those settlements in the desart soon rose into the rank of members of the great commercial league.

At Cologne, in 1364, was held the first general assembly of deputies. This assembly gives an extraordinary idea of the extent and power to which the association had arrived in an age antecedent to nearly all the chief discoveries of European science, to all regular polity, and to all general knowledge. It represented the principal cities of the immense shore spreading from the Scheldt to Livonia. The cities of the interior eagerly solicited leave to send deputies, and the assembly laid down the laws of commercial empire. It is on this occasion that we find the phrase of Hanse Towns first applied to the league. In the Low Dutch, *hanse* signifies a *corporation;* and the word itself is presumed to be a corruption of *hands,*—the natural and common emblem of united strength or fidelity. It had been used before by Hamburgh and Lubeck, in the charter granted to their factory in London, by Henry II., in 1267. But it was now applied to the whole association, and henceforth superseded every minor title.

The assembly had been summoned by the necessity of providing for war against Denmark, once the head of the piratical states, and now evidently extending its ambition to the overthrow of the Hanseatic privileges, and, as the natural consequence, to the seizure of northern sovereignty. All history is but a repetition of the same men and things; and Valdemar the Third, the King of

Denmark, might have been a prototype of Napoleon, in his love of conquest, his successes, and his double flight from his throne. Valdemar had found Denmark fallen from its ancient supremacy, and he haughtily determined to raise it to a supremacy still higher than it had ever attained. But, in a realm intersected every-where by great waters, he could do nothing without a fleet; he created one. Wisby, a city in the Isle of Gothland, had grown to singular opulence by being the depôt of the chief trade between the Hanse Towns and the North. It had acquired a still more honourable distinction by being the cradle of that code of maritime law on which the chief codes of commercial Europe have since been constructed, and which has earned the praise of all the great civilians. But the pirate king saw nothing in this celebrated spot but its wealth and its weakness. He made a sudden descent on the coast, under pretext of assisting the Swedish king, whose yoke the citizens had thrown off; the place was stormed, the people were mercilessly slaughtered, and Valdemar carried off a booty, which, in those days, was equivalent to the possession of a kingdom. But a just and formidable reverse soon followed. In the destruction of the city, every commercial establishment of the North had felt a wound; their goods had been carried away, their merchants and agents slain, and their privileges insulted and annulled. The whole Hanseatic alliance instantly prepared for war. Holstein, Bremen, Lubeck, Hamburgh, the Prussian ports, the whole great trading republic, strained every effort for retribution. They sailed for Gothland with a large fleet, and swept every thing before them. Gothland was taken, Wisby was freed from the presence of the pirates, the Danish fleet was beaten in sight of its own capital, and Valdemar was driven to the ignominious demand of a treaty.

But a new source of alarm roused the war again. Valdemar, despairing of the seizure of the Baltic by arms, attempted it by intrigue; and gave his daughter, the famous Margaret, the Semiramis of the North, to Haquin, heir of the crowns of Sweden and Norway. This extraordinary union of power in the hands of an enemy, so active and inveterate as the Danish king, would have exposed the Free States to imminent hazard. The merchants of the league had already become warriors; they now became diplomatists. Their first act was to raise an insurrection in Sweden, which finally deposed its king. Their next was to prevent the elevation of his son to the throne, by giving it to Albert, duke of Mecklenbourg. Their fleet put to sea at the same time, and Valdemar, thus cut off from land and sea, had no resource but to fly for his life.

Human nature must rejoice in this triumph, for it was the triumph of intelligence, manliness, and a sense of right, over plunder, cruelty, and wrong. But the vigour which man learns when left to the natural workings of his own understanding, was still more conspicuous in the progress of the war. Valdemar had fled to the Emperor, Charles the Fourth, and a succession of haughty decrees were issued against the League. But the merchants persevered in defiance of the Imperial authority. The pope launched his bulls against the League, and excommunicated all who bore arms against the will of Charles. Yet, in an age of profound superstition, when the pope was supreme monarch of Europe, and when its kings were proud to hold his stirrup, the bold traders of the Elbe and the

Baltic listened with disdain, or answered with open defiance, to the anathemas of a throne which never forgave, and which combined in itself more of the elements of power than any sovereignty ever before witnessed by man.

It was to counteract the imperial and papal hostility that the celebrated conference of Cologne was summoned, and the Hanseatic League first assumed its complete form. Seventy-seven cities subscribed to the declaration of war against the king of Denmark. The declaration was followed with military promptitude. While their troops and fleets pursued Valdemar with open war, their money and influence raised insurrections in his territories and those of his allies. The League, inflamed by victory, at length loftily declared their determination to dismember the Danish kingdom, which still extended largely over the provinces to the south of the Baltic. They sent expeditions against the coasts of Scania and Zealand, took Copenhagen by storm, and laid it waste, seized on Elsineur, and were thus complete masters of the entrance of the Baltic. But while war thus thundered round the shores of the inland sea, and

threw Sweden and Denmark equally into terror,
a new fleet swept the Danes from the ocean, ranged
the coast of Norway, where Haquin now reigned;
landed at all points, and ravaged the whole sea line.
Two hundred towns or villages were burned; and
hostilities were pursued, until the king, on the
point of seeing his capital fall into the hands of
those bold and irresistible avengers, renounced his
right to the Swedish throne, recognized Albert of
Mecklenbourg as king, and submitted to all the
commercial claims and privileges of the League:
Valdemar fled from Denmark, and was driven, like
a mendicant, to solicit subsistence from the German dukes. The regency of Denmark gave up
the fortresses of Scania as an indemnity for the
plunder of Wisby, and Valdemar, as a last humilia-
tion, subscribed to this treaty, before he was suffered again to set foot within his kingdom. Emergencies often make men, and among the most
honourable testimonies to the spirit of commerce
was, that it had made officers and councillors, who
without the usual training of camps and cabinets,
were found capable of conducting the greatest transactions of public life. The fleets of Lubeck were

commanded by two senators, Attendam and More. Their general, Warendorf, was the son of a burgomaster. He fell gloriously in the moment of victory, and his countrymen raised a monument to him in one of their principal churches, where he stood for many an age, an ancient hero, in a Roman helmet and cuirass, and with a fame not unworthy of the distinction.

Nations are sometimes driven by necessity to the discovery of principles which long elude philosophy. One of the latest doctrines of political œconomy is, that the most profitable traffic is the one nearest home. The first efforts of the Hanseatics had been exerted, to share the splendid profits of Venice and Genoa in the Mediterranean trade. They soon succeeded in obtaining a share. But it was found that the length and hazards of the voyage were more than equivalent to its advantages. The vessel, sailing from the Baltic or the Elbe, did not return for a year. It thus became necessary to find a nearer port. The Low Countries, in their liberty, industry, and commercial habits, offered the true site for this central establishment, and Bruges was finally fixed on for the grand depôt of the Baltic and the Mediterranean.

But the history of commerce is a detail of all the improvements that have shaped the modern mind of Europe. Perhaps two of the finest expedients of civilization are insurance and bills of exchange. Yet the former of those was in activity in Bruges even in the beginning of the fourteenth century; and the system of bills of exchange, a simple yet admirable effort of human ingenuity, from which the principal liberties of Europe arose, and which, beyond all other human inventions, gave the invaluable power of escaping from the hands of a tyrant; was brought almost to its perfection within the walls of this Flemish town.

Before the middle of the fourteenth century the League had risen to the highest pitch of prosperity. But, it was destined to feel the symptoms of decline long before its close. On the death of Valdemar, his daughter Margaret had placed her son Olaus on the thrones of Denmark and Norway. An insurrection against Albert, the unpopular king of Sweden, drove him from his throne, which the nation offered to Margaret. The League, dreading this new accumulation of power in one line, immediately armed; and, in their rage, singularly forgetting

the first principles of commercial polity, let loose
a barbarian swarm of pirates upon the dominions
of Margaret. But those robbers, who were
named *Vitalians*, or the Victuallers, from their
having been originally employed in provisioning
the besieged towns, soon turned upon their masters. The Hanseatic ships offered a spoil which
was not to be looked for among the meagre cargoes
of the impoverished ports of Sweden; every day
brought accounts of some new excesses; and the
League was finally forced to a compromise with
Margaret, in order to stop a war which was destroying themselves. Albert, deserted by his last
support, was now forced to abdicate, and by the
memorable " Union of Calmar [1]" the three crowns
were supposed to be laid on one brow for *ever!*

The brevity of those " eternal " arrangements in
politics is proverbial; and the death of this great
princess threatened her system with immediate
dissolution. Her policy had been bold, but temperate; that of Eric, her successor, was at once
feeble and violent. The Swedes, by nature a

[1] 1397.

singularly restless people, soon pronounced themselves neglected for the Danes. The Danes, pronounced that they were robbed with impunity by
the Hanseatic monopolists. The Norwegians
were jealous of both, and demanded why they
should pay obedience to a king who scorned their
crown, and who never visited their capital? As if
only for the purpose of embarrassing himself in-
extricably, Eric now made war on the Count of
Holstein, by whose military skill he was perpetually
baffled. He next provoked the Hanseatics by im-
peding the herring fishery, and he finally alienated
the German princes by the alternate indolence and
rashness of his character. The internal dissensions
of the League alone prevented them from instantly
wrenching the tyrant from his throne. But he
was not to escape the natural fate of weakness and
guilt in high places. The Swedish revolt was renewed under more active auspices. Denmark declared itself beggared by his wars and personal
waste. Eric in vain attempted to save his crown,
by making peace with Holstein, after nine years of
ruinous hostility. With equally fruitless effect he
abandoned to the League all their monopolies. The

cry of his people still arose, that he was unfit to reign; until with his mistress, Cecilia, not less obnoxious than himself, and with whatever wealth he could seize, he retired into Gothland. Denmark gave its crown to Christopher, Duke of Bavaria, a son of Eric's sister. The exiled monarch, in wrath, poverty, or despair, turned pirate, and robbed all nations in his exile, as he had robbed his subjects on his throne. This career could not be suffered long: he fled from Gothland, and shortly after died in Pomerania, obscured and scorned.

The League had already shown that it was equal to the highest efforts in the struggle for its own rights. But there was reserved for it a yet loftier display for the rights of others. Sweden, whose remoteness from the stirring scenes of Europe, and whose barrenness, have never saved it from the whole wild game of ambition, intrigue, tyranny, and war—Sweden, the country of revolution, was now suffering under the sternest calamity which can afflict the heart of a proud and gallant people. Christiern, the Dane, who, even among his own people, had earned for himself the title of

Christiern the *Bad*, had suddenly marched an army of mercenaries into Sweden, surprised its forces, seized the young heir to the throne, Gustavus Vasa, and mastered the country, which he delivered over to the savage licence of his soldiery.

But, for the honour of human nature, there is an inevitable point at which oppression works its own ruin. The peasants met in their morasses and mountains; the nobles, as each could elude the vigilance of the tyrant, joined them; insurrection burst out, and, to complete the peril of the Danes, the young Gustavus escaped from the place of his confinement, and was declared leader of the patriots of Sweden. But the true source of this heroic resistance was to be found in the counting-houses of the League. Hatred of the tyrant, fear of the result of accumulating the power of three crowns on his head, and not less the natural compassion which men of intelligent and civilized minds feel for undeserved misfortune, were motives which roused the whole energy of the Hanse Towns. They sent a fleet into the Baltic, assisted Gustavus in his escape, supplied him with money, and were rewarded for their efforts, by seeing the dreaded Union of Calmar [1] totally and finally dissolved.

History has no nobler office than that of showing the triumph of manliness and justice, however humble their origin, over bloated insolence, let its rank be what it may. The proud king of Denmark and Norway, the despot of the north, and conqueror of Sweden, the brother-in-law of the first monarch of the continent, Charles the Fifth, found himself at war with the clerks of Hamburgh and Lubeck, and baffled by them! Wherever his fleets or armies appeared, they felt this daring enemy on their track, and were forced to fly. Christiern, reduced to extremity, fled to Charles, and attempted to rouse the imperial wrath against the traders. But Charles had been taught, by his experience with the free German cities, that it was perilous to disturb men armed for their rights and properties. An unfortunate request, which Christiern made, hastened his catastrophe. He had asked Charles to give him the city of Lubeck. The emperor justly treated the request as that of a

[1] 1520.

madman.   Christiern, in a fit of rage, tore off the Order of the Golden Fleece, which had been given to him by the emperor, and dashed it on the ground.   But Lubeck heard the request, and determined deeply to punish its insolence.

Gustavus had already driven the Danish troops from the open country of Sweden, but they still possessed the three strongholds of Stockholm, Abo, and Calmar.   Against those walls the insurrectionary army, ill provided with money or military means, must have wasted its rude valour.   But the spirit of Lubeck and its allies was roused, and it poured in troops, provisions, and money, until Gustavus was monarch of Sweden.   After having placed a king upon the throne, its next office was to extinguish a tyrant.   The general rendezvous of the Hanseatic fleets was fixed at Copenhagen[1], and on the first attack Bornholm and Elsineur were taken, sword in hand.   The outworks of the capital thus seized, the capital must next have fallen.   But the Danes, weary of expending their blood, and seeing their fleets and cities burnt, for a prince

[1] 1522.

" who should long since have fatted the region kites with his offal," revolted against Christiern, and conferred their crown upon his uncle, Frederic, duke of Holstein. Thus Gustavus and Frederic equally owed their diadems to the sons of trade. But Christiern had not yet felt the last vengeance of the republic. Its fleets pursued him through every corner of his dominions, and conveyed the Swedish and Danish troops with a rapidity which he could not elude, until Norway too, disgusted with the spectacle of a fugitive king, abjured him, and gave her crown to Frederic. The League was now paramount, its services were acknowledged by both sovereigns: at the decision of their claims it was chosen umpire, and at the famous conference of Malmœ[1] its ambassadors acted as the general mediators!

Christiern was now crushed, and an exile. But he was not destroyed, and for six years he spent a life of perhaps the greatest misery that the spirit of a proud man can suffer,—a life of solicitation at foreign courts for assistance to recover his

[1] 1524.

dominions. The jealousy of Holland against the
Hanse Towns at length enabled him to obtain a
fleet from the States, with which he sailed for Norway. But his indefatigable enemy was still upon
his steps. The Dutch fleet was suddenly assailed
by the Lubeckers, and after a desperate resistance
destroyed. This was the final effort of the tyrant.
In attempting to make his escape, he was surrounded, seized, and thrown for life into the dungeons of Sunderbourg, leaving to the world nothing
but a name, which in his own country still points
many a tale of terror.

The fortunes of this great League had now reached
the meridian, and from this period they were to
decline. The history of all republics is the same.
By the simplicity and directness of their earlier
councils; by their riddance of the weighty expenditure which overwhelms monarchies with debt;
and still more by their utter rejection of that spirit
of patronage which encumbers old governments
with imbecility and ignorance in office; and which
altogether renders desperate, or crushes men of
talents born in the inferior ranks of life, they suddenly outrun all their competitors. In their ope-

rations there is no reserve for waste; their whole vigour is called on, and thrown directly into the struggle. Their finance is applied exclusively to the purposes of the state. And where eminent ability exists, it is stimulated to its full development by the consciousness that the most dazzling of all prizes is within its reach, and that if it fall short of the highest wealth, power, and fame, the failure is altogether its own.

But the fall of a republic is as certain as its rise. It contains within itself the principle of inevitable ruin. The popular energy which raised it, undermines it, and the volcanic fire does not more surely hollow and eat away the soil which it covers with preternatural luxuriance, than the power of the multitude shatters the foundations of the national prosperity. Lubeck, by its maritime prowess in the Danish war, had risen for a time to the head of the confederacy. It was the first to feel the symptoms of fatal decline. George Wullenwer, a trader of Lubeck, had forced his way up to the highest rank in his country by the exhibition of great public talent. His element was struggle; and after he had obtained all that ambition could demand at home, the office of bourgomaster or chief of the republic; he was driven by his vigorous and daring nature to seek it abroad. The disturbances of Sweden and Denmark, still agitated by a turbulent noblesse, an impoverished, unruly populace, and the rival claims of pretenders to the throne, offered Wullenwer the natural field for fame. But while he held the reins of government, he required a soldier capable of putting his designs in execution. This ally was soon found in Meyer, who, from being a locksmith at Hamburgh, had sprung into celebrity as a first-rate soldier. On this man he conferred the military command of Lubeck; and then, to render himself monarch in all but name, haranguing the populace on the vices of the old senate, and the general errors of the old government, he proposed to *renovate* the constitution. The oration was successful, the populace applauded, the golden days were come when all was to be freedom, peace, and plenty; and with the words on his lips, this type of Cromwell marched to the senate-house, expelled the senate, placed his creatures in their room, and was lord of the republic.

Wullcnwer's plans of conquest were worthy at once of the brilliancy and the rashness of his ambition. He felt that Lubeck, restricted in her territory to the narrow district at the mouth of the Trave, must perish at the first attack by any of the great land powers. He now projected the perpetual possession of the Sound, which would give him possession of the Baltic; and the perpetual union of Denmark with Lubeck; or if he failed in obtaining the whole Danish territory, including Norway, he looked to at least the dismemberment of provinces sufficient to make a solid territorial power. In the last resort, the fertile brain of this politician thought of obtaining the aid of our Henry VIII., and even of Francis I., by offering to them successively the crown of Denmark.

A fleet and army were raised, and the command given to the Count of Oldenburg, one of those roving German princes whose trade was war, and who were ready to fight any quarrel for their pay. This powerful armament fell irresistibly upon the naked coasts of the Baltic. The principle of the war was revolutionary. There is nothing new under the sun; and the French fraternity and equality of the eighteenth century were anticipated by the proclamations of Lubeck in the sixteenth. The Count of Oldenburg every where declared that he came only to restore their rights to the people, to extinguish the tyranny of the nobles, to teach the suffering nations the way to peace and freedom, and to spread commerce and independence through the north. Those promises were fulfilled alike in both cases. The Count's republican army robbed, burned, and slaughtered with the vigour of the oldest abuses ; roused the peasantry to reform their government by slaying their masters ; and by the double scourge of insurrection and invasion, covered the unfortunate land with fire and blood.

But this violence wrought its own extinction. The Danish nobles had chiefly fled to Jutland, another La Vendée, where the tenantry were yet unenlightened with the new doctrines of public prosperity. They put at their head Christiern, Duke of Holstein, son of the late king Frederic; summoned their retainers, and learned in the war of adversity and exile the lessons by which they were to reassert the rights of their country. The

young prince was fortunate in having for his con-
temporaries Henry IV. of France, and Gustavus
Vasa, two of the most extraordinary princes that
Europe has seen ; and who, like himself, were forced
to fight their way through rebellious subjects and
powerful invaders to the crown. Christiern is said
to have even resembled Henry in his romantic
valour, his brilliant resources, and peculiarly in
that animation and buoyancy of heart which never
failed him in his lowest depression ; and which to
the leader of a popular army is of all qualities the
most invaluable.

The aspect of the war was suddenly changed:
Christiern, at the head of his desultory levies,
ranged the country, attacked the invaders unexpectedly, harassed their communications, and while
every skirmish cheered his rude soldiery with vengeance, or with the spoil of troops loaded with the
plunder of Denmark, he broke the spirit of the
Lubeckers—tired of fighting in a wilderness, and
longing to return and enjoy their plunder at home.
But the catastrophe was hurried by more than the
sword of the young king. While every courier had
brought details of triumph, the people of Lubeck

had sustained the war with national pride.   But
when the news of defeats came, accompanied with
urgent demands for troops and money, the question
of profit and loss fortunately awoke their sensibi-
lities. The merchants angrily and despondingly computed the sums which peaceable traffic would have
brought in, while they were expending millions of
florins for the empty honour of distributing kingdoms.   But higher considerations may have opened
their eyes, for the spirit of commerce is one of
justice and goodwill to man.   The opulent merchant, in his luxurious mansion on the banks of
the Trave, must have thought of the " looped and
windowed nakedness" of the unfortunate Dane or
Swede, with whom he probably had long personal
intercourse, and whom at least, he must have felt
entitled to the claims of a common nature.   A
counter-revolution commenced.   The former senate
were restored.   Their first act was to return to
the peaceful maxims of their ancestors.   They
proposed a truce.   A congress was held at Hamburgh [1], and the war of Lubeck was at an end.

[1] 1536.

The Count of Oldenburgh, who had flattered himself with the hope of seizing a territory in the general dismemberment, still held out in Malmoe and Copenhagen. But he was pushed vigorously. Famine finished both sieges, and Christiern the Second made his triumphal entry into Copenhagen, on a day which is still recorded as the second birth of the throne [1].

The fate of the " regents" of Lubeck, Wullenwer, and Meyer, is but a sketch of the customary pencil of popular ambition. Those men, who had been idolized in the day of their prosperity, had suddenly become objects of the fiercest aversion. All the misfortunes of the war were heaped upon their heads, their splendid talents and services were forgotten in indiscriminate calumny, their noble expenditures for the state were imputed to avarice. Their intelligence, valour, and grandeur of design, which had raised Lubeck to the summit of the League, were bitterly converted into presumption, rashness, and personal cupidity. Their fate may be easily conjectured. They had raised a spirit

---

[1] 14th July, 1536.

which was too strong for them to lay, and in making the populace the arbiters of the republic, they had signed their own death-warrant. "They were," justly says the historian, " undoubtedly no common men. They had given proof of great courage, and of genius firm, vast, and daring. They clearly belonged to that class of mankind, fortunately a small one, which possesses all qualities for the overthrow of established things, and for the termination of their own career on either the throne or the scaffold[1]." The " regents" died by the hands of the public executioner.

The establishment of the Factories was one of the most characteristic and effective conceptions of the League. Among the jealous and half-barbarian people of Europe, the merchant was always an object of mingled envy and contempt; and the Hanse Towns had found at an early period that an unprotected commerce was only an allurement to plunder. Their only resource was, to form large communities in the principal countries, capable of giving protection to their traders, of receiving their

[1] Mallet. Histoire de la Ligue.

cargoes directly, and by their superior knowledge of local circumstances, fitted to avail themselves of all the peculiar advantages of their position. To those who recognize a Factory under its modern aspect, the solemn and formal rules of the ancient school of commerce must appear singularly forbidding. The age was one of cloisters and chivalry, and the Hanseatic factories curiously combined the spirit of both. The factory at Bergen, the model of them all, was at once a fortress and a convent. Its tenants were at once knights, and recluses. Its buildings spread over a large quarter of the city, and its walls were regularly mounted by guards attended by dogs of extraordinary ferocity, trained to fly equally at friend or foe. No person was permitted to pass the gates after nightfall. To prevent the influence of external manners or interests, all alliance with the people of the country was strictly prohibited. Its inmates were all unmarried, and they were prohibited from receiving the visits of any female. To satisfy the governors of the fortitude of their younger members under this cloistral discipline, all aspirants underwent an ordeal scarcely less severe than that of old ap-

pointed for criminals. The three species of proof
were the trial by smoke, by water, and by the
scourge. Those were so severe, that it was not unusual to see the aspirants die under the operation.
Still the certainty of making wealth in time, the
eagerness of youth, and perhaps even the mystery
of the life, attracted such crowds of young men from
all parts of the continent, that it was constantly
found necessary to increase the difficulties of admission by still more barbarous penalties. This
ordeal, which was called *The Games*, annually
attracted an immense concourse of spectators to
Bergen. The severities of the exhibition were
followed by a carousal, dances, masquerades, feasts
and revellings of all extravagant kinds. The
factory was mad, till the Carnival was over. Then
the gates were shut, silence prevailed, every man
was bent over his ledger, and the grimness of a
den of Carthusians succeeded to the revelry of a
German hostel. The close of the ceremony was
announced by the appearance of a jester or fool,
who proclaimed, " Long life to the Games," and
proposed a general health to the prosperity, the
honour, and the trade of the Hanseatic factory.

The second factory, but the most productive in point of trade, was that of Bruges. The early progress of the Flemings in the possession of public rights, had long made them eminent in every art cultivated by the free labour of man. While France and Germany were turned into deserts by the perpetual quarrels of their masters, and while their people, exposed to the extortions of all, lost the spirit of economy and industry,—for who will toil for the robber and the oppressor?—The Fleming, secure that what he earned would be his own, and fearless of power while he could take shelter under the wing of a constitution, had turned his country into a garden, and built manufactories like citadels, and houses like palaces.

The wool-trade of Europe, like all other trades, had naturally devolved into the hands which could best pay for it; and the beauty of the Flemish stuffs, the richness of their dyes, and peculiarly the splendour of their tapestries, which, to the eyes of the half-savage German and Russian, must have looked scarcely less than miraculous, commanded the wealth of Europe. A Flemish tapestry was a royal treasure, and no sovereign hesitated to strip his exchequer for so singular, and certainly so beautiful, an evidence of the skill of man. The Hanseatics filled their depôt at Bruges with the produce of the extreme north, timber, iron, hemp, canvas, cloth, and especially wax, which had an extraordinary sale, at a period when the Continent was overwhelmed with churches and cathedrals, when perpetual lights were burning in them all, and when sins were atoned in proportion to the thickness of the sinner's candle.

Another of their great factories was established in the heart of Russia. It must seem strange to us, that in the country of Europe which now exhibits the model of the most unrelieved despotism, one of the freest and most powerful republics existed, so far back as the eleventh century. This was one of the many miracles of commerce. The situation of Novorogod, on the Wolchof river, and at the head of one of the great inland waters of Russia, directed its attention to trade, on the first cessation of the Tartar wars. From a place of refuge for fishermen, or the few wandering traffickers who still survived in the desert, it rapidly rose into a city, the wonder of surrounding barbarism. Its duke or sovereign was soon forced to limit his tyranny, and was finally compelled to surrender all but the shadow of power into the hands of the general assembly of the citizens; by whom the hereditary succession was changed into the elective, and the barbarian despot into the limited and responsible magistrate of a republic. With wealth, its commercial enterprise, its population, and its rank as a government, rapidly increased, until, in the fifteenth century, its population was said to amount to half a million; its fairs were the emporium of Asia, and the north of Europe; the German, the Italian, and the Chinese, met in the streets of this famous and flourishing city; and the admiration of the surrounding provinces, to which its strength and opulence must have looked like something fallen from Heaven, could find no other language than that of idolatry: " Who can resist God, and the mighty Novorogod?"

But the usual fate of republics was not to be averted. The citizens, grown ambitious as they grew opulent, fell into faction, and were surprised by the wild invasion of the neighbouring barba-

rians. Ivan the Fourth, a brutal savage, looking
with a greedy eye on the arts and wealth, which
he had neither the taste to cultivate, nor the industry to acquire, suddenly rushed on the city
with a host of savages, as furious, greedy, and
blood-thirsty as a life of savagery could prepare
for plunder and massacre. The overthrow was
complete. An immense multitude were destroyed
by the indiscriminate havoc of the Russian pike.
A still greater multitude fled from a spot where
nothing but security could have reconciled men to
the ungenial climate, and the remoteness from the
general intercourse of Europe. They never returned.
The furious feuds of Russia, thenceforth alternately
torn by revolt, and trampled by the Tartars, extinguished all hope of personal safety, and Novorogod never recovered the blow. The transfer of
the seat of government to the mouth of the Neva,
by Peter the Great, and the change of the route
of commerce to the cities on the Euxine, were
new impediments, which even the tendency of all
great places of commerce to resume their original
strength, was not able to resist; and Novorogod
has long since dwindled down into a provincial

city, with a feeble and idle population of a few thousands.

The Hanseatic Factory among ourselves would deserve a history of its own, from the singular vigour of its system, its perpetual encroachments on what, even in the darkness of the middle ages, we had already discovered to be the rights of British trade, and the perpetual and stubborn resistance with which its monopoly was met, and by which that monopoly was finally abolished. The whole detail would give a striking proof of our early sense of justice, the clear-headedness in commercial principles which distinguished the British merchant, and the public and personal evils that must result in this country from any system of favouring strangers at the expense of the nation. While the English monarchs continued poor, and their thrones unsteady, the Hanse Towns continued lords of the trade of England. But as England began to feel her strength, the privileges of the foreigner declined. As her kings became more secure, and were less compelled to lean on foreign influence, the natural rights of their people took the lead, the cessation of the York and Lancaster wars pre-

pared the Hanseatics for their fate, and the last
privileges of the Factory were abolished by Eliza-
beth [1], when, in the closing years of her reign, she
had at last fixed the unsettled throne of her ancestors on an immoveable basis, and had built
round her empire the impregnable walls of liberty
and religion.

The same causes which repelled the League at
so early a period in England, began to operate on
the Continent in the following century. The general European system had gradually assumed a
consistency, which gave comparative security and
peace to the people. Elective monarchy was replaced by inheritance; and commerce, no longer
compelled to take refuge under the protection of
strangers, established itself nearer home. The
Hanseatic League then declined. Its purposes
had been accomplished; and they were admirable and almost providential purposes. But
its necessity had passed away, and other sub-
stitutes less cumbrous, and more consistent with
the immediate good of nations, were to assume

[1] 1597.

its office. The allied towns gradually broke off their connexion with the once famous League, and before the close of the seventeenth century it was but a name.

CHAPTER XXVII.

***

THE BATTLE OF BAUTZEN.

MAY 26. Consternation again. Intelligence
has been just received, that Napoleon has routed
the Allies, has driven them on Silesia,—a country
where they must be starved or surrender; has
mastered all Saxony, and may now order the
municipality of Berlin to be hanged up beside the
senators of Hamburgh any day he pleases. Every
body is of course in infinite terror. The very atmosphere is thick with rumours, and in the confusion, it is difficult to ascertain any thing, but
that Napoleon has sworn vengeance against all
rebellion. Then we shall have our neighbours of
Altona on our hands. The natural result of an
unsuccessful struggle on the part of our friends,
must be, to make our half-friends enemies, and
our enemies insolent and intolerable. If the

French have really gained the day, all is over with
the slippery neutrality of Denmark.

———

The accounts of the battle clear up by degrees.
From Lutzen, the allies had begun to practise
the manœuvres of the Russian campaign. They
continued retreating slowly, as the enemy's columns
took up more advanced quarters; avoiding general
actions, but still keeping up a formidable front.
Their task was a delicate one; for they have been
for some time bidding against Napoleon for the
Austrian alliance. A decided defeat, or a decided
victory, would be equally fatal to the purchase;
unless, indeed, the victory were of that nature
which swept Napoleon from the face of the earth
at a blow. The Austrian policy is palpable; both
the belligerents are fighting its battle from hill to
hill, and from river to river; the Austrian cabinet
lives by jealousy; the balance in its hands is worth
all the swords in Europe; it is the lawyer of the
Continent, and thrives by the quarrel of the more
boisterous blockheads, having had sufficient experience of the folly of undertaking suits of its own. Its

empire grows sleek by the surrounding pauperism;
and until mankind shall grow weary of firing away
their gold and silver in shot and shells, and raising
fools from Picardy to Provence, to shoot fools raised
from the Rhine to the Polar Ocean; until nations
are starved, ravaged, beggared, and massacred, into
a general peace, the plumpness of Austria will never
go down.   Her card is now to be the arbiter of the
Continent: the stiff neutral, until she can be the
sullen sovereign.   But the popular feelings are
against this tardiness.   The Austrian peasantry
remember the terrible tithe in which the French
mulcted them.   The nobles are indignant at the
insults of the French rabble of commissaries and
field-marshals.   The emperor himself, son of peace
as he is, has a bitter memory of the four millions
sterling! which Napoleon made the first fruits of
his invasion in 1809; and, above all, the soldiery
long for an opportunity of coming to blows, and
wiping off the heavy arrear, from the day of Marengo to the day of Ulm and Austerlitz. A month
or two will settle the question.   Metternich will
resist, in his usual style, until the moment when
he finds it unpopular to resist any longer; and

then, in his usual style, he will discover all the merit of giving way. Maria Louisa, for whom nobody cares; and whom the higher minds of Austria scorn, as having allied herself to the scion of a regicide republic, will be thrown overboard; and Napoleon will find himself for once outwitted in bargaining against German brains for the souls and bodies of men.

Such are the speculations of the time. Yet an hour may turn them all into thin air; a shot from some Tyrolese rifle may send the fiery spirit of the Corsican into the clouds; or a fit of his hereditary gout may displant the pacific Emperor, for the warlike Archduke; or Metternich may fall in love again in his grand climacteric, marry his chambermaid, and flee from domestic slavery to the gentler irritation of foreign war. Clouds and darkness are lying every where upon the future; and happy is the man, who, contented with his own share of troubles, escapes those of the regulator of kingdoms.

Napoleon's manœuvres exhibited all his cus-

tomary scorn of human life. He every where
threw his conscripts full into fire. Yet this exposure may have been from the well-known military
maxim—that with young troops any thing is better
than to stand still. And, of all troops, the French
require this tactique the most. They will fire for
ever, move from morning till night in the face of
an enemy, run under or over batteries; but stand
still they cannot. The famous Lord Stair said,
" that the British were the only troops he ever
saw who could go into fire, and *out of fire*, at the
tap of the drum." The latter point was the perfection, and it still remains with the British. But
no troops can go *into* fire in higher style than the
French. Their advance is proverbially one of the
finest things imaginable.

Napoleon's battle of this day was all marching.
He passed the Spree on the 20th. The allies still
moved on before him; covering their movements
with large bodies of horse, in which they have a
most important superiority. He rapidly pushed on
to Bautzen, a considerable town, where their infantry had taken up a strong position. From this,
however, on the sight of Napoleon's tirailleurs, they

retired to a still stronger in the hills overhanging the town. At the foot of those hills the French halted for the night, with the determination of *culbuteeing* both Russ and Prussian by the dawn.

One of the singularities of perpetual campaigning is its suffering the mind to ramble into all kinds of ideas. Men become accustomed to battle and bloodshed, until they actually look for excitement to any thing else. This dreadful slaughter is described as a "model of the *picturesque!*" The movement of 125,000 French in the sunset, the columns diverging and converging through the forests, until they met at the foot of the mountains, and, after glittering in all the colours of the sunset, lighted their own illumination, and propagated a circle of fires extending for nine miles; all figure in the story, until they efface the recollection that on this showy spot torrents of blood were to be poured out, and the fate of Germany or of Europe was to be decided.

The position of the allies rendered the march one of the most perilous operations of the war. In the rear of Bautzen a fine range of hills rises amphitheatrically, covered with forest, broken only by

corn and meadow. A few valleys of no great depth
separated some of the allied divisions, and here was
the first defect of the position. The hills on the
right trended gently to the plain, and here was the
second; for here the position might be turned,
though the strong ground of Klein Bautzen in its
rear was within gun-shot, and a few battalions there
might make any movement on that side extremely
hazardous to the attacking force. But the true military value of the whole position was, that it afforded
a retreat under all circumstances. To force it must
inflict a waste of lives, which might have all the
effects of a defeat, and paralyse all the future objects of the enemy; while, in the rear, opened
among the heights several precipitous gorges leading inward to the mountains of Silesia.

By day-light the French were seen manœuvring
in a parallel line to the allied front. The allies
were posted on the amphitheatre of hills, the Russians on the left, and in a position nearly secure
from attack; the Prussians on the heights descending to the plain. Partial skirmishing occurred
from three in the morning; but the main bodies
remained for some hours looking at each other.

Napoleon's inactivity was afterwards explained by his waiting for the signal from Ney's guns, whom he had sent through the mountains the evening before, to turn the Russians. The engagement began about noon, by a series of attacks on the strongest part of the position. Those gradually decayed; and while the allies were in some degree perplexed by the manœuvre, its object was discovered by a general movement of the enemy's line to the left. Towards evening, heavy columns of the enemy were seen moving out of the woods in front of the Prussians. The whole disposable force of Napoleon was now evidently gathering for a final attack on this quarter. The firing, which had languished along the line for some hours, suddenly grew heavy. The allied officers now felt the disadvantages of a position, which though in some points impregnable, yet rendered it difficult to assist each other. Troops were, however, moved from the left, but the difficulty of the mountain-road was so great, that but trifling reinforcements could come up in time. In the meantime Napoleon's old manœuvre of bringing his whole artillery to play upon one point had been practised with terrible effect. The slaughter on the right began to be ruinous. The allies, exhausted by a day of incessant fatigue, felt that they must soon give way, unless they could overpower this accumulation of fire. There was still a short interval of success. The Prussian centre, under Blucher, Kleist, and D'Yorck, hurried down from the heights in rear of the right wing, and the French columns were brought to a stop, in the moment of victory. The slaughter was here retorted on the enemy, and was probably the greatest of the day ; for wherever the Prussians were they fought with desperation. But, as the chimes of Bautzen were tolling five in the evening, an order came for the general retreat of the troops through the Silesian gorges. It had just been ascertained that Ney, with a powerful force, was in their rear. An hour more would have placed the allies between two fires!

Other accounts, since received, increase the numbers engaged. The allies are said to have had 130,000 men in the field, and Napoleon his usual superiority, little short of 200,000. This extraordinary force he had gathered by calling in garrisons, and by the levies of conscripts who had been hurried forwards from France. His object was to finish the campaign at a blow.

Yet, he has been evidently foiled in this point. He has gained the battle; but by it he has gained nothing more than forcing the allies from one position, while they have a hundred others in their rear. The allies have lost ground, but they have lost neither guns, prisoners, nor colours. The French loss has been tremendous, for their line was exposed to the whole fire from the heights, and all their attacks were made upon strong positions. They are said to have had five or six thousand killed, and the usual frightful proportion, or about twenty thousand, wounded. The allied loss was probably less than two-thirds of the number. Such is war; ten thousand human beings that were in the full vigour of life in the morning, clods of the valley in the evening—thirty thousand bleeding, mutilated, groaning, and dying on the ground; and all this for a bulletin and six miles of rock and quagmire!

CHAPTER XXVIII.

CAROLO SCOPELLO.

THE Germans are the most soaring of genealogists; with them every great man of the earth draws his courage, his generosity, and his herald's coat, from the days of the deluge. They might as well follow it up to the fountain-head, and re-establish the old relationship of the sons of Adam and Eve. But Napoleon is now the great absorbing principle. The genealogists, as good Germans, hate him; as men fear him; but as explorers of pedigree, are consuming lamps and eyes in every province of the Teutonic world, to convince themselves that so supreme a soldier could *not* have been the simple son of a Corsican solicitor. With some he is the descendant of the refugee Vandal princes, who hid their heads in Corsica from the sword of Belisarius. With others he is the son of a Saint Napoleon, who

6

has long fallen out of the calendar. Napoleon himself is prodigiously amused by those heraldic flatteries, and persists in saying, that " he is the first great man of his family:" adding with historic fidelity, that he is the only one; and, with prophetic sagacity, that he will be the last. In this dilemma we are entitled to look for the truth wherever we can; and if it should be found lurking among the rocks and copses of the Mediterranean, we may not reject it, even for its coming from Corsica. It is only to be premised, that if the tale which follows contain more truth than compliment, nothing is more notorious than that Napoleon is not popular in Corsica. His countrymen were proud of him, until he betrayed that he was not proud of them. They now only imagine themselves a superior race to the nations who were foolish enough to be hood-winked by the son of their village attorney; or cowardly enough to be frightened into laying crowns and sceptres before a sallow youth, whom any one of their mountaineers could have outswum, outrun, or outshot; who if he had remained in their island, would have been at this hour only a poacher, or an attorney; have grown grey in the prison of the French police for apophthegms against government; or died of a rival's carbine in the courtship of the postmaster's daughter.

Carolo Scopello.

On the back of Cap Corso, the most genuine model of the Corsican of the last century was to be found two years ago. He was a fine old man, full of recollections; for he had first fought the Genoese, and kept, to the end, the sword-knot of a Genoese colonel, and the cockades of two of the captains of his *legere*, whom three several discharges from the family trombone had dismissed from war and the world together. He had next fought under Paoli, whom he pronounced to be the greatest of Corsicans, a phrase equivalent, in his estimation, to the greatest of the human race; and had reserved as his trophies the snuff-box and curling-irons of the French brigadier commandant, who had fallen by his marksmanship in the skirmish of the olive grove behind Montegrosso, a well known scene of French discomfiture. Those, however, he showed only by particular request ; as he had soon discovered that the French were remarkably jealous of their military fame, and had no hesitation in hanging the very best marksmen in Corsica.

But Carolo had other accomplishments ; at the age of eighty-one he danced, he could play a gavotta on the flute, he touched the mandolin, as indeed every body does in the island, and melancholy music they make of its hard, dry tones ; he could go through a day's shooting over the hills with his son or his grandson ; and the report went strongly, even to the last, that a hare or a stray fawn from the governor's preserve was not safe within some miles of this gallant old specimen of the Cyrnœi.

But his politics were anti-Buonapartean in the bitterest degree. He hated the French, but he hated them the more for their having made the son of Carlo and Letitia a general, a king, any thing. He remembered Marbœuff's coxcombries, gallantries, and tyrannies with scorn, but he scorned the Count less as a Frenchman, and hated him less as a governor, than as the reputed father of Napoleon, as his acknowledged protector, and as the

man who had sent him to a college in France.
" This," said the old man, " was the direct way to
ruin him ; from that moment I knew all that would
happen; he would forget his country; he would
think only of being a colonel or a general in
France, and he would be a Corsican no longer."
The German genealogist who took down Napoleon's
story from the lips of the old patriot, had been employed for thirty years, at the usual German
allowance of sixteen hours a day, in deciphering
the Herculaneum MSS. He had succeeded at
length to the full extent of his ambition. He had
unrolled a papyrus, which wanted all the pages
but the first and the last; the former acquainting
him that the treatise was upon the art of proving
by metaphysics that " out of nothing came nothing,"
and the latter concluding with the experience of
the author, Epicharmis, the son of Diodorus, the
Samothracian, that " the gout and the toothach
were evils," and that, after all the experiments of
philosophy, from Thales downwards, " eating and
drinking were among the best contrivances for
keeping soul and body together." With this treasure the German sailed homewards in the cheering

certainty of being made decipherer-general to the sovereign of the three villages adjoining his native town. But on the coast of Corsica his ship impinged, his portmanteau, weighty with his literature, went to the bottom; and, lost to glory for ever, he had nothing to do but to copy the old Corsican's angry tale. Carolo's resentment had a personal cause: on Napoleon's elevation to the consulate, Carolo had been urged on all sides to offer himself to the sight of his distinguished countryman. He came all the way from his island, and walked into the palace with his hoary hair about his shoulders, his upright Herculean form, his startling mountain *patois*, and his family fowling-piece in his hand. Such a sight had never before been seen in the Tuileries. But he made his way through them all, embroidered chamberlains, feathered aides-de-camp, and diamond-starred and epauletted generals. All the world stared at Carolo, as if he had dropt from the moon; but the brave old Corsican gave them stare for stare, and pushed on. He found Napoleon " Premier Consul de la Republique," in the centre of the circle of ambassadors, going his rounds, with Rapp and Lavalette his aides-de-

camp taking step for step on the outside, and
watching the movement of every ambassadorial
muscle that might be raised against the life on
which, as all the poets and philosophers of France
averred, hung the salvation of Europe. Carolo,
nothing daunted, raised his voice, and announced
his own arrival. Napoleon started, and was ashamed
of his emotion; saw his wild countryman, and was
ashamed of his country. With an expression of
wrath at the chamberlain who had admitted the
Vandal! he broke up the circle, instantly retired to
his closet, and made old Carolo Scopello his enemy
till his dying day.

Tale of the Generations of Napoleon.

*   *   *   *   *   *   *

" Who has not heard, read, written, or dreamed,
of the bay of Naples? Of its morning sun show-
ering it with pearls and roses, and of its evening
sun exchanging them for topazes and tulips! Of
its being at one time a mirror in which Aurora
dresses her ringlets, and at another a prodigious

cathedral window, stained with all kinds of heavenly things, before which Phœbus goes to vespers."

It was one of the finest evenings that ever shone
on the shore of Naples.   The sea lay under the
sun-beams like a huge golden *plateau*, bordered
with the innumerable buildings of the city and the
suburbs, that looked like incrustations of silver
round its edge.   Music from the various boating
parties, and even the sounds of the city that came
up, softened and mingled by the sea breeze, filled
the air with harmony.   The eye ranged from Mi-
senum, with its bold purple promontory overshadowing the waters far and wide, to Vesuvius, sitting
on the opposite side of the bay, like a gigantic
guard of this fairy region.   On that evening the
giant too was in his gala robes. He was crowned with
a double diadem of cloud and fire.   All the heights
were filled with travellers from all corners of the
earth, enjoying the magnificent landscape; even
the peasantry, accustomed as they were to the
sight, remarked on the peculiar richness of the
sunset, stopped on their way home up the hills,
and prided themselves in their having a country
which had the finest sun, sky, sea and volcano, in the
four quarters of the globe.

But in the midst of all this beauty and exultation sat a man, who seemed neither to see the one
nor to share in the other. He was evidently young,
and as evidently under some misery of mind; for,
as he sat on the side of the Solfatara, he was observed to start up frequently, and hurry forwards,
as if he had forgotten the hazardous height, or had
intended to throw himself down the precipices, on
whose very edge he was treading. He would then
lift his eyes to heaven, beat his forehead, and tear
his hair with the violence of Italian passion. Those
extraordinary gestures naturally caught the eyes of
the strangers on the different points of the mountain; but the difficult spot on which he had fixed
his seat repelled the generality, and those who at
last reached him received such repelling answers,
that they soon left him to himself.

The general eye, too, was now fixed upon a more
amusing object; for there was a felucca race from
the Mole to the point of Capri. The king's barges
were on the water, followed by a large train of the
nobility in their boats, and the whole glittered
along, springing and shining like a swarm of flying-
fish. But as they came towards the centre of the
bay, a boat with a single rower suddenly took the

lead, beating all the ten and twenty oared cha-
loupes, barges, sparonaroes, every thing.   The sea-
breeze had now sprung up, and all the feluccas
hoisted their sails as they came into the wind:
they were not a foot the nearer; the strong rower
alone kept them behind, and yet, evidently did
not exert half his strength. As he came nearer the
shore, the thousand telescopes that were pointed
to the water had but one object, the extraordinary
boatman.   All the Lazzaroni on the Mole were in
ecstacies, and swore by every saint up to St. Jan-
uarius, that the world had never produced any
thing like it. The boatman certainly seemed to
be prodigiously at his ease; he scarcely touched
the oars, but sat throwing an occasional look back
at the crowd of gilded vessels that were heavily
ploughing the sea into foam far behind, then dip-
ped his oar into the water, and then laid it down
again, or stood up, waved his cap, and huzzaed to the
huzzaing multitude; while the boat absolutely shot
over the surge.

Night falls rapidly in the south; the scene below
had been gradually darkening for some time, and
the boatman had scarcely darted in and disappeared

under one of the little wooded hills at the foot of
Puzzuoli, when the whole royal show sank in shade,
and, but for the innumerable lamps that twinkled
on their tops and rigging, would have been invisible. But they were still at some distance from
land, when the cloud that had sat heavily during
the day, wreathing a blue and sulphur-tinged
turban round Vesuvius, moved towards Capri, and
began to discharge its thunders and lightnings.
Rapidity and fierceness are the style of a Mediterranean storm; the breeze had now become a
wild succession of gusts, that tore up the very bottom of the waters. The butterfly navy of Naples
was in danger; guns of distress followed; cries of
distress were heard from time to time, but all
earthly sounds were speedily extinguished in the
incessant roar of the thunder. The hour was terrible to the fresh-water sailors of the ante-chamber.
As the storm deepened, the only light was from
the long flashes that burst along the horizon,
throwing a blaze of peculiar and ominous redness
over the earth and sea.

But there was one to whom the storm produced
no terror. The young Italian gazed from his

height on this war of the elements with strange and desperate delight : it seemed to have renewed life within him; he wildly stripped his bosom to the rain as it burst round him in torrents; he tauntingly lifted his arm to the burning and serpent flashes that hissed and whirled round his head, as if to bid them do their worst; he cried aloud through the roarings of the wind, as if to challenge and defy the storm in his despair. And, he seemed to have been answered. The cloud which had been rolling heavily along the bay, at length wheeled round, and overhung the pinnacle of the Solfatara; the sulphurous vapours of the hill caught fire, a yellow flame rushed round it like a garment; and the last look cast towards the frenzied Italian by the multitude who had fled in terror towards Puzzuoli, showed him sitting calmly in the midst of a circle of conflagration, evidently awaiting his fate with the courage of frenzy.

*   *   *   *   *   *   *

" Ho ! friend, will you sleep for ever? Here, take a drink of this, and be a man again." The

Italian opened his eyes, and to his astonishment found himself in a low chamber, evidently hewn out of the rock; and his surprise was not diminished when he saw standing over him the boatman of the evening, holding some cordial to his lips! It was evidently to the activity and courage of this bold rower that he owed his preservation. His last perception had been that of the clouds stooping deeper and heavier round the spot where he sat in gloomy longings for death; a broad burst of intolerable light had flamed across his eyes, he felt smote by the flash, and felt no more! He now attempted to thank his preserver, but was answered roughly by, " Come, come, no words, I have no time for talking now. Here you are, safe for awhile against every thing, but starving. The Douaniers will look twice before they come after their old acquaintance, Maldimondo." The Italian recognised the name as that of a famous contrabandist, who had either eluded the vigilance, or defeated the force, of the officers of the customs, for many years.

" Maldimondo!" he repeated in surprise.— " What?" said the boatman, " you know Maldi-

mondo then ?   Do you expect to get the information money for giving me up to the knaves in the
king's pay? But, no; though I defy them, the
rascals generally contrive to keep clear of me;
and when, now and then, we have come athwart
each other about the bay, I think I have given
them pretty good cause to steer another course in
future.   I suppose you saw the dance I led them
this evening?" The Italian expressed his astonishment; though he acknowledged that he had been
too much absorbed in his own feelings, to have
looked long. " Aye, that" said the boatman, "was
a specimen of what I could do any day in the week,
the wind on an end, or larboard or starboard, aye,
or in the teeth, it is all the same to Maldimondo
—all the same to Maldimondo! winds, hours, seas,
shores, night and day, years, centuries; alas! alas!
he struck his huge hand fiercely upon his forehead
—then burst out into a bitter laugh—" aye, aye,
all the same to Maldimondo!"

The repetition of the word came with a tone of
voice which struck the Italian as the most peculiar
that he had ever heard—but in what the peculiarity
consisted he was unable to define; it however

roused him out of the half slumber into which
he had fallen from exhaustion, and made him look
in the man's face. "Maldimondo!" said he, with
an effort of recollection; "is it possible that I see
before me that prince of smugglers? I have been
hearing of him since I was in the cradle, and then
they talked of him as an old man: he must be
ninety or a hundred by this time."—The boatman
laughed out loud. "Aye, those are Neapolitan
stories; give the honest people in that ants' nest
there," and he pointed with a contemptuous gesture to the city, "enough of sunshine, macaroni, and
nothing to do, and they will find tongue for the
world. Look at me: do you take me for ninety
or a hundred?"

"Quite the contrary," said the Italian, "you
look scarcely older than myself; but I have had
troubles enough to make me old at thirty; and I
have found, that it is ease of mind, after all, that
keeps one young. Yet you are miraculously active,
strong-looking, and fresh-coloured."—"Aye, ease of
mind," muttered the boatman, and his countenance lost its broad, bold expression,—" words,
words," said he bitterly, " human folly! but this

is no talk for us. Come, let us see what provision there is on board." He now pulled down a few stones from the side of the cell, and showed a rude receptacle of wine-flasks and sea-stores. " There," said he, " is the true receipt for good looks of all kinds. Look at the sallow faces of Naples; the nobles lolling in their coaches, the citizens stuffing themselves with every beast of the earth, fowl of the heaven, and fish of the sea, without taking an hour's real labour to give them an appetite in the four and twenty! Though money is not a bad thing in its way, nor title neither; but if men were not three-fourths fools, there would be no physicians in the world. I would not have the gout or the dropsy for all the strings or stars that ever glittered on the Chiaja; no, not for a pile of gold as high as St. Elmo. Drink, friend, and thank your night's work, bad as it is, that you have the pleasure of being both hungry and thirsty."

The Italian acknowledged that he had gained at least an appetite; and the sour wine and salt fish appeared to him delicious. He remarked the singular pleasure which he felt in this simple fare, and acknowledged that hunger and fatigue were the true secrets of enjoyment after all. " Yet," said his jovial entertainer, " an hour ago you would have tossed yourself down the side of the Solfatara, or jumped into Vesuvius supperless. You see the advantage of waiting awhile, in the worst of times; you would have been a cinder already, but for my luck in seeing you as I stept out of my boat. I had amused myself long enough with the king and his laced coxcombs—long enough to bring them in the way of the gale, as it happened; and if the gale does not give a handsome account of them, it is no fault of mine." He laughed long and loud at the idea. " Aye, by to-morrow morning there will be something besides fish to be caught in the bay, and something to be seen in the palace yonder, besides bowing knaves covered over with tinsel and rascality. I saw, aye, it was the very last look I gave them; I saw," said he, bending forward in a burlesque affectation of a whisper, and with one of those strongly derisive gestures peculiar to the Neapolitan populace—" I saw one crown-wearer the less in the world."

The Italian started, and exclaimed " The king

lost!"—" Well," said the boatman, " and where is the wonder? there are heirs enough to follow him. When his time is come, what is to hinder his going, in the way of quiet, like yours, or mine—" He broke off at the word, and writhed on his seat, as if shot through with an internal pang. " No, not mine! no, never, never!" He plunged his forehead on his knees, and remained awhile convulsed, but in silence; then recovering, suddenly and completely, he said, with a flashing eye, and a reddened cheek, " Come, another flask, brother, and let me hear what brought *you* on the hill. I found you, on my way to this den; the lightning had, I at first thought, put an end to all your troubles; but as I felt motion in you still, and you seemed to be pretty much in my own condition, an outcast, though I now and then see good company too, aye, and the first company, I thought you might be 'the better for a cup of Maldimondo's home-made wine. Come, no thanks; confess who you are at once: spies are not in fashion here."

The Italian hesitated: " Oh, you think me a bad confessor; trust your friend for once," said the boatman, lifting up a heap of clothes that lay in the corner of the cell, and showing a capuchin's habit. " I have been a confessor myself, and within these four and twenty hours too. Nothing is to be done in our trade without it. The douanier's wife knows more than the douanier all the world over; and what she knows, the capuchin knows. But, if you doubt me, I can tell you more than that : the unlucky king might have been this night safe and sound in his bed, in spite of thunder and lightning; but he had a friend at his elbow who gave him a sleep, that will never trouble him with dreams. I confessed, not three days ago, the wife of the excellent and trustworthy prime minister, who plunged him over the poop. To-morrow the Count Fernando Filicino would have been brought to book for robbing the exchequer, and seen the sun rise through the bars of St. Elmo; but to-morrow he will be appointed prime minister to the new king, for reasons best known to them both, and to the bay of Naples."

" And you kept this horrid treason to yourself!" was the Italian's exclamation. " And why not?" was the reply. " If I had told it, I should not have been believed; the guards would have kicked me out of the palace ; the courtiers would have marked me for a fellow not to be trusted in an *emergency;* the king would have never troubled his head about a lazzarone like me. But Count Fernando would have had me assassinated,—half a ducat would have done the business ; and if I escaped his bravoes, the capuchins would have thrown me between four walls, with leave to live as long as I could, upon half a loaf and a pitcher of pond-water. Excellent thanks, *per Bacco !* I should have had, and deserved them too, for meddling with matters out of my line. But, you see I can keep a secret, at least when there is nothing to be got by telling it, and that is monk's law all round the world. And now for your story."

The Italian had been startled by the reckless familiarity with which crime was thus talked of. But the customs of the confessional were notorious; the man before him was his preserver, and he himself felt too much out of sorts with life to care about concealment. His story was, in fact, but brief and common. He was an advocate in one of the royal courts of Naples, and in the receipt of a moderate competency for his standing; but he had

H 3

been for some years soliciting a superior appointment in the court; and it had been successively promised to him, and given away to higher interest, until the disappointment had worn out his patience. With every occasion of its being snatched from him, the place had grown upon his imagination, till it seemed equivalent to death or life. He had at length mustered up all his interest for a final effort; he had touched the very verge of success, he had even seen the appointment made out for him, and had received on that very morning the congratulations of his brother advocates. But, on returning to his home, rumour reached him that it was again given away. In a fever of anxiety, he flew to the chief of the tribunal; he soon ascertained that the rumour was true; it had been given to an inferior advocate, whose brother shaved the minister's valet. The disappointment was intolerable. He felt his brain turn round—he flew furiously to the minister; he was invisible. He flew to the palace, to fling himself at the royal footstool, and bring down the royal vengeance on the criminal minister. He was beaten from the portico, and had a narrow escape of being run through by one of the halberdiers on guard, for the eloquence of his wrath at thrones and tribunals. He had then rushed up the mountain, determined never more to associate with human beings; the storm had come like a friend, it seemed to offer him an easy way of escaping from all his anxieties at once, and he availed himself of it with fierce philosophy.

" Well," said the listener with a smile, and stretching his large and athletic limbs across the cell, " If I were not too sleepy, I think I might put you in a way of getting the place after all; but I take it for granted you have lost all inclination for it now." He looked inquiringly into the visage of the Italian, which kindled with sudden passion. " I have a friend or two about the court," said his entertainer; " for I must contrive to have friends in all kinds of places—who I think might, in time, get you the appointment, if you felt inclined to bestir yourself." The Italian unconsciously clenched his hand, as if it held a dagger.

" So," said the boatman, grasping the hand, and strongly preventing the awakened Italian's effort to draw it back from the giant grasp; " I do not know, sneered he, "but that yours may be the best way among a thousand; it is, at all events, the shortest. The stiletto saves an infinity of trouble, and one half of Naples would eat the other but for it; *per Bacco!* it is your true peace-maker. Why not stab the rascal who has tricked you out of your livelihood, your right, your actual property?"

The Italian obviously shrank, and remained wrapt in thought. "No;" he murmured, almost forgetting that he was not alone, "I must not commit murder." "Ha! ha!" burst out the boatman, "you are a rare Neapolitan; yet I believe you to be an honest fellow at bottom. No, you must not commit murder; leave that to the nobles and the monks; we, though we cut up the king's customs a little now and then, never do any thing of the kind; all is fair fight, and as little of that on both sides as we can. The officers are shy of us, for we give them nothing but the best Leghorn powder and ball; and we have no liking for losing our time, when we should be landing our cargo. But here, sorrow calls for a bumper, whenever it is to be got; and I have not yet let you taste my capuchin wine."

He brought out a large cup, evidently gold, magnificently chased, and sparkling with jewels. It flashed a sudden light through the cave, as he took it from its case: to the Italian it seemed an altar cup, and he felt a strong reluctance to drinking from a vessel, which might have been sacrilegious spoil. The boatman saw this, and held it closer to the lamp: " What offence is there in my cup?" said he, laughing, " it does not come at least from Loretto." The Italian had no answer to make. The chasing, which, at a distance, had seemed to represent sacred subjects, was obviously, on the nearer view, taken from Ovid's Metamorphoses; and what had appeared crosses, and virgins in the clouds, was now seen to be banquetings, huntings, and dances of forest nymphs. But the sculpture was incomparable: and the Italian, a man of native taste, broke out into loud admiration of its beauty. " Well, then, since you like my cup," said the boatman, " you must in all good fellowship taste my wine. I tell you, however, before I draw it, that it is heady; and with some people, of weak brains and tender consciences, has played strange tricks: but you have no fears of that kind."

The Italian had already taken more wine than was usual with his temperate countrymen, and he felt no reluctance to further hospitality. In a kind of frolic of acquiescence, he raised the empty goblet to his lips, when, casting his glance to the bottom, he saw it, to his astonishment, covered with sculptures resembling an incantation; a young figure naked was kneeling in the centre of a circle of fearful forms, and above him stood a colossal shape, with its lower extremities covered with clouds; a fiery crown was on its forehead, whose flashes seemed pointing down to consume the victim. The flashes looked so vivid, that the Italian thought he saw them actually blaze, and felt their fire. He set down the cup with a trembling hand. " Why, friend, what is the matter now?" exclaimed Maldimondo; " you look as white as my main-sheet. Come, get up your spirits, and try my wine." He held up a large golden flagon. " The cup! the cup!" muttered the Italian; " I dare not touch it—look in the inside."—" Folly!" said the bold boatman, " you have not had wine enough to bring back your senses yet. My cup! what could you see in it, but the reflection of your

13

own frightened face? its inside is as smooth as the queen's hand—look again." The Italian still drew back, but the strong hand of Maldimondo was suddenly pressed upon his forehead, and he was compelled to glance in. The inside was, to his wonder, perfectly smooth—no figures, no flashes were to be seen. While he was still gazing, a dash of a rich Burgundy-coloured wine was flung into it from the flagon above his head, and the draught was all but forced upon him. He swallowed some drops —the flavour struck him as peculiar, but incomparable. He tried it more largely. " This is no native vintage," said the Italian, almost breathless; " but wherever it has been grown, it is the finest I have tasted in the course of my life. Whence does it come? what is its name? or where can any more of it be had for love or money?"—" Try it again," said Maldimondo. He complied; and acknowledged by San Januario that for colour, fragrance, and flavour, he had never seen its equal. He now drank deep, and delighted.

" Now, Mr. Advocate," said the boatman, filling the cup gaily to his health, " since you have found the use of your tongue at last, I will treat

you as a friend, and tell you, in the first place,
that whence this flagon came is a profound secret.
But don't take me for a churl about a bottle of
wine.   You have only to give me your address in
Naples, to have a little consignment of it sent to
you whenever you want it.   The truth is, the wine
is first rate, and first rate we have always found it,
for our business.   Maldimondo's vintage is as well
known in the court of Naples as the king's wits,
and between ourselves, I have known them go together.   Now, a bumper to all your hopes and
mine, and then let us talk of business."   They
drank to each other.   " I must drink no more,"
said the Italian, "it gets into both head and heart.
I feel myself fit for any thing, good or evil, now.
That wine is absolute temptation."—" I don't
know, that if we were thinking a hundred years,
we could find a better name for it," said Maldimondo, in a half whisper; " but to your affairs,"—
who is this fellow who has supplanted you?"

" He is deputy treasurer of the first royal Tribunal."

" And, of course," interrupted the boatman,
" as, in Naples, the principal never does any thing,

the deputy is the acting man. A cheat too, we may fairly presume ?"

" No, I believe, honest, as the world goes."

" Well, but if he was supposed to filch the tribunal money,—and I'll lay my life he does it every day,—the lawyers seldom like to have the tables turned upon them, and be under apprehension of being robbed. Now, a little insinuation to that effect—nothing direct—but a mere hint, a look, a gesture, has done good service before our time; and besides, ten to one but the fellow is, from his trade,—I beg your pardon, Mr. Advocate,—not remarkable for clean hands already. Now, listen to me. Let your conscience be quiet. I happen to know the very man; I know him to have fingered the public money once; and we may be pretty safe in saying, that when once a man begins with that, it is a long time before he tires of the amusement. I know him to be a knave. Denounce him to the minister, and you are sure of his place, and you do a public service besides."

The Italian's countenance flashed with the thought, and he lifted his eye to Maldimondo's, which he found fixed on him with a strange intense-

ness. Under his dark brows it looked like a fire-
ball from the skirt of a cloud.

"It will be disingenuous, nay, be thought dis-
honourable in me, of all men, to turn his accuser."
He hesitated. "Besides, I have no proof," said
the Italian.

"Proof, folly! suspicion is enough, where the
public purse is concerned. The fellow is of course
too cunning to leave proofs to be picked up in the
streets against him. Come now, I take an interest in you. You have been atrociously treated in
the whole business. Leave it to me to find proofs.
In the meantime all you will have to do will be to
write a note, anonymous if you like, to the minister, warning him of the rascal whom he has to deal
with. Leave the rest to me: and now for a health
to his successor." The cup was filled again.

*   *   *   *   *   *   *

Five years after, the Italian was sitting at twilight in his cabinet, surrounded by books and
papers, when he heard a low knock at the door,
and a stranger entered, who seated himself without
ceremony, and addressed him by his name. He
was altogether unconscious of the acquaintance.

" Do you forget your old friend, Maldimondo,"
said the stranger.

" You Maldimondo! Heaven forbid! impossible!"
exclaimed the Italian, starting from his seat in terror. " I had certain intelligence of his being taken
up by the Inquisition, and dying in his dungeon.
Besides, friend, you are at least fifty years older;
he was in the prime of life, but you—"

" I *am* what I say, Signor, and I am not what
I look. Five years of hard weather and tossing
about the wide world, sometimes half starving, and
sometimes half roasted alive under a tropical sun,
would be enough to make some alteration in a
man's outside. Why, I don't think even you look
much the better for your staying at home; you
don't seem to have half recovered the fright on the
Solfatara yet."

The Italian shuddered at the name. It led him
into bitter recollections. It led him too into the
full conviction that the decrepit being before him
was the boatman. But, how changed! The black
and curling hair was now thin, and white as snow;
the florid complexion was jaundiced, the jovial
countenance care-worn and wrinkled; he walked

with extreme difficulty; the athletic limb was shrunk; the whole noble figure was dwindled and diminished into that of one on the very verge of the grave.

" Accursed be the memory of that night," exclaimed the Italian, " better I had died. From that moment I have been a miserable man."

" But you got the deputy treasurership, and have it still, I think?" said the stranger.

" Aye, that letter which you persuaded me to write in drink and madness, did the business. I was never asked for proofs; but I might as well have stabbed the wretched man at once; the suspicion was enough: he was turned out of his office, and in despair—"

" Went up the Solfatara," said Maldimondo, with a loud laugh.

The Italian shuddered, and with his eyes cast on the ground, said, " The unfortunate man died by his own hand, died in this very room." There was silence for awhile; he then resumed: " You may have heard the rest, or if not; the place was given to me without any solicitation. I would have shrunk from what I must look on as the price of blood; but refusal must have been suspicious, perhaps fatal. I soon after married. The emoluments of my new situation were considerable. I launched out into life, as is expected from every man in office. My wife had her expences too, and I became embarrassed."

" But the public funds were in your hands; you might have relieved your difficulties, and replaced the money at your leisure. The thing is quite official," said the stranger, calmly.

" Dreadful expedient! But I need conceal nothing from you. Was I to go to a dungeon? was I to see my name disgraced, my family undone? utter, helpless, desperate ruin?"

" I hope you were not such a fool," said Maldimondo. " Come, I know it all. You acted like a man of sense then; and rather than go to the galleys, what do you mean to do now?"

" Holy San Januario, what was I to do? I was led on step by step. You know all. You have some strange power over me. Well, then, I *have* been in the habit of employing that expedient; and till now all has been safe: but this very day I have received an order to pay up my balances to the minister, who is fitting out an expedition against the Algerines : and I am not at this hour master of a zechin. He is a villain, and I know it ; but he is merciless to inferior villains, and I am undone !"

" What, Count Fernando ! *My* old enemy, and your's too, my dear comrade. Oh! for an ounce of opium in his soup to-night! it would be but justice to you, to me, and to all mankind ! I swear it by the majesty of evil!" exclaimed the old man, in his indignation springing up from his seat with the vigour of manhood. " Have you thought of nothing to save yourself? I know the villain well; he is corrupt to the very bottom of his soul: still he is powerful, vindictive, unprincipled. Ah! my good friend, how soon, if he were in your situation, would he extinguish all his fears: the tiger would have your blood. His stiletto would be in your heart before he laid his head upon the pillow to-night."

" And yet, Count Fernando," murmured the Italian, " is not wise in being too hard upon me. I know some of his proceedings that might ruin him. He and I have had private transactions, for he has been constantly in want of money; and if I am not altogether mistaken, he is at this moment engaged in a desperate design. I am even convinced, that nothing but the urgency of the Algerine expedition could make him press me now for the money, which he must know I cannot raise, if I were to hunt the world for it. He is, at least I have strong suspicions that he is, at this hour a traitor."

" Then, why not inform the king of it at once?" exclaimed Maldimondo. " You thereby serve your country, save yourself, and extinguish your persecutor at a blow. You may remember, the Count has had the life of one king to answer for already. Smite the traitor, and get yourself the name of a patriot—it is the most thriving trade going; and if you then want to have the handling of the public gold, you may have it to your heart's content, and have all the honour and glory that the rabble can give you besides. Why, man, who knows but you may yet be minister yourself."

" Absurd!" said the Italian, with a sad smile; " but, if I were to denounce him, how is it to be done? Of late all access to the king's presence is impossible. The Count has kept him constantly

surrounded by his creatures. The result of a movement on my part would be an order for my hanging
before sun-set.   No! all is lost ! I am inevitably
a ruined man."

While this was uttered, Maldimondo had been
gazing upon a pair of pistols, imperfectly hidden
on his entrance, among a mass of papers.   He
took up one of them, and pressed its muzzle sig-
nificantly to his forehead.   The Italian faintly
smiled.   " You are determined that I must have
no secrets with you," said he ; " those things are
sometimes good friends ; they pass a man's accounts,
when nothing else can ; you see you and I agree
at last."   He took up the fellow pistol, and began
to examine the priming.   Maldimondo sat steadily
gazing at him as his eye glanced into the barrel.
" One touch of this trigger," murmured the Italian, " and all is over."

" Then you would be a greater blockhead than
your predecessor," exclaimed his visitor, seizing it
from him.   " Shoot your enemy, your destroyer,
the public enemy, the king's enemy, if you will ;
nay, if you have 'a sense of common duty about
you ; but, as to shooting yourself—" he sank back

in his chair, with a roar of derision. " Would you make yourself the sneer of all Naples, only to oblige *him* ? Pho, pho, man! put up your pistols, and listen to me with both your ears. I have, from particular circumstances, a strong hope of bringing that villain to justice."

" Justice!" exclaimed the indignant Italian; " it is now *you* that are the madman. Justice in Naples! Justice with a bigotted government, a besotted people, and every soul in the tribunals bribed, from the lowest huissier up to the supreme judge! No; the only chance for me would be the tyrant's instant death. Heavens !" said he, casting his hollow glance upwards, " where are your fires? are there no fevers, no pestilences, no lightnings ?" He rose, and walked restlessly about the room. Maldimondo followed him with his dilating eyes. " Are there no opium draughts, no *aqua tofana* drops ?" whispered the old man—" Is there no *doctor* in the whole length of the Toledo? If I recollect Naples right, I think that I could find one—a *safe* one too. The pill would be rather more to the purpose—shall I inquire ?"

The Italian heard him, but returned no answer:

he continued wildly pacing the room. Maldimondo watched his movements with a smile. A
loud knocking was suddenly heard at the outer
door. The Italian glanced out of the window, and
starting back, flung himself on the floor in agony.
" They are come," said he, " the officers of the
tribunal, to take me before the minister,—my disgrace will be public : I am beggared—outcast—
shamed—crushed to the dust for ever." He writhed
upon the floor.

" At all events, you must not be left in the
hands of those hang-dogs," said the old man, attempting to lift him. " One word for all,—give me
carte blanche, and let me save you; there is but
one way." The wretched treasurer, still upon the
ground, paused in his agony, and threw up a melancholy look of doubt on his preserver. " What
I say I can do," whispered the old man; " but the
Count must *die.* Let me have only your consent.
You need not trouble your conscience. *I* have
sworn it long ago. My own injuries, and not
yours, call for it; but I also would desire to save
my friend. In fact, I came to warn you that you
were to die on a scaffold. Have I your consent to

my crushing your murderer? to my at least making the trial?" The knocking redoubled. "All
—any thing," said the shuddering Italian: "do
what you please!" The old man absolutely sprang
from the ground—he uttered a scream of fierce exultation, waved his withered arm with a gesture of
wild triumph over the head of the unfortunate
being still stretched beneath him, and was in an
instant gone.

* * * * * * *

The fleet of the King of the two Sicilies was
standing into the Bay of Naples, after a successful
co-operation with the imperial forces, against
Venice. The city was in an uproar of rejoicing.
The whole magnificent range of the houses on the
Chiaja were illuminated; and fêtes of the most
costly description were going on in the mansions
of all the principal courtiers. But the most costly
was that celebrated in the palazzo of the Count of
Manfredonia, first minister, and acknowledged to
have displayed the most distinguished abilities in
his administration. The Spanish alliance had been
negociated by him in the face of difficulties innumerable; and the late conquest of the Venetian

terra firma was due not less to his diplomatic sagacity than to his personal enterprize. The brilliancy and power of his talents was unrivalled; yet
he was more respected than popular. His life of
anxiety and occupation had given him secluded
habits; he mixed but little among the nobles, and
then the melancholy of his very handsome features
argued either inveterate sorrow or hopeless disease.
On this evening he had retired early to his portfolio, leaving all the pomps and splendour of almost
royal feasting to the crowd that filled his stately
apartments. He was sitting wearied and head-
ached, in a small but superb cabinet, that looked
out upon the waters; and where the slight sounds
of the sea-air, and the subsiding waves, were the
only music. He had been for some days waiting
for despatches from the imperial governor of Milan, on matters involving all his fortunes; and their
delay had increased his natural irritability. This
evening was to be the crisis. He waited, watching
every boat through the twilight. At last a page
had announced their arrival. The courier was an
officer of rank, in the uniform of the imperial
Hungarian guard. When they were alone the

officer delivered a personal letter from the court of
Vienna, announcing him as in its entire confidence,
and empowered, under the name of a bearer of despatches, to negotiate in the fullest manner with
the Neapolitan minister.

Manfredonia feverishly opened the despatches,
and read them with evident and eager satisfaction.
" All is as it should be," said he; " but Signor
Colonel, why was this delay? The business was
on the point of discovery; another day, even an
hour more, might have been fatal."

" The delay was inevitable," pronounced the
officer firmly; " precautions were necessary; they
take time; and the court was to be put off its
guard: but now we must proceed to execution."
Manfredonia passed his hand across his forehead
anxiously and often, as the officer perused his detail;
" The archduke was actually within three hours'
march of Naples, with a strong column of cavalry;
the Genoese fleet was only waiting for a rocket
from the roof of the Count's pelazzo, to come
round Miseno; ten thousand Austrian infantry
were in the rear of Spalatro." The showy
Hungarian closed with, " And by this time to-

morrow the fools who now fill the throne and
the palace will be on their passage to Africa; and
you be proclaimed prince and governor of the Calabrias, a throne for yourself and your posterity!
You may depend on the archduke's honour."

" Honour!" repeated Manfredonia, with a bitter
smile: " well, so be it.   I am *forced* to this line
of conduct.   The king has insulted and injured
me beyond human forgiveness.   I have even certain intelligence that I have grown too important
in the public eye to be endured by the low jealousy of the race that infest the court.   Colonel,
take a lesson from me of the life of courts.   I am
convinced that I have grounds for saying, that before
this night was over I was to have been arrested,
and probably sacrificed in my dungeon."   His
voice failed him.   He turned away.   " Accursed
ambition!" he soliloquized.   " Would that I had
never known you; sin of the fallen angels, it is
still their deadliest temptation to miserable man."
He bowed his head on the casement, and even
wept.

The Hungarian made no observation; but a tumult of gaiety outside now attracted him to the

casement. The torches of a passing pageant enlightened the chamber, and first drew Manfredonia's eye to the figure before him. He was a remarkably handsome man, in the very flower of life, tall, and martial looking, and the rich costume of the imperial guard covered with jewelled orders gave the stranger a most conspicuous and brilliant appearance. Yet in the handsome countenance, bright as it was with manly beauty and intelligence, he seemed to recognize some traits with which he was familiar. As the Hungarian listened, there was a glance of deep fire, at times, in his eye, to which the Count had never seen the equal, but in one man. " I think, sir," said he, at last, " we must have met before; at least, you have the most striking likeness to a person whom I have not seen these five years. Yet, his excessive age—a Neapolitan too—obscure—the thing is impossible—have you had any relations in this country?"

" *I* am the Count de Scharnau Holtzberg," said the stranger, proudly drawing himself up, and dropping his hand strongly on the diamond-studded hilt of his sabre. " I have the honour to be of the imperial guard; none but Hungarian blood, and that the noblest, can wear this uniform. But we waste time: is all ready? Here's to the success of our enterprize." He poured out some wine from a flask, which he produced from his sabretache; then, taking up the fire-work which had been agreed on as the signal to the Genoese, he planted it on the edge of the casement. Manfredonia felt the sudden sickness of heart that has been so often experienced by the most powerful minds, when the blow is to be struck that makes or mars them. He swallowed the wine; and the thought flashed across him, that its taste strongly resembled that strange draught of the Solfatara, which had never left his recollection.

The Hungarian was now about to apply the match to the signal, when he paused, and turning round said, " In five minutes after this is seen, the Genoese will answer it, and there may be some alarm in the palace. If there should be resistance, we must be prepared to defend ourselves."—" Why, yes," said Manfredonia, with an attempt at firmness. " But *if* the king, the royal family, come in the way?" said the Hungarian, half drawing his

sabre as he spoke, and holding it suspended.   The
gesture was not to be misunderstood.

" Heaven and earth ! you would not let slaughter, indiscriminate slaughter, loose in the palace ?"
exclaimed Manfredonia, shuddering, and looking,
as if for help, in the haughty soldier's countenance.

" They or we," pronounced the Hungarian
fiercely.   " Self-defence is the first law.   How
can it be helped, if they are mad enough to court
their fate ?   But consent to this.   It may not be
necessary ; it *will* not be necessary ; *you* need do
nothing ; but, at all events, I must have your authority for using my discretion in the business,
and this moment ; or I leave you to—aye, to the
scaffold."   He pronounced the word sternly, and
dashed the sabre into the sheath with supreme
scorn.

" Is there no alternative ! What is to be done ?
They or I—an ignominious sentence—the rack—
death—or—"   The minister's voice died away.

" Or safety, honour, wealth unbounded—the
undoubted principality of the Calabrias," was the
quick reply.   Manfredonia could not speak: his

throat was filled; his tongue was tied; but, stooping his cold brow upon the marble of the casement,
which was not colder, he convulsively gave a token
of acquiescence with his hand. The rocket flew
into the air, and it was instantly answered by a
shower of lights that illuminated the whole horizon. " They are coming," exclaimed the Hungarian, in a voice of thunder; " I knew that they
would not fail. Victory!" The voice seemed to
have found a hundred echoes in the earth and air.
Manfredonia cast one eager look towards the bay,
on which a huge crescent of ships of war, with
lamps in their bows and rigging, were advancing,
like a floating rainbow, or a host of new-fallen
stars. " Victory!" he cried. But, at that moment
the door burst open behind him—he was grasped by
the throat, and a crowd of the king's guard filled
the room. He was undone!

*   *   *   *   *   *   *

It was a night in the month of November; the
weather was stormy; and the chillness of a Neapolitan winter night is often such as to try the hardihood of men accustomed to the coldest climates :
yet through that entire night, the Chiaja was filled

with the thousands and ten thousands of the Neapolitan multitude, to see the preparations for an
execution of the first rank. A scaffold was raised
in front of the mansion of the celebrated and unfortunate Count of Manfredonia. He had been
tried in secret, and was now consigned to the dungeons under Saint Elmo. His crime was not distinctly divulged; but he was charged with some
strange offences that apparently belonged to the
tribunals of the church, as well as of the state—an
attempt to place an Austrian prince on the throne,
by a compact with, as some believed, evil beings.
Traitor and magician, together compounded a
fearful charge; and the city was in a state of universal confusion.

The bells of the citadel roused the unhappy
Manfredonia from a broken slumber; and a few
minutes before day-break the governor of the castle
entered his cell, attended by the confessor, to give
him notice that his time was come. The Count
received the announcement with feigned com-
posure, but unspeakable terror.

The confessor remained with him to do his office.
" Holy father," said the miserable man, " spare

me now. I have but one sin to confess; but that one
the mother of all—ambition." The monk solicited
him, until he had disclosed the whole singular succession of events, which had led him on from obscurity
to rank, and at each step had loaded him with an
accompanying crime. " But had you no adviser,
no accomplice in those acts of guilt? no tempter?"
said the confessor. The word struck keenly on
the unhappy man's ear. " Aye, too surely I had.
But my chief tempter was my own hatred of obscure competence; my insane jealousy of the
success of others; the satanic passion for being first
in all things; yet—" and his voice died away to a
whisper, " evil was the day I first met thee, Maldimondo. In that hour heaven was shut upon me."
He sank on his knee in broken prayer.

" Have you no lingering desire to see that
tempter again? or have you piously and solemnly
forsworn all connexion with him?" asked the confessor.

" From the bottom of my soul I have forsworn
him," was the answer of the penitent.

" Then, more fool you," sneered the monk,
throwing back his cloak; " Come; once more be

a man, and your life is saved. Make that prayer to me."

The wretched criminal looked up in astonishment. Maldimondo stood before him! but with his former handsome countenance darkened into gloomy rage. "Hear me, fool!" he exclaimed; "that look of horror is absurd: I can save you:—nay, you can save yourself. You have played your cards badly; not from too much ambition, but too little. You plotted for a principality. You would have been safe, if you had plotted for a throne. You plotted to make a thick-headed archduke a king. Why should not a crown become the forehead of an Italian man of genius just as well?" He took a lamp from his bosom, and opened a small trap-door in the pavement. "Under this stone," said he, "is the powder magazine. The king and his laced and liveried race are now on the parade above our heads, waiting to see you set off for the scaffold. I have a key to every door of the prison: we can escape in a moment, and the next moment may see the fort and all that it contains blown into the air. Vengeance, my friend, glorious, complete, magnificent vengeance. But command me to lay this lamp upon the train. A single word, and the whole dynasty are cinders. Remember, the extinction of your enemies would leave the world clear for you—from a dungeon you might in the next five minutes be in a palace—instead of a scaffold you might mount a throne. One word and it is done. That head, instead of hanging by the gory hairs in an executioner's hand, might be receiving the homage of princes."

The monk waved the lamp before his eyes; and the sudden thought of vengeance and mighty retribution, the whole filling up of the whole of human ambition, smote through him like lightning. The conflict was maddening; he sprang on his feet; the trap-door was open before him; he grasped the lamp, and felt that he had the fates of a dynasty in his hand. But an inward voice, such as he had not heard for many a year, seemed suddenly to resound in his soul. He hesitated—his grasp was like that of a child. He dropped the lamp on the ground— "No more blood—no more blood!" was all that he could utter; as, faint and half blind, he laid his hand upon a goblet in which some wine had remained, and hastily put it to his parched lip. To his measureless astonishment, he saw it suddenly covered with sculptures of the same strange character that had startled him in the cave of the Solfatara. The incantation was there : the kneeling victim, the fiery radiance. The truth broke on him. " Leave me, Maldimondo—man, or dæmon, leave me!" said he, as he dropped the cup on the table. " I deserve to die; life is distasteful to me. Yet I have my folly still; even now I would avoid the stain of a public execution!"

" Then drink," said the tempter, pouring wine into the cup; " shame will never reach the man who drinks this liquor." The perfume of it filled the cell.

" Never, out of that cup—that cup of crime !" groaned the victim.

" Worship me, slave!" echoed in thunder through the air.

" Leave me, fiend !" was the scarcely audible reply from Manfredonia's lips.

" Then die !" The form snatched up the cup, and dashed its draught in his forehead, as he knelt in remorse and agonising prayer. He felt it like a gush of fire—uttered a cry, and was dead !

* * * * * * *

The tempest of that morning is still remembered in Naples. The wind unroofed many of the principal mansions along the shore, tore the scaffold into a thousand fragments, and utterly dispersed the multitude. The sea rising committed great damage among the more exposed buildings, and swept away the smaller vessels, and every thing that is generally loose about a beach. The scaffold was gone totally into the Mediterranean. In the burst of the hurricane on St. Elmo, the first care had been to secure the ammunition and other important stores of the fortress. In this confusion the distinguished criminal was partially forgotten. When at length the governor and the guard entered his cell, they found him on his knees. His only son, scarcely more than an infant, who had been brought for the parting interview, was found kneeling with him—the hands of both were raised as in prayer; but the count was cold as a stone. His countenance was calm; but, on lifting the cloak that had fallen over his forehead, they found a deep red impression of a cross burned through to the brain. His death was attributed to the lightning.

The child was conveyed away by some friends of

his unfortunate father to Corsica.   He had the genius, the melancholy, and the ambition of his father. But there were no crowns for him to rifle in Corsica, and the fiend loves places where there is more gold.   This infant was the ancestor of Napoleon in the third generation. He was on his death-bed, when Letitia Ramolini brought her babe and laid it in his aged arms.   " Boy," said the patriarch, " you shall be the first of your line in renown, and the last in shame ; the first in power, and the last in helplessness; the king of all nations, and the slave! I bequeath to you your forefather's ambition, his genius, his restlessness—and his devil."

CHAPTER XXIX.

—————

THE BULLETIN.

WE have become sceptical in all that relates to bulletins, invisible armies advancing to our rescue, and the perpetual victories of irresistible deliverers, who are always retreating. Let the following scene find believers or not, as it may deserve.

During the days of French supremacy in Hamburg, when generals lived like epicurean deities, and commissaries kept tables of fifty covers; a dinner was given to a large party of the staff and the agents of the vassal courts then gathered to learn their fates from the footstool of Napoleon. The Russian campaign was the universal thought. A noisy French general made it the universal topic. "He is no true Frenchman," said the Gaul, "who calculates on the emperor's failure. He has five hundred thousand Frenchmen with him," added the general ; " and how is it possible that he could be beaten ?"

The times were delicate, and diplomacy delicately held its tongue. The general repeated the question, and turning to an old Prussian baron, famous for his knowledge of whist, an accomplishment which had probably introduced him to public life at the Russian court, where he had enjoyed some appointments; inquired, whether, from his knowledge of the country, he thought it was in the nature of things that Russia could resist a French invasion? The old man had now come to Hamburgh in the Prussian service, a transfer not unusual among foreign diplomatists. He answered dryly, " Russia has forty millions of subjects !"

" Sacre !" exclaimed the general; " but will they fight ?"

" Every man of them," said the baron. " They will fight you in the field, in the city, in the cottage, and in the forest. Or, if you drive them from those, they will fight you in the wilderness."

The Frenchman laughed; " Well, let them fight; but before they know a howitzer from a pipe, the emperor will be in Moscow."

" I am not Russ enough to wish he ever may see it," said the baron.

"*Mille tonnerres*, M. le Baron, what is to prevent him ? Would Alexander wish to see the French hussars mounting guard on his palace, his princesses flying into the desert, and his capital given up to a three days' plunder ?" asked the Frenchman.

" I don't know who would," replied the baron ; " but listen, Monsieur le General ; " a French soldier, without ammunition, food, and clothing, is not more than a man after all. Now, the Russians bury their provisions, hate their enemies, and can cut down a tree, or a cuirassier, at a blow ; Alexander beside is sovereign over some millions of square miles ; and you must beat him to the wall of China before you find him signing a peace. Your emperor should have stopped in Poland."

" And lose a whole campaign," sneered the general, " drilling the Poles, and teaching those human bears to know their right hand from their left ; while he might have been sitting on the throne of the Czars. Pardon me, Baron, the very idea is Russian. No ; the next bulletin will announce the annihilation of all the detached corps of the

12

enemy; the concentration of the Grand Army in front of Moscow; a surrender, or a battle, which is much the same; the arrival of an aide-de-camp from St. Petersburg to ask for peace; a new demarcation of Europe; and the peace of Europe triumphantly settled for ever."

" Under the Napoleon dynasty, of course;" said the Baron, with a smile; "yet as all this will take up time, I repeat, that I wish them well home before the first snow. Moscow is a terrible distance from Paris; and on my last journey, though it was only from Moscow to Wilna, I was frozen enough through all my furs, to form a tolerable estimate of what the journey might be to a man who added fatigue, fighting, nakedness, and hunger, to the pleasure of being frost-bitten whenever he uncovers his ear, finger, or nose. No! your emperor should have stopped in Poland, talked to the brave fools there of liberty, which not a man in the country ever did, or ever will understand; promised to give them a Polish king, whom they were never able to maintain; and filled them with dreams of military glory, which will be performed only when they lay their bodies in some Russian morass, or are blown to dust in front of some Russian battery.   No! he should have raised all Poland, carried with him two hundred thousand infantry, sent a hundred thousand of their lancers to keep the Cossacks from his flanks, and then made his push for St. Petersburg."

" *Voila*," said the general, " a fine plan of campaign ; but Monsieur le Baron," and he fixed his eyes on him with an expression of contempt, " do you actually persist in saying that the emperor will never arrive in Moscow ?"

" It is quite possible that he may ; but the point is, whether he will ever get back," said the Baron.

The Frenchman was offended by the tone in which his contempt was answered ; and he more than intimated to the old man, that his opinions might bring him into personal inconvenience. The Prussian bore the menace quietly, and returning the remark, told him that " having been asked a question, he had merely given an answer."

But the matter had now become so grave, that the master of the entertainment, and the guests in general, interposed, and begged that the subject might be dropped. The Frenchman now recovered his politeness, if not his good humour ; and laying a diamond snuff-box with a portrait of Napoleon on the table, said, " That box was given to me by the emperor the day after the battle of Wagram; yet I will stake it that Napoleon is now master of Moscow." The faces of the company involuntarily showed how little they relished the intelligence; but the old Baron, taking a box of considerably superior brilliancy from his pocket, said, " This box was given to me by the Czar, on my retiring from his service; yet this box I will stake that Napoleon is *not* master of Moscow."

The matter had again become interesting, and the company gathered round the disputants. " Come, come, Monsieur le Baron," said the general, " I must not accept your challenge, for the truth is, *I* am sure of my point. I have had despatches on the subject this evening." He beckoned to an aide-de-camp, who left the room, and returned in a few minutes with a packet. The general triumphantly read the bulletin, which he had received express from Paris, and which detailed the battle of Borodino, or of the Moskwa, as the French term it; dated from the first Russian position at the village of Moskwa, nearly between Ghijet

and Mojaisk.   The despatch concluded by saying,
that the Russian army had entirely disappeared
from the Moscow road; that the patroles had found
nothing between the French camp and the city;
and that a corps was already on its march to " take
possession of the ancient seat of the Czars."

The company now waited for the old Baron's
acquiescence; but he simply said, " General, Napoleon is *not* master of Moscow; there is not a
single Frenchman in Moscow, but as a prisoner, and
there is not a man in the French army in Russia
who would not at this moment wish that Napoleon
had never passed the frontier.   But I shall deal
fairly with you, *I* speak on information."

The general rose in great wrath, and denied the
possibility of the statement; haughtily observing,
that if such rumours were scattered through the
country, it was by individuals who had motives in-
consistent with the honour of France.   " Even,"
said he, " Monsieur le Baron, I know not but that
I am betraying my duty to the emperor, in not
ordering the individual who utters such sentiments
in these times under arrest."   All stared at the
denunciation, which might, during any period of

the French rule, have alarmed the boldest; but it seemed to make no impression on the old man, who answered in his quiet tone, " I am not a subject, sir, of your emperor, and therefore I owe him no allegiance. But, as your language puts an end to courtesy, I ask you again, do you stake your box on your view of the affair?"

" Bah! *quelles sottises,*" exclaimed the general; "I should stake fifty boxes. Have I not shown you the last bulletin ?"

" No, sir," was the answer, as the Baron drew a paper from his pocket, and read : " On the 14th, the Russians set fire to the exchange, the bazaar, &c. On the 16th, a tempest arose; three or four thousand robbers and assassins set fire to the city in five hundred places, by order of the governor, Rastopchin. Five-sixths of the houses were built of wood; the fire spread with prodigious rapidity, it was an *ocean of flame.* Churches, of which there were a thousand, above a thousand palaces, immense magazines, nearly all have fallen a prey to the flames. The Kremlin has been preserved. Above a hundred of the incendiaries have been apprehended and shot; all of them declared that they acted under the orders of Rostopchin, and the director of the police."

"Falsehood!" exclaimed the Frenchman; "I insist, sir, on having that paper in my possession, and on your surrendering yourself, as the propagator of news, which will bring you under a military commission."

"Well, sir, so be it," said the Baron rising, and handing the famous 24th bulletin to the angry Frenchman. "There, you see, my authority is your master's own; and I appeal to the company whether I have not substantiated my statement." There could be no denial; and the old man, without another word, took up the two boxes, and put them in his pocket. Then turning to the general, who was absorbed in the bulletin, which he rightly felt was ruin, said, "Sir, I am now at your disposal."—"Sacre!" was the reply; "go with my aide-de-camp; he is answerable for you, till the commandant summons you to-morrow." The Baron made his bow to the table, and withdrew along with the aide-de-camp. The party, sufficiently startled at this summary display of vigilance, instantly separated. Nothing more was uttered next day on the subject of the bulletin, for espionage rendered all communication dangerous. But all looked for the process against the old Baron. Yet, day after day passed, and still he was not mentioned.

At length, on the retreat of the French, a letter was received by the gentleman at whose house the circumstance occurred; informing him, that "his old friend the Baron" was living, like another Cincinnatus, in the midst of his corn-fields in Silesia, having made his escape from the French surveillance, within the first twelve hours of his arrest; and requesting to know what had become of the angry general, as his box was again at his service, with a recommendation against being too positive in the matter of French invasions in future!

Paris is still the spot to which every German eye turns; not, as of old, for the fashions of coats and curls, but for the newest style of revolutions. An impression prevails here, that Napoleon's government is more likely to fall in Paris than in Germany; and that a conversazione, or a club in the Rue St. Honoré, will be more fatal to

his diadem than all the swords of all the myriads
of this warrior land, armed in proof, and led by all
the Frederics and Alexanders. I fully believe it.
The Germans have stumbled on a fact; they never
walked, climbed, or winged their way to it, or any
other. But, from time to time, in all nations,
there is a general impression of some truth, which
is inevitably soon vindicated by the reality. Thus,
the full conviction, that Napoleon will be sooner
outplotted in his own council, than outgeneraled
in any field of Europe, is with me no acquiescence
in a popular prejudice, but the recognition of an
established result of a solid principle. He is now
the sultan of Europe ; and, like the sultan, he will
be deposed by his own viziers ; lucky if he is not
hanged by his own mutes. Mallet's conspiracy is
ominous.

The following particulars are curious, they
are new, and what is more to the purpose,
they are authentic. Napoleon was charged with
poltroonery for leaving his army at Wilna. Yet, it
was Mallet's attempt to overthrow his throne, that
brought him back. It came like a thunder-clap;
and, like a thunder-clap, it made men think, for

the first time in a quarter of a century, that there were other sources of power than the bayonets of the grand army, or the knife of the guillotine. It awoke all Germany to the instability of that throne which France had so fiercely proclaimed to be immoveable by all the strength of earth, or perhaps of Heaven. Mallet was but a tool after all; a half or a whole madman, actually taken from a receptacle for the deranged. The true conspirators [1] will never be known, till they are in the grave, that great revealer of secrets, which to atone for its panegyric on the tomb-stone, lets out all the bad of every man, for the general behoof of the community.

But Mallet had qualities which fitted him for public explosion. He was a Jacobin of the true old school; a revolutionist of the golden age of revolution; a soldier, robber, orator, and cut-throat of 1793. When Napoleon was raised to power, Mallet, like all the Jacobins, was thrown into the background; for Napoleon had resolved

---

[1] One of those on whom public suspicion turned, is since dead. The other survives, in high station.

that there should be but one successful Jacobin in France. Mallet, in the true spirit of his creed, formed a conspiracy to murder him. But Frenchmen, if they are the most ready of all conspirators, are always the most luckless. They *must* talk, they must go to the coffee-house, they must have some fair object of their attentions, be she seventeen or seventy, be she secret as Harpocrates, or a notorious pensioner on the list of the lieutenant of police. The conspiracy is known day by day, it is known to the mistress, to the maid, to the Swiss at the gate, to the garcon who brings in the *deux plats* from the next *traiteur's :* it is known to fifty, to five hundred. The police at last think that the affair is mature enough for their exertion. They seize the conspirators at the soirées of their several *confidantes ;* and send them to the galleys, the guillotine, or to the mad-house, like Mallet. Mallet's conspiracy had been, of course, detected. But Napoleon was then in his hour of triumph. He was Cæsar forgiving all his enemies. He laughed at the folly of a dozen Jacobins dreaming of the overthrow of the master of the directory, the conqueror of Marengo, the tutelar genius of victory. But he sent Mallet to a mad-house, where he remained for ten years.

But the Russian retreat had begun to make men doubt of the perpetual triumph of Napoleon. The marshals were growing old, they all were rich, and all willing to enjoy their plunder. Out of the twelve, six had been beaten desperately by Wellington, and sent home to France, completely shorn of their laurels. Of the other six, some were in disgrace, and some toiling homeward through the Russian snows, with the Cossack lances in their rear. All were angry, all disgusted, and all longing for the time, when life would be made up of a drive to the levee, or a dinner at Tortoni's, a parade or a promenade. " If this war goes on, we shall all be killed !" was the *naïve* expression of one of their intercepted letters. And this feeling, however unheroic, was universal. The fall or imprisonment of Napoleon would long since have been a day of rejoicing to every marshal of France.

There were others, and in high places, to whom the dispatch that announced the last sleep of Napoleon in the Beresina, would have made the fortune of the courier. The great officials of France, in perpetual terror of the caprice of their master in his best moments, looked forward to his arrival under defeat, as a new commencement of insult, violence, and tyranny. But, for slaves what resource is left, but the weapon of the slave? On the ruin of Napoleon depended the security of their titles, their peculations, and perhaps of their heads. They could no more trust to his consideration, when he should come back, stript of his troops, his fame, his means of universal dominion, and his spell, than they could trust to the consideration of a tiger irritated by the sight of his own blood.

The people too were sick of the war: it sent them no more pictures; it gave them no more fetes; it fired no more cannon in the park of the Invalids; it flourished no more praises of Frenchmen in the journals.—But it gave them three conscriptions of eighty thousand men each in one year; it tore the bread out of the Frenchman's hand, in taxes; it filled the hospitals with mutilated wretches, and covered the high roads with beggary: finally, it consummated the national calamity by a shape of evil which France has never been able to endure; it gave them no news!—the old rapidity of battle, march, and capitulation, which fed the journals, and filled up the day of the thirty-two millions of statesmen in France, had been brought to a stand. Napoleon's fertility of bulletins was evidently exhausted: no man better knew its value with the subject blockheads, from whom he exacted in return only their money and their lives; and the exhaustion was felt to be an omen of undoing. The last bulletin had left the "Grand Army" commencing its terrible travel through the wilderness. Since that time, not a syllable had transpired: all that was known, was from the Russian reports of armies pouring down on the French line of march from east and west, north and south, a conflux of living fire, the hostility of half a world, summoned from all its heights and depths, inflamed by victory and vengeance, and raging round the unfortunate remnant of the army of France. For five and twenty desperate days, no bulletin had arrived; and the only hope in which any man could indulge, was, that the whole invading force had fallen into the enemy's hands.

In this interval, Mallet, the lunatic, saw his

dungeon unaccountably opened before day-light, a
field-marshal's coat lying on his bed, and six hundred men of the guards of Paris at his service! He
got up, dressed himself, and marched at the head
of his new army to the military prison, where he
found two generals, Guidal and Lahorie. To them
he announced himself as the commandant of Paris,
commissioned to extinguish the imperial government, and proclaim a republic.   The two generals instantly followed him.   From the dungeon
he marched to the hotel of Savary, the minister of
police; Savary was dragged from his bed, and sent
to the military prison, to take the place of the two
generals.   The prefect of police next made his
appearance; he too had been dragged from his bed,
and he too was put into a cell.   Hulin, the governor
of Paris, was still to be captured: Mallet found
him also in bed.   The dialogue was one of revolutionary brevity.   " General, I have orders to
make you my prisoner."—" What! is it you, Mallet, where do you come from? what brings you
here?" said Hulin.—" The Emperor is dead, and
the government is changed," was the answer.   Hulin prepared to follow, when a suspicion struck him.

" Show me," said he, " the order of arrest." But this was no time for discussion. Mallet answered the question by firing a pistol at his head. The bullet stunned him, and he fell. Mallet, thinking him dead, left him where he lay. He then crossed the street, entered the chamber of the chief of the staff, told him that he came to announce his promotion to a higher grade; and ordered him to follow. All was hitherto successful; so successful, that all seems to have been prepared. A single oversight changed the scene. Mallet had hitherto taken some of his people with him to make the arrests. Into the chamber of the chief of the staff, he went alone, probably for the sake of special conference. The door suddenly opened, one of the heads of the police entered, and unexpectedly seized Mallet: the policeman had previously, with some of the gendarmerie, liberated Savary and the prefect. The whole transaction was ended. Mallet and his officers were thrown into prison, and shot, to the number of about twenty. The revolution was begun and finished in three hours!

Mallet talked to the last the jargon of twenty years

before. He oratorized on Brutus and republics, on dying for liberty, and making France the chosen temple of freedom. In short, he talked like the madman that he was. But there were others behind the curtain, who had the skill to pull the strings of the puppets, yet keep themselves out of the supervision that might have cost them their lives. A mysterious note received early on that morning by one of the imperial officials, declaring that the empire, or rather, the Emperor, was " extinguished," shows that the conspiracy reached deeper than the crude outbreak of a lunatic, and a few discontented soldiers.

The overthrow may be still delayed, or be finally due to nobler hands; but the German theory will have its consummation yet. The pillars of the throne are half sawed through already. The political dry-rot has found its way into the Tuilleries. The alienation and resentment of France are already ripe. Ground by taxes, instead of being pampered with plunder; torn up by conscriptions, instead of adding nation to nation, and fighting her battles with the servile population of Europe: and soundly beaten, instead of gasconading it through the world ; France is at this hour in all the indignation of a shrew, who has discovered that she has indulged her meekness too long, and can turn the weapons upon her husband. A single reverse in the field will leave the grand Napoleon without the sympathy of a poissarde.

CHAPTER XXX.

NAPOLEONIANA.

NAPOLEON has fairly vindicated his character for personal intrepidity in this campaign, if it is to be done by running the risk of being carried off by cannon balls. He has played *le petit caporal* even with a rashness unsuited to his own responsibilities; his army, which lives but through him, has thus been hazarded like the last stake of a desperate game-ster; and the destinies of his wicked and magnifi-cent empire have hung upon the trigger of the first sharpshooter who could mark the *redingote gris.* He has been found on all occasions hazarding his person in fire. Wherever the allied rear-guard, in their march from Lutzen, made a halt, he galloped forward, scolded his engineers, placed the guns, and sat exposed to the enemy's batteries, until he saw the effect of his own. His pursuit of the allies was so close, that he was in Dresden on the same day in which the Emperor Alexander and the King of Prussia had quitted it. The deputies, who came with the keys to meet him, were prepared with a long compliment; he cut them short, with " Who are you? Have you bread for my army?" The whole affair was one of breathlessness.

The Russians had burnt the bridge of boats over the Elbe. Napoleon reconnoitred it, accompanied by Murat, *alone*. They were fired on, but he persevered, until he had completely examined the ground. There are but two ways for a general to reconnoitre; one with a portion of his army so large, that the enemy cannot distinguish between a reconnoissance and the preparation for actual attack; and the other so unattended, as to be altogether unsuspected, if not unseen. Napoleon would take ten thousand men to a reconnoissance, or but one; the latter was his usual mode. He left his staff and escort under cover of some village or thicket, and went out with an officer, both wrapt in their cloaks, and at a little distance undistinguishable from the peasants.

At Dresden, while the allies were in the neighbourhood, he was up at day-break, toiling like a
captain of engineers. While the staff were con-
structing a bridge in place of the one burnt by the
Russians, he took his stand beside a building which
had served for a depôt of ammunition. The Russian fire was drawn upon this point, and a shell had
nearly closed the campaign; it burst over the spot
where he stood, struck the side of the building,
and dashed a large fragment of wood or stone at
his feet. While all round him were alarmed at
his hazard, he coolly turned the fragment over,
and observed,—" a few inches nearer, and it would
have done its business."

––––––––

At the close of the battle of Lutzen, Napoleon
was in the most imminent danger of being killed
or taken. The Prussian brigade of cavalry, which
rushed forward so unexpectedly after night-fall, and
when the engagement seemed to be entirely over;
threw the very battalions among which he was
riding at the moment into great confusion. They
however formed squares, which in the darkness

fired in all directions, without knowing at what they were firing. His suite all dispersed, equally to avoid the Prussians and their own men. The firing and the galloping continued in the meantime, and the Emperor was no where to be found. If the Prussians had followed up their charge, they might have taken him and half the general officers of his army; or, if they had been more strongly supported, they might have cut off the wing, and broken up the army itself. But it was a mere dash of their brigadier; and on discovering that the French were again under arms, they reined up, and retired. When all subsided, Napoleon was found—he had been galloping about in the confusion, looking for his staff, under a shower of balls.

———

At Bautzen the day was lost simply by Napoleon's superiority of force. The French fought remarkably well, but the strength of the positions which they had to attack would have occasioned so formidable a loss, if attacked in front, that the assailants must be unable to move for the rest of the campaign. The march of Ney's corps alone made the retreat necessary. It is observed that Napoleon, though a first-rate tactician, and unrivalled in the variety of his resources, has one favourite principle, one favourite instrument, and one favourite manœuvre. The principle is, that perseverance is the secret of success; that while little is to be expected in the beginning of a battle; every army, after half a dozen hours of marching and fighting, is glad of any opportunity of getting off the ground; and that then is the time to throw in an additional force, and finish the day at once.

The instrument is artillery : he absolutely encumbers his column of march with guns; always preferring those of the heaviest calibre, and, when the grand impression is to be made, parks them, and opens a weight of fire on some particular point, where he tears his way, and clears the ground for his infantry. " Fifty guns, Berthier; a hundred guns, Duroc," are his common order; and the effect of so vast a body of fire is incalculable.

His manœuvre is, always to have a detached army ready to fall on the rear of the enemy's movements. A day or two before the battle he marches a corps of from twenty to fifty thousand men to the left or right, with orders to advance on the sound of his guns. The enemy are then attacked in front, and held in play until the period of exhaustion arrives, and a general attack can be made. The result is secure : the enemy suddenly see a new army in their rear. They must then either retreat at once, before the roads are closed up ; or if they resist the attack in front, they are liable to the attack in rear by the fresh force ; or if they are beaten in front, they must be driven directly upon that force.

Such is termed the Napoleon theory ; and it has been practically successful in the German campaigns, almost without an exception ; yet it obviously requires a great numerical superiority ; and in case of a decided failure in front, it is attended with the extreme hazard of losing the whole detached army. A retreat of the main body leaves it behind ; and its defeat must be fatal, if the enemy have force enough to spare for the pursuit and the attack together. The whole manœuvre is founded on the desperate, revolutionary system, in which Napoleon was taught his first art of victory, and which is to this moment the foundation of all his success. His science is risk; his war violent disregard of life; and his deity the most insolent and capricious form of fortune [1].

———————

Napoleon pays the greatest attention to ground; he has always inspected the enemy's position in person, if possible; but this hurried inspection was not enough; *after* the battle he inspected it again, and with extreme minuteness; rode over it foot by foot, and left not a nook unexplored. His first point gained by this was a nearer guess at the actual numbers opposed to him. His next was probably an insight into the principles on which their generals acted: he thus got the key to the cypher of their tactics. Another advantage was, his ascertaining the mistakes which had been made by both

———

[1] It is remarkable that in his final campaign he tried the same manœuvre, in detaching Grouchy to the flank of the allies. If the Duke of Wellington had been forced from the field, Grouchy would have been in Brussels before him. But the Great Captain had met his conqueror at last.

parties, the points on which the attacks should have been forced, and those on which he had formed erroneous conjectures—the whole forming a fine military lesson.

———

It is the custom among the officers of high rank in the continental armies to follow the marches in carriages. The custom seems effeminate; but it has sufficient reasons in its saving the fatigue of riding on horseback, which on long journeys would exhaust the mind along with the body. Frederic the Great constantly used his carriage on campaign. Napoleon ate, drank, and slept in his carriage; corresponded, diplomatized, dictated the route, and planned the battle, in his carriage. When the engagement was about to commence, he got on horseback, and galloped through the lines. A British officer lounging in a carriage would be laughed at, and one of the first acts of a Hyde Park general is to prohibit every supernumerary horse and conveyance in his army; but common sense argues, that in all instances the less the officer, even to the subaltern, is fatigued, the better for the men: he

is the fitter to take care of his men on their arrival
at quarters for the night, and the fitter to conduct
them in the field—they want neither his legs nor his
arms, but his understanding ; that a tired general is
of no more use than a tired serjeant; the more riding
officers the better ; and that one of the most useful provisions for a campaign would be any system
of conveyances by which the whole of the officers
should be saved from all *bodily* fatigue whatever.

The French extend this principle even to the common soldier: their forced marches are often made by
the help of the country carts, and twenty thousand
men may thus be moved fifty miles between sunrise and sun-set: a movement which might decide a
campaign. Where they cannot thus convey the
men, the next attempt is to convey their muskets
and cartridge-boxes. This decided the fate of
Austria in 1805. The Austrian generals had calculated the movement of the French grand army
from Boulogne at ten miles a-day. Napoleon ordered them to throw their arms and ammunition
into carts, divest themselves of all burthens, and
march as fast as they could. They hurried on like
a party of peasants going to a fair, singing, shout-

ing, and playing upon each other. But they marched thirty miles a-day! Two hundred thousand Frenchmen were in the heart of Austria a month before they were expected to reach the Rhine; found the Austrians quietly gathering by brigades and battalions; captured a third of their army on its way to head-quarters; beat the remainder, in one fierce fight; and extorted a peace from the monarch of thirty millions of men, and half a million of soldiers, in a three months' campaign. A few hundred carts overthrew the Austrian empire, and their hire was handsomely paid for by the conquered. Napoleon mulcted the imperial treasury in a fine of four millions sterling!

But, from the beginning of this campaign, he has evidently felt that his task is commencing again; that if he has not to make a character, he has to preserve a crown; and that, to conquer the new spirit of liberty in Germany, he must re-act the old republican soldier of France. He is thus seen constantly among the troops; he harangues; he runs hazards; he laughs at them, and with them under fire; and he abjures the carriage, and makes his marches on the charger. In the late engagement he had rode up to a spot where some of the Italian regiments were giving way before a heavy discharge of one of the enemy's batteries. A shell fell near him, and burst. He did not move. The enemy probably observing him, tried the range again, and missed him, but the shell rolled forward along the front of the battalions. Those sons of Parthenope and the Tuscan vales immediately felt the love of life strong within, and began to break up their files. Napoleon galloped after them, laughing, and roaring out, " You rascals, you rascals, it can do you no harm." *(Ahi, cujoni, cujoni, non fa male!)*

The loss of the French in general officers has already been heavy in the campaign. It had become the etiquette to expose themselves: Bessieres was killed unnecessarily at Lutzen, in heading a mere battalion of tirailleurs; and Duroc was now killed, by a shot which had nearly finished the war. He and General Kirchner were riding and talking a few yards behind Napoleon, on the day after the battle, when a turn of the road brought them within view of a Russian field-piece, moving with the rear-guard. It threw a shot into the midst of the party; the ball whizzed by Napoleon's head; but he bears a charmed life. It took more fatal effect on his unlucky officers. In a moment Kirchner was seen knocked off his horse, motionless; and the grand marshal of the palace lying beside him on the ground, rolling in agony. Before the aide-de-camp in his alarm could call out to Napoleon, Kirchner was dead. Duroc was a hideous spectacle—his bowels were torn out.

No death that had occurred during the war so evidently affected Napoleon. He was deeply struck by the intelligence, and remained for some time silent, and with his eyes fixed on the spot from which the gun was fired. He sat up the greater part of the night, after visiting the unfortunate marshal; gloomily gazing on his camp fire, while the troops lay on their arms round him. Duroc was a gallant soldier, but of those there were enough in the imperial army. He was besides a man of graceful acquirements, and polished manners, and even Napoleon's half-savage roughness was pleased with him. He tried to encourage him with the hope of life; but Duroc was aware that his wound was

mortal, and he was in too much pain to wish to
live.   He died on the next day.   Kirchner was a
distinguished and scientific officer; he commanded
the engineers.

Napoleon's manner in the field is cool and composed; but he sees every thing.   His decision is
prompt; his orders are remarkably brief, thus of
course leaving a good deal to the quickness of his
officers;   but their brevity prevents them from
being mistaken, the usual source of failure in extended movements. His orders are *principles;* the
application belongs to others: and the orders once
given, he seems to think his part done.   He then
alights from his horse, and walks about, like an un-
concerned person; or sits upon a hillock or a stone,
with his telescope in his hand, gazing on the country, as if he were an amateur sketching the landscape.

Perhaps there never was an instance of a general
so completely master of his troops as the French

Emperor. They rail at him, they make songs on him, they curse him, but they cling to him; and so far as the savage soldier, with all his innate savageness inflamed by perpetual habits of blood and rapine, can love any thing, they love him. Other generals may have equalled him in military science; but none have ever equalled, none probably ever will equal, him in the science of the Man of France. He knows the melo-dramatic spirit of the people, and he makes every thing a melo-drame. He is a mountebank, like all foreigners, but of all mountebanks the most splendid. His battles, his negotiations, even his journeys, are all *tours de scene.* All his campaigns commence with a thunder-clap; there is no lingering about head-quarters; no tardy diplomacy; no lazy lounging in courts; no bewildering parade in the field: all is electric—a manifesto, that sounds like a sentence of fate, a tremendous battle, a whirlwind rush on the capital, and all is done! He is never heard of, till the whole cloudy weight of devastation is gathered, and ready to descend with a touch. " The Emperor is come !" strikes upon the universal ear at once, like the sound of a trumpet, and like the sound of a trum-

13

pet it is the signal for instant battle. With his army success and Napoleon are identified; he carries the war along with him.   He is not a general, but the genius of generalship; not a victor, but victory!

CHAPTER XXXI.

———

HAMBURGH.

I HAVE just returned, after a ramble among the villages. The mother city looks best from the outside. The villages are little, wild, odd things, with a primitive look, yet with some kind of gaiety. They put us in mind of a group of young Quakers, with the blood of youth contending against the inveteracy of the drab; or the unwilling formality of a family circle in the presence of the venerable and forbidding grandmother of the household. The brown roofs and ponderous steeples of the city are seen from every dell and thicket for miles round, looking gravity, and frowning down the light propensities of the rising generation of villas.

The contrast, to one returning from the country into the sudden gloom of the streets, renders all their evils still more unpalatable. Whatever bet-

ter times, or another generation, may make of the
city, it is now dark, intricate, and miry, to the full
republican measure.   Republicanism may have its
advantages, but it never paves, sweeps, lights, or
whitewashes ; the sovereign people feels the value
of its independence too profoundly to suffer any
intrusion of authority in the shape of public comfort ; cleanliness is a breach of privilege, and the
order to hang up two lamps where but one twinkled before, would be an insult to the genius of the
constitution altogether unheard of.   The result is,
that there is not a stone in the streets of Hamburgh
which has not been suffered to settle into its place
by the laws of gravity ; not a spout which does not
irrigate the passer by, and seem to be employed for
that sole purpose ; not a crevice which does not
widen into a pool ; not a pool which does not widen
into a gulph ; and, in a huge city of ravines of
lanes, and cut up with foggy canals, not a light
much exceeding that of a moderate cigar.   The
senate know all this, and are alternately laughed
at and libelled for not smoothing their pavements,
stopping up their pools, and lighting their streets.
But what can any citizen-senate on earth do more

than groan over the commonwealth; draw up mag-
nanimous resolutions, and throw them into the fire,
through fear of offending the freeborn sordidness
and patriotic putrescence of the state; and leave the
rest to destiny and the general conflagration.

I honour and esteem the spirit of Hamburgh in
its resistance to the French, but all my respect
cannot disguise from all my senses, that the city
would be infinitely the better for a good, active
bombardment. But an earthquake would be the
true benefactor. Any thing would be good that
would bore, batter, scatter, and prostrate some furlongs of those streets, that, wild and winding as the
shafts of a coal mine, seem nearly as dark, narrow,
subterraneous, and unwholesome. After having so
lately renewed my recollections of fresh air and
open sky, I feel doubly incarcerated among those
endless piles of old houses, like so many German
barons, bowing round me with stiff decrepitude.
The city has some memorable old buildings, but the
republican spirit, which forgets every thing but
its crabbed rights and peevish privileges, leaves
them to the common career of men and buildings;
and there they stand or fall, proud with established

squalidness, and solemn with the sacred dirt of ages.

Such opinions are, it must be acknowledged, *lese majeste* here, for the citizens are delicately alive to the honour of their city; though their delicacy does not extend, or stoop, to its ablution. But all the anger under the stars will not rail the seal off the bond; and, with all its virtues, the Englishman, at least, will find it intolerably miry and murky; find every sense of the *propre* startled by its unexpected developments, and rejoice every night to find, that he has miraculously returned to his hotel with sound limbs, however with tortured nostrils. If the Russians have not yet impaled the man who said that Moscow was like an enormous palace surrounded by its stables and pigsties; may not the traveller be suffered to live, who compares Hamburgh, public and private, only to an enormous King's Bench, surrounded by its Rules?

Still the city is a fine old gloomy relic, of fine old gloomy times; when, whatever might be the wickednesses of this world among the satrapies of the Continent, there was a spirit of grandeur, Gothic as it was, moving among mankind. I never tread my swampy way under the shadow of those fierce old buildings, that seem to scowl over the degenerate race of modern traffickers; without doing homage to the phantoms of sovereign commerce which still linger round the comptoirs, like ghosts round the spot they loved. In the massive doors I see the barriers that once guarded the wealth of the world from the vulgar eye. In the looped walls I honour the fortress of the bales of silk from the farthest Orient, the chests of ingots from " the rich Peruvian shore," and the jewel boxes, that left the turbaned kings of Afric and Ind reft of their lustre, to dazzle the earth besides. In the "sublime obscure within,"—an opacity compounded of solid stone, as thick as the chambers of a pyramid, passages almost as complicated, and dust almost as immortal, I see the shape of the lordly burgher of the sixteenth century, with his helmet side by side with his ledger, corslet on throat, and pen in hand, ordering at once the march of a " plump of gallant spears," and the opening of a freight of spices, from " Taprobane;" a portly and bold defier of princedoms, broad as one of his own bales, haughty as the holder of the

universal purse, and fierce as every man who fights
for his own; gathering the money of all nations
into his mighty grasp, to pour it out again in a
flood of pictures, gorgeous manuscripts, ponderous
plate, and imperial cloth of gold; a daring, lavish,
speculating, sweeping, magnificent monopolist;
stirring up the ends of the earth to feed him with
perpetual gain; holding the potentates of the land
in fee; defying the wilderness and the tempest in
the chase of wealth, and then, reclining at home in
a solemn and solid luxury, a rich and grave study
of enjoyment, a calm and corpulent Sybaritism, a
" sober certainty of waking bliss," worthy of a
burgher of Hamburgh, or an Epicurean Jove!

But this famous city makes a better figure from
the country. Her ramparts will flourish no more
in tales of chivalry; but they bear long lines of
fine trees, look green in perennial turf, and are a
prodigious addition to the view. They are also to
Hamburgh, what the parks are to London; the
lungs of the city, the infusers of fresh vitality into
the melancholy lanes, and steaming alleys, the
Stygian labyrinths and Acheronian pools, of this
huge hive of squalid human life.

Yet, in this world there are few goods or evils without their compensation. Those ramparts, it is true, shut up the city; and, let the increasing population be what it may, there is no hope for its breathing a fresher air than the supply of the ramparts, strained through ten thousand hovels; or finding other space than the little narrow alleys which are now compressed to the last degree of compression. But then comes the compensation—beyond the ramparts all is country. The merchant, the weary artizan, the pale-faced dweller in the hut, which he calls a warehouse; or in the shop, which he might call a dungeon; steps but outside the gate, and, within a yard of his hovel, finds himself at once in the midst of fields; all round him is verdure. And in sight of his own shingly roof, that seems the antipodes of all things vernal, the unwashed and unshorn son of the arts sits down, breathing primroses, and filling his sensorium with the sight of cattle feeding, children at their gambols, and birds playing their happy antics on blossomed bushes and garden bowers, glowing with the promise of pears, peaches, and grapes, incalculable. Yet men will dispute even upon those points. If you say,

L 4

how much better is all this, than the intolerable
size of London, that measureless diffusion of building which covers the land with brick, makes a
morning visit a day's walk, and a country walk
a march through five miles of houses to reach but a
high road at last; the German will tell you, that
you are at once too rich, too powerful, and too free,
for any thing else; that in Germany, the people can
easily get into the country, because, in the first place,
their cities might be stolen out of a suburb of London, and five minutes will here take a man from
'Change into the heart of the wilderness: and, in the
next, because no man, in his senses, will build any
thing outside the " old town;" that in Germany,
they have war every ten years, on a fair calculation ;
and every city, every meagre town, every mud village,
may expect to find itself bombarded, stormed, and
starved, sacked, or burnt down, in due season.
Unquestionably, the building propensity must be
powerful, if it be not taught a little moderation
by this.   But if it were as unteachable as a mar-
grave, the civic wisdom would prohibit the perils
of having the good town shot at from batteries,
made of peach walls and melon beds.   The

town engineer, who generally knows no more of the range of a mortar than the flight of a comet, yet knows a great deal relative to knocking down windows and wainscots; and if he find but a dove-cot within a thousand yards of the glacis, the building ambition is sure to be knocked on the head, and the builder is fortunate if he escape without damages for giving him the trouble.

If you attempt to panegyrise the cheapness of the popular amusements, and the general easy propensity to be amused; your panegyric is probably rejected, and you are told, that English amusements are dear, because money is cheap; while German amusements are cheap, because there are as many guineas in England, as there are florins in Germany; and that the populace study amusement, and spend all that they get, on it: because money is of no further use among them. This is unhappily true. In Germany, there is but little hope for any man of being better off than his fathers, except in having more money to spend: while, in England, the very first result of money, is to raise the man in society. The Englishman turns his money into rank for himself and his family: he makes it the instrument, not merely of appetite or indulgence, but of honour. He pushes himself forward in life; he, in the course of time, becomes a member of the legislature; perhaps a peer, and thus secures a permanent distinction of the most exciting kind, by the possession of opulence, directed to generous and manly objects by a manly and generous ambition. It is this access to honours that has preserved England so long from the excess of personal profligacy, or the excess of faction. Abolish the peerage, or malign it, until, like the French order of St. Michael, it is worth offering only to the hangman; and you instantly abolish the only safe object of opulence. Great wealth will be accumulated at all times by great commerce, or hereditary possession; but what escape can it have, but in personal grossness, or public excitement; but in boundless licentiousness, as in France, or perpetual faction, as in America. Wealth will inevitably act, and act with power; but in the one instance it will act as a poison, and in the other as a firebrand; and the only difference will be between its converting the land into a lazar-house, or a bedlam.

THE world begins to look brighter on us; for our weather is intolerable. This may sound like paradox; but the solution is, the islands are flooded. The famous piece of tautology, for which Addison has been so perseveringly laughed at,

" The sky is overcast, the morning lours,
    And heavily in clouds brings on the day,"

and which in its two lines tells the same tale three times over, is the very reverse of ill omen to us: for we exult in every shower, as an auxiliary, and a much better one than Russ or Tartar. We hear the wind rushing in at our doors, and the rain bursting against our casements, with patriotic calculations of the number of the enemy drenched *à l'outrance* by the fog of the islands, swamped in their mire, or stagnated, to all intents and purposes, horse, foot, and artillery, by the little, turbulent branches of the river. Yet this is terrible weather. An English rainy day is bad enough; but the German rain is like every thing else German: it *bores* through its business incomparably. It comes down with a quiet, grim resolution, a plodding pertinacity, a *vis iner-tiæ* of wet, that would irrigate the deserts of Arabia.

The visible horizon is contracted to the round of the umbrella; the sky is merely a grave, gloomy roof, a little higher than the chimneys; day is visible only by the help of candle-light; the air is nearly as thick as the earth, and both air and earth are but diversities of quagmire. This is dreadful for *Jean Tigre-singe*, who carries his aquatic propensities no further than the stream of livid abomination that runs through every street of all his cities. Of all soldiers, too, the Frenchman is the least supplied with the means of defence against such a specimen of climate: he never has a tent, except when he carries it off from some German magazine; a second pair of shoes waits for the chances of war, or the requisition on some luckless village, where the sabots of the peasantry happen to fit French feet; a water-proof cloak is not made within the limits of France; and with an outside of rags, and an inside fortified only by Corporal Trim's specific, brandy and ditch water, the Frenchman trusts to fortune.

But this is also uneasy work for ourselves: the duty of the town is harassing; our regular troops are too few to be of any use but as patroles; and

our volunteers take the charge of the posts, and
are sinking under it : they are now compelled to
remain under arms, night and day. I see them,
with regret, lying in their little temporary huts
in the bastions, on straw or whatever they can
find, to keep them from the ground. They bear
it as cheerfully as they may ; but it is out of all
question, that they can bear it long. Gentlemen
may shoulder their muskets, eat barley broth, and
fight ; but rain, cold, and want of rest, will wear
down men accustomed to such lives as they have
led hitherto. Even those on the bastions are still
better circumstanced than many of their brethren.
Some of our guards are posted in the low grounds
along the river, where their couch, if they lie down
at all, must be in mire. The overflow of the river
sometimes suddenly covers the whole ground; and
if this weather last, I should not be surprised to
see half our camp navigating its way, on a spring-
tide, down to the Northern Ocean. To sleep,
would be difficult, in such bivouacs; but even the
attempt to sleep, is often next to impossible ; from
the teasing hostility of the enemy, who now seldom
let a night pass, without sending in half a dozen

shells. The first sound of the guns naturally sets every man upon his feet; then the question of slumber is settled for the night; for who can tell how soon a general assault may be expected: guards are turned out, battalions paraded, matches lighted, cannon manned, every soul who has a musket is on the alert; and after standing for two or three hours, listening for the march of the enemy, watching every candle in a cottage window for ten miles round, and comparing notes on every bark of a dog, or sound of a horn—and by some odd fatality of the time, dogs are barking, and horns sounding, why, the fiend and the French only know, from sunset to sunrise—they receive the report of their patrole, and turn into their straw, shivering, wet, and with every bone tingling with ague.

May 27.—News from the armies, gloomier than ever! Napoleon is still hunting down the allies: all their bulletins cannot make them conquerors. They fought well; but their scale has kicked the beam, and there it clings. The French are driving them, like wolves after sheep, from hill to river, and from river to hill. They halt only to fire a few shots on some adventurous regiment of *chasseurs* or *chevaux legers*, that pounces upon their sour-krout breakfasts; then comes the word for re-treat, and they fly over the hills again. Schweid-witz, famous in the wars of Frederic, is said to be the next fighting position.

The Berlin Gazette scoffs at all this, invokes the days of the Great Frederic, and swears by the shades of the Teutonic knights, that the French have been so crippled by the late battle, as to be deprived of all power of locomotion. But the princesses of Prussia, in that case, are more fortu-nate than the French; for the same Gazette states, with a minuteness worthy of the event, that they have just left Berlin, in six post carriages and four. In Silesia, too, all is declared to be in the proud-est security; yet it suddenly transpires that every man in Silesia is packing up his household, and preparing, like the princesses, to escape, full speed, from this immoveable enemy; in the mean time, we are inevitably, and beyond all controversy, ruined. Our old city cannot make wings to itself,

13

and flutter out of the reach of the French cannon balls. I see the scoundrel *garçons* in every café, already brightening up their cups and visages for their countrymen.

There are sanguine spirits among us still, who are determined to believe in the magic of *the* cause, and protest against the possibility of the Lady of the Hanse Towns wearing French papillotes, or wrapping the tri-colour again round her ransomed limbs. But a few hundred German dragoons would be worth all the figures of speech. Hamburgh *must* fall! The negligence, or the feebleness of the allied cabinets has here recklessly abandoned a most powerful source of northern influence. It has sacrificed a great city, which common sense might have converted into a great national bulwark, and which the enemy *will* assuredly convert into a great fortress, without delay. It has sacrificed the still more important bulwark of the cause, that was to be found in the patriotism of one of the first cities of Europe; and it has even soured that patriotism into a warning against trusting to them and their tardiness any more. Such is war,—terror, misery, confiscation, and exile. Ruin has here been brought into a large, honourable, and flourishing community, and for nothing. A few regiments of their idle landwehr, a few squadrons of their rambling cavalry, and half a dozen of the field-guns that are now rotting in their parks at Berlin, if managed by hands which knew how to make any use of them, would enable the people to resist, until they were sufficiently disciplined to take the defence of the city upon themselves. Another month's exercise, with half that month expended on the fortifications, and Hamburgh might be impregnable to fifty thousand Frenchmen, " armed in proof," and led by the profoundest plunderer in France. It might have been made the head of the northern movement, the *appui* of the northern armies, and invaluable, as the point of direct communication with the firmest, and the most effective, the only effective, of all allies,—England.

But we have still our tower of strength, our six or eight hundred Cossacks, and not a soul more; and even those we have spoiled. We have fed the savages into a plethora, till they have lost

their national physiognomy, and their nature together; and both man and horse have become
thick-winded, fat, and lazy—the whole pulk completely aldermanized.

CHAPTER XXXII.

NIGHT.

NIGHT, after a day of incessant rain. The storm is raging among the old gables of the city, like the potentate of the air, thundering among the tall steeples, and whirling away vanes and tiles into the wilderness. The shower is dashing against my casements as if it were determined to weary out the solid framework that has lasted since the days of Charlemagne. And here I sit, in the midst of a general assault and battery of the angry elements, waiting only for the moment when my citadel shall be stormed from the clouds, and the garrison forced to surrender at discretion, or drowned. This would be the true temperature for some magnificent feat of magic, some huge conspiracy, or startling regicide; a Macbeth night, when—

> " The chimneys were blown down : and, as they say,
>   Lamentings heard in the air, strange screams of death,

And prophesyings, with accents terrible,

Of dire combustion, and confused events,

New hatched in the woeful time.   The obscure bird

Clamour'd the livelong night,—some say, the earth

Was feverous, and did shake."

Yet nature, in all her aspects, has something
that reconciles us to her, something in even her
repulsion that attracts, something in even this
hurly-burly of the storm, that is not altogether
without its echo even in that narrowest nook of the
heart where its pleasures are hid.   It certainly
does not require Zanga's stimulant, to " like this
rocking of the battlements."   The secret may lie
in the sense of power ; beyond all doubt a source
of high interest at all times ; and which every man
will discover to be such, who will but take the
trouble to put the question to his own mind.
Lightning and thunder, roaring seas, and heaving
forests ; the palpable subjection of those vast solid
things of nature, which man can no more control
than he could create them—promontories sub-
merged, mountain tops splintered and swept away,
volcanoes lighted up to heaven, continents shaken
and torn to the centre, fill the mind with a sensa-

tion, in which it takes an inevitable and instinctive
delight; a fearful one, perhaps, but certainly a
most absorbing enjoyment, the sense of power.
The Lucretian principle is wrong: the sense of contrast, the *suave mari magno,* is too feeble, too rare,
and too selfish. Nothing can account for an impression as universal as man himself, but an original feeling, a great, arbitrary impulse, a stamp
upon his spirit, fixed by the same hand that fabricated him. We can go no higher than his birth,
but to that we must ascend.

The English are laughed at, and libelled by the
laugh, as eternal talkers " about" the weather;
they do not talk the tenth part that foreigners do,
upon that topic or any other: yet what topic can
be half so natural as the state of things which come
home to every man's heart and bosom in every
hour of the twenty-four, which turn every man into
a walking barometer and thermometer, and trans-
mute his blood alternately into bile and icicles. Hail,
rain, and snow are the secrets too that make the
Englishman the man he is; if they sour his politics
they sharpen his invention; if they shut him up a

prisoner half the year, and fill his brain with blue vapours, and his lungs with carbon, they give him comfort, cleanliness, and a subject on which he may be discontented till doomsday; they make him the handicraftsman of mankind, the very prince of moralists and manufacturers, the most devoted worshipper of the household gods, and the best blacksmith in creation.

———

Midnight.—Rain still, in all its shapes; gushes, bursts, sheets, cascades. This would be the night for the Wierd Sisters. I hear in every gust that bounds, breaks, and howls through the old castles of houses, the roar of the Hartz. Every witch of their pandemonium is abroad in full incantation; and Hanover, the primitive soil of innocence, and sand, is deluged with wit and wickedness. The Lucretian principle is wrong; yet there is something in contrast still: and here, in the midst of torrents that might sweep away the face of a mountain, and gusts that might blow out the moon, I sit in a pavilion of glass, with a Parisian lamp burning before me, unshaken by a breath, with books and papers and gossamery things on the table, all the fine frailties of the finger of man, that a touch of one of the furious elements without, or of the fiends that ride them, would scatter to the poles: yet here I sit, like a Persian prince, in the midst of vases of roses, French and artificial though they be, pictures of heroines and heroes in their robes of chivalry and state, and sunshine landscapes, blooming as the eternal cheeks of a maid of honour; or, like an Indian necromancer in his magic circle, defying the dæmons, that flourish their fiery tails, and impregnate the atmosphere with storm and sulphur within a foot of his impassable dominion.

But what a night must this be in the North Sea—all rocks and shallows and yesty waves, with nothing to anchor upon between the Baltic and the Pole?—what in the sands, the snows, the forests of the wilderness? And what if the desolation of the night were made more tempestuous by the desolation of the mind? Of all the thoughts that ever shaped themselves into magnificent poetry, to me the most magnificent, the most natural, and the most overwhelming, is Lear's oratory in the storm:—

> " Let the great gods,
> That keep this dreadful pother o'er our heads,
> Find out their enemies now!"

The appeal to the self-condemned has the inten-
sity of an avenging spirit.

> " Tremble, thou wretch,
> That hast within thee undivulged crimes,
> Unwhipt of justice.   Hide thee, thou bloody hand;
> Thou perjured; and thou simular of virtue,
> That art incestuous: Caitiff, to pieces shake,
> That, under covert and convenient seeming,
> Hast practised on man's life : close pent up guilts,
> Rive your concealing continents, and cry
> These dreadful summoners' grace!"

But, to stoop to matters more " akin to th' time."
If this weather go on, Hamburgh will be but one
huge pond, as it is now but one huge shower-bath;
the Jungfersteig, with all its casinos, will be but a
branch of the Elbe, and our patriotism and our
city will be dissolved into futurity together.   But
what must the islands, in the very bosom of the
flood, be ?   A mist as solid as midnight has sat upon
them since break of day.   The work of sap and

swamping has doubtless gone on there in its full vigour. I have missed the usual booming of the French guns to-night: the cannoneers are themselves besieged, or where " their bones are coral made ;" gone to the Alarics and Attilas, where they will never spunge howitzer more ; and their guns will be dug up some thousand years hence to adorn some new theory of the deluge ; and prove the dexterity and madness of the " world before the flood."

Yet nationality takes so many odd shapes, that it might be a delicate point to insinuate to a German that this was a wet day. In all my rambles through mankind, I have never seen any man but the Englishman superior to the absurdity of being sore about the face of his skies. Frenchman, Italian, and Spaniard, with his visage as adust as his own sandals, make their broiling sun, their scorching wind, and their torrents of rain, that when they come, come with a vengeance that pays up all arrears, matters of personal quarrel ; and there are fellows whom I now hear floundering home through the streets, soaked and drenched through every pore, who would probably resent the calling this

" German weather" as a call to the pistol and schlager.

Yet they can tell historic truth in other realms. I remember, some years ago, in London, as I was hurrying through the Strand, in one of the worst nights of our worst November, with the rain coming down in a steady flow, that blackened the streets in spite of all their lights, and depopulated them down to their last watchman; to have heard a passing voice mutter from a huge German cloak, " Ah, ha! dis be vara fine wedder in Yarmany." The speaker accidentally looked up at a half-drowned lamp; and the grey, granitic face told me, beyond all possibility of mistake, in what soil it was fabricated. He then double-clasped his cloak, plunged on, and was lost in a minute, perhaps melted into water, like a he-Undine.

Nature supplies every animal with some kind of defence against its peculiar evils; and German nature has resources against those frowns and scoffings of the elements, those " knittings of the brows of Boreas and Auster," as one of their poets has

pictured it, which prove that Germans were born
to be drenched.   But what can a stranger do, to
whom those resources are no more resources than
wings to a beaver? who cannot doze away his cares
in tobacco, drown them in beer, or dream them
away over the most tiresome novels of all that ever
abused the name; one who is sick, beyond all expression, of the loves of the Ildegondas, let their
locks be ever so yellow; and the leaps of the Hilde-
brands, let their steeds be ever so bold; who loaths
eternal descriptions of mawkish passion, and adventure divided between the silly and the mad;
maidens, all simplicity and impudence, with the
bluest eyes and the most capacious hearts on
earth; and heavy horsemen, who do all impossible
things for their well-fed charms!

Theatre in this city there is none, and if there
were, there is no vehicle to take one to its doors
but a *stuhl wagen*, a colossal wheel-barrow, open to
all the winds of heaven; a swimming jacket would
be just as dry, and much more suitable.   But of
the German stage, what portion exists that could
dispose a rational being to stir from his fire-side?
What is there in the interminable dreariness of

Lessing, the pert profaneness of Kotzebue, or the bewildered and dreamy feebleness of the whole tribe of the Mullners and mystifiers, to excite a rational interest, or even amuse a natural curiosity.

What is there in the whole dramatic horizon of Germany to fix the eye, much more, to enlighten the national darkness, with the single exception of Schiller? a man of talent undoubtedly, a bold, forcible, and opulent master of dramatic language; yet still but in the second rank; a builder on other men's foundations; a man who could not swim a minute without being held up by the chin by Shakspeare; a mind of strong native proportions, and altogether a fine specimen of the barbarian; but dressed from head to foot in the cloth of gold of our noble old dramatists, and showing the barbarian through it all. It is impossible to refuse him the praise of genius; but it is genius so often obscured, so desultory, and so flagging, that we often doubt whether we have not been deceived after all, and mistaken the stilt for the wing, the ambitious and temporary effort for the natural supremacy, the mountebank spring for the easy and secure elevation of the master mind.

Far be it from me and mine to speak carelessly of such a son of the Muse. Whatever he may be in other lands, in his own he is a leader; and so forward a leader, that he has left his army at a prodigious distance, even totally out of sight, behind. But as far be it from me and mine to sacrifice one iota of the just fame of the most manly-minded and intellectual of all countries,—England, to the folly of propitiating the vanity of Germany, or any other soil. In the gloom of Germany Schiller is a national light; but whether he be an *ignis fatuus*, or a beacon, he utterly dwindles away before the dramatic blaze of England. He is at best but a satellite of our own great luminary; a moon, utterly extinguished in the broad sunshine of Shakspeare.

Even the newspapers fail the Briton here; for who, but one born in the land, can toil through the mixture that covers the four sides of the little clay-coloured sheet before me; one half protocols, and the other half anecdotes of every trite and vapid frivolity that can enter into the mind of man? Stories of miraculous dogs, horses, and captains; biographies of illustrious councillors and chamber-

M 3

lains, the human dust and cobwebs of the little courts, never heard of till they are swept away; actual amatory tales, of the silliest species, figuring side by side with bulletins, the latter nearly as much the work of fiction as the former; and anecdotes of " national" wit and wisdom, that meet us with the instant loathing of that most wearisome of all recognitions, an old story! As to intelligence; continental news is nothing, and can be nothing, while, if the editor should happen to let slip an unpalatable fact, the Emperor of Austria might throw him into the dungeons of Olumtz, or the King of Prussia send for his head in a charger. The *Correspondenten* itself, which built its reputation on its courage, and once boasted of taking emperors by the beard, is not an atom more heroic than the rest of the cravens: all write with the fear of the provost-marshal before their eyes. The frown of the senate may have lost its powers, but it must be allowed that the knout on the spot, and Siberia in the back-ground, are no very vivid stimulants to political courage. And even if our Russ commandant should spare the national weapon, there is a fearful witness of the pen; the dark eye of Napoleon, vigilance itself, registering every paragraph, and for every slide into truth, sure to exact, soon or late, a deadly retribution.

But night grows apace ; the cathedral chimes toll duller than ever through the mist, like the bells over Lethe, a knell to the departing honours of the city, where they have jangled through so many hundreds of lazy years. But, " *Invida terra madescat.*" What man can look upon the world kindly in a day like this, when the very air is saturated with the spleen? Let me turn to the moon. To see her on a night like this, in the lulling of the tempest, lifting up her horned front in troubled majesty, through piles of solemn vapour, that roll and swell round her in shapes and grandeurs innumerable and unspeakable, continents of cloud that look like the upbreaking of some superior world, is a noble exchange for the dripping earth below. Of all the idolatries that ever beguiled the imagination of man into substituting the things of the Divine hand for the great invisible King, the worship of Selenè was the most imaginative. Waning as she is at this moment, what can be more lovely than to see her rising, like a spirit from the grave, from depths of darkness that seemed made to bury her for ever; then adding lustre to lustre, till she stands, like the risen spirit, clothed in her full light, the splendid denizen of the blue empire of suns and stars above.

But no Italian moonlight for me—no sheets of unspeckled azure—no night, when all unstained,

> " The glowing planets roll,
> And not a cloud disturbs the solemn pole."

Give me the night of clouds, and of clouds in their wildest commotion. Is it only in her rule over this turbulent royalty that the moon shows herself the true sovereign? Who can doubt that half her original honours, as Hecate, arose from her dominion over those " wild creatures of the element?" She is the true light, limner, creator, of the great landscape, that reaches from one end of heaven to the other. What are the purple pavilions of the sunset, and the highways of pearl and diamond that lead to them, compared with the grey Mont-Blancs, and unfathomable valleys, and myriads of apparitions that I now see moving over them with pale and ominous banners, like a general insurrection of the tomb? Dian, Luna, Hècate, the Terge-mina! is the true " cloud Compeller" after all; the mother of shades; the mighty wizard touching airy nothing into castles of ivory and pyramids of phosphor; brightning giddy vapour into " shapes unutterable, nameless, dire," phantom hosts, and superb monsters. At this moment she is flooding with sudden silver, right over Russia, the pinions of an eagle ninety degrees from point to point, with Sirius flashing like a burning diamond, for its eye, and a beak heavy with thunder.

Let me worship the new symbol of supremacy; *Die Russiche Swartz Adler!* which Napoleon protests on all occasions is the true glutton, to which he and his Frenchmen are but playful epicures; the predestined all-swallower of Europe; the wholesale, insatiable feaster on that field of human mortality where not armies but nations shall be ranged in battle array; and where the prize shall be not kingdoms or continents, but the dominion of the globe.

THE RUSSIAN BLACK EAGLE:

A NIGHT VIEW.

THE trumpet of the storm is blown,

The thunder wakes upon his throne.

Through the vapours damp

The moon's sad lamp

Seems lighting funeral shrouds;

And a giant plume

Stoops through the gloom

Of the thousand rolling clouds.

That head is crown'd with many a ring!

I know that fearful eagle-wing!

Fierce, broad, and black,

It hung on the track,

From Moscow's towers of flame,

O'er hill, and plain, and tide,

Chasing the homicide,

Till France was but a name.

Thou eagle-king! I know thee well,

By the iron beak and the deadly yell.

It was no forest prey

Thou wentest forth to slay;

Whole armies were thy food,

Earth's crown'd and mighty men:

Thy haunt no forest glen,

But kingdoms, slaughter-strew'd!

Dark spirit of the mystic North,
When sweeps thy sullen pinion forth,
Like a cloudy zone ;
What fated throne
Must sink in dust again !
Com'st thou to wreak
Old vengeance for the Greek,
Giving him blood to drink like rain !

Or shall thy gory talon sweep
O'er the pale Propontic deep,
Where sits the Sultan-slave,
His throne beside his grave !
Gathering his vassals wan ;
And with shrinking ear,
Seems in each blast to hear
" Death to the Ottoman !"

Or from thy tempest-girdled nest
On Caucasus' eternal crest,
Shall thy consuming eyes
Glance where trembling India lies,
Offering her jewelled diadem,
Another, to thy many-circled brow !
Or shalt thou too be low,
Thy grandeur like the rest—a dream !

Or shalt thou revel till the storm,
When the avenger's fiery form

M 6

Bursts from his midnight skies,

And mankind's trembling eyes

See the last thunders hurled?

And thou, and thy wild horde,

Are in his hand the sword,

Destroying, and destroyed but with the world!

CHAPTER XXXIII.

_____

THE CAPITULATION.

May 29.—IT is certain that the French have not altogether the most comfortable quarters, strong as they are on the left bank. The peasantry lead them many a dance through mire and sand, for not a potatoe will they surrender, but at the point of the bayonet. This compels them to scatter a good deal, and they suffer in consequence; for the Russian horse and the German partizan corps watch their proceedings narrowly, and when they can catch them napping, make fearful work with the conscripts.

A few days since our crests were brightened by the rout of a body, of all the most obnoxious to the " good German," a whole posse of *douaniers.* They were marching to post themselves in one of the little towns on the Hanoverian side; why,

there are a hundred versions; some say, to prevent
smuggling, or to smuggle on their own account;
some to plunder the town, which is perfectly probable; some to plunder the town, and then hang
the principal inhabitants, banish the rest, and finish
by setting fire to the houses; which would be perfectly probable too, if they could find any thing to
be got by the more complete proceeding.   But information of their march was rapidly communicated
to the Hanoverian General Walmoden, who dispatched some hussars to find them out.   The French
were " seen, followed, and conquered."   The affair
was lively.   The whole enemy's corps made head
for awhile, for they showed cavalry and infantry,
every douanier besides being at all times convertible into a soldier; and the broken nature of the
ground, and the shelter of a grove, afforded some
opportunity for taking up a position.   The firing
became heavy, and the Germans were kept outside
the wood.   The hussars galloped round and round
in vain; for they could not unearth those foxes; and
a Frenchman behind a tree is dangerous.   At length,
however, they made their way, broke down the
barricades, and plunged upon the copse, which the

douaniers had fixed on as the " key of the position." The conscripts who, like all Frenchmen,
would fire for ever, if their enemy would stand to
be shot at; were confounded by the sight of the
bayonets and sabres flashing so near their faces,
totally broke, and attempted to make their escape
across the plain. But this was utter ruin, with
the hussars ready to pounce upon them. The result was, that the whole corps were taken or
destroyed, to the infinite joy, as may be supposed,
of the little town for which their visit had been intended; and which but for the gallant hussars, might
have been a scene of shooting and hanging before
the day was done.

We were again rising to the point of security;
having actually sent a deputation to Bernadotte,
either to implore his advance, or to threaten him
for his tardiness ; but the news has come that we
are left without a regular soldier ; and the news is
true. The Crown Prince has done thus much for
us ; and with a whole army of French, looking at
us, hour by hour, and waiting only for the opportunity to cut us up, we are left to our own bayonets. However, before the French come, we are

making an effort to do the best that we can, and, like Cæsar, die decorously.   We are raising a *levée en masse*.   At five this morning I found the whole populace under arms; a motley assemblage enough, and armed with all sorts of weapons, from the musket to the pike and the pitchfork.   But it would be unfair to laugh at even the rough preparations of those honest fellows.   Mars and Bellona in their trim never deserved half the homage; and I confess that all the well drilled and close buttoned guards of all the emperors of the continent—and I have, by one accident or other, seen most of them— never seemed to me worthier of respect than the ragged heroism of this morning's parade.   But the *Correspondenten* has just settled all doubts for the day, by the following notice :—

" *May 28.*—Yesterday some battalions of Prussians and Mecklenburghers arrived here, to replace the Swedes, who have taken a strong position near Bergedorf.   The works on our ramparts approach their completion, and are prosecuted with the more diligence, as even in case of the most vigorous offensive operations, which will most likely soon be employed against the French, it seems to be the intention of his Excellency General Tettenborn to make Hamburgh a place of strength, conformable to its importance in other respects. The enemy at Wilhelmsburg have suffered very much from the continued wetness of the weather, and a part of the island has been laid under water by the late high tides. In those circumstances the French will be under the necessity of deferring their views on Hamburgh, the water, as it is well known, not being their favourite element."

A German bulletin concluding with a witticism, is worth recording; and but for this the bulletin was worth nothing. The wierd sisters themselves never contrived any thing more calculated to keep the word of promise to the ear, and the ear alone. Every statement in it turns out to be as shadowy as if Katterfelto, or Napoleon himself, had held the pen. The Prussians have come, but to go; the Swedes are gone, never to come back. Tettenborn has packed up his baggage, to his last moustache, and is on the wing. The French are openly in movement in all directions; and at this hour Cossacks and couriers are flying about the country, with horn and hurrah, to gather up all the troops that can be gathered, for the purpose of driving the enemy back again over the Elbe! for it is now notorious that they have landed on *our* bank, and are probably in full march at this moment over the bodies of the Prussians and Hanseatics, to take possession of the gates. A heavy firing has been heard all the morning up the river.

About noon I went to the Borsen halle: its steps were crowded with anxious faces; every one was asking for news, but news there was none; even the invention of the Borsen halle had failed. Not a syllable was to be heard, but " curses, if not loud," deep, on the tardiness of the allies. At length, one of the Hanseatic troopers came in, in full gallop, and, giving signs of having good tidings to tell; we crowded round him, but all that I could learn, was, that " affairs were going on well—that there was an *action*—that there were prisoners—that the general was there—that all the Hanseatics fought like heroes; and, again, that every thing was going on well." This intelligence was received with great congratulation.

But unable as I was to hear the whole, for the crowd was large and clamorous; I heard some misgivings, which induced many to think, that they might act not unwisely in having their passports ready for all emergencies; they acted accordingly, and on my way homewards, those misgivings were confirmed by my seeing a considerable number of the citizens going to the passport office. *I found the office quite full,* and full of as anxious an assemblage of countenances as could easily have been congregated. A painter would have found a capital study in the eager, the angry, the terrified, the dejected; the rich, who were frightened for their property; the beggars, who were frightened for their lives; the notorious Antigallicans and Russian partizans, who well knew the bitterness of Napoleon's vengeance; and the general mass of the people, who knew only that the next change must be famine and free quarters. One old Spaniard at my side, with a long, la Mancha visage, and who might have passed for a discontented Don Quixote, could utter nothing but " Mala epoca, Senor, mala epoca." All was struggle to get possession of the passports as fast as they could; escape from the city being clearly the general expedient. It must be acknowledged, that the clerks seconded this eagerness to the best of their power; they were startlingly active and obliging. This phenomenon I had never witnessed in the course of my travelling experience before, and I unequivocally set it down as a sign of the times; all clerks in Government employ on the Continent being proverbially among the most insolent, nonchalant, and leisurely personages in existence, and the passport clerks generally bearing the palm in those qualities from all their brethren.

But on this occasion the " law's delay and insolence of office" were postponed; the passports were showered on the heads of the crowd, and a comprehensive touch of the pen despatched the drawing of our portraits, that most frivolous and offensive, even among the fooleries which the foreigner calls wisdom; and which amounts to nothing more than an impudent pretence for subjecting the traveller to a caricature, and degrading a gentleman to the level of a fugitive felon. The solution of the wonder was, that the clerks had the dungeon or the *fusillade* as clearly before their eyes, as the rest of their countrymen; or even in a peculiar degree, for it was a well authenticated maxim of the Napoleon code of war, that the clerk who, on any French reverse, took office under the enemy, though that enemy were his king, put himself in imminent hazard of being hanged on the first opportunity : these are delicate times for subjects.

Evening.—Hamburgh droops! The news of the morning's affair up the river is now clearing itself; and the truth is evidently, that we have had the worst of it. The French are too many for our scattered people; they have the power of attacking when and where they please, and the necessary result is, that they must finally succeed. It appears that they had landed in force on Ochsenwerder, an island some miles above the city; and that our troops, though re-inforced by some Prussian battalions, have not been able to drive them back. Still, rumours are to be heard, that the enemy are breaking up their camp at Harburg; that a strong column of the allied troops is in march; that the Danes are about to embark in active hostilities on our side, &c. &c. And those ten-times detected absurdities are still swallowed; for there was no absurdity ever hatched in the cowardice or presumption of man, but would find the multitude open-mouthed to receive it. But, without arms, discipline, a leader, or a government, what can be done!

One thing there is that may give us some hope, as the patient sometimes recovers by the flight of the physician. All our *diplomats* are gone: they have been gradually disappearing since times began to frown; and the last of them, the little pragmatical secretary, who seemed born to burlesque even the burlesque diplomacy of this land of envoys, has been met this morning, ten leagues off, flying, as fast as a pair of horses could carry him, towards Stralsund. If we had got rid of those charlatans a month ago, Hamburgh might not be now at the mercy of her enemies. For it was the promise without the performance, the constant expectation of troops from Sweden, troops from Silesia, troops from the moon, constantly kept up by the quackery of those fellows, that disabled the honest Hamburgher from the use of his natural means, tempted him to rely on strangers for the defence which he might have best found in his own stout sinews; and, by making Hamburgh a feeble

dependent on a feeble system, a dismantled out-post of a great unwieldy camp spreading from the Baltic to the Danube, deprived her of the concentrated strength, and bold, civic spirit, that would have made her impregnable in a war of her own.

Whether in a month, a week, or a day, the French must become masters of the city; and they have already taken measures to prevent the escape of the inhabitants, and especially of the English. They have blocked up the Elbe—at least so strong is the impression among the authorities, that the English post-bag makes its tours backward and forward through Holstein; and the wisdom of the British Senate thus comes to us nightly smuggled in base alliance with horse-bean coffee and cabbage-leaf cigars.

The difficulty of an escape by land is, that it is next to impossible to know whether the first step of the traveller may not be into the very jaws of capture. Every movement of the armies is masqued by cavalry; and in the late campaigns cavalry have been employed to an unusual extent. There is always a fringe of hussars spread for miles round the march of the infantry; and the unwarlike tra-

veller who at night conceives that he knocks at the
door of an inn, finds that he has roused a barrack.
The fairest road may lead him into the centre of a
platoon of chasseurs; or the most smiling harvest-
field surprise him by a dropping fire from the pistols of a patrole of horse.   Resistance is of course
entirely out of the question, flight is nearly as much
so, and if not shot, he is sure to be plundered of
every florin, and sent to the next depôt, to be sent
into France, from which he will never return, while
Napoleon can chain, starve, or sink him into the
grave.

About sun-set I walked towards one of the batteries on the river's side.   A considerable number
of the citizens were in little groups along the bank,
gazing anxiously enough at the islands.   Some
Prussian officers, who had probably been sent to
ascertain what the enemy were doing, were lounging carelessly in front of a café, with much the
look of the Irish philosopher, who when the ship
was sinking, disclaimed all interest in the matter,
" as he was only a passenger."   But all specula-
tion was turned to the islands, where with the
naked eye little could be seen but the yellow lux-

uriance of the advancing season. The effects of the tempest were scarcely visible but in the broader and more rapid current.

A hot sun had dried up the ground, and the French were already reconstructing their howitzer battery. However, it was at last obvious that there was level with the ground something more than its shrubs and corn. I borrowed a telescope, and saw that what I had mistaken for a honest corn-field was actually a French bivouac, or rather a French prostrate parade, a *ventre à terre* manœuvre, apparently for the purpose of avoiding our cannon-shot, which had them completely within range; but which, in this position, might have as effectually fired at the fish in the river. The men were lying down in long parallel lines, fully equipped, with their muskets beside them, and their knapsacks under their heads. A few mounted officers were leisurely moving about from corps to corps: there seemed to be several hundreds of them, but their grey great-coats, and the quantity of thicket that darkened the ground, prevented any accurate view. Why they exhibited themselves at all was a problem, and the only answer which we could devise was, that they must be waiting only till night-fall, to make a " start," and cross over to the city : and for this, too, they had by some unaccountable means obtained boats, which we saw lying in the little creeks of the islands.

From the spot where we were standing the view was extensive, and often as I had observed the contrast between the landscape and the sullen work that was doing, or about to be done, in the heart of it; the impression was never so forcible as on this evening, from the direct and obvious preparation of the enemy. On my right, as I looked towards the setting sun,—and he was bathing in a flood of amber glory that seemed melting the Hanoverian wastes into its substance, an evening apotheosis of the hills and forests,—lay Altona, with all its old angular roofs and copper-sheeted spires, looming large, and looking, in the imperfect light, like the misty towers and battlements of some feudal fortress or groupe of castles. To the left the eye ranged up the river along a vale of such prodigality of vegetation as might be expected from abundant moisture, a summer sun, and the garden-loving toil of the German peasant. Below, the river, much broadened and swelled by the late rains, rolled on, dappled with every colour of cloud and sun, at my feet. Before me stretched the islands in green fertility to the left bank, one luxuriant level, now just dipping into that gentle dusk, which gave them all a touch of purple richness. All looked the quiet bounty of nature; all calmness, gentle profusion, and composed beauty: and in the midst of this, under our eyes, was the very instrument of desolation, the concentrated evil of all evils; murder, burning, rapine, all the wild and hideous passions and violence of our nature, ready to be let loose at a word; the spirit of the devil himself visibly before us, in his especial agent—war; waiting only to burst upon us, and before that sun rose again, to turn all that the eye now rested on, in almost sacred gratitude and enjoyment, into a scene of horrors, a howling wilderness, covered with embers and the dead.

As I walked towards Altona I could see a considerable bustle in the islands opposite the Danish shore: large boats were passing and repassing, which seemed to be for troops; they were certainly capable of being applied to that purpose. French

officers also were on board; and I understood that
this intercourse had been peculiarly going on during
the day; the general opinion was, that the governor
of Altona had recommenced his negotiation with
the French, and that the Danes were finally trafficking for the surrender of the city.

It may be now the part of wisdom to take my
departure while I may, and leave Hamburgh and
its troubles far behind.   But the ruin has been so
often threatened, and has been so often postponed,
that I feel disposed to doubt it still, or at least not
to take it for granted all at once: besides, all is the
chapter of accidents; before to-morrow an order
from Napoleon may send Davoust full gallop back
through Hanover; Wittgenstein has been circling
the French in Magdeburgh, and he may be on the
march to the mouth of the Elbe at this moment;
the crown prince of Sweden has certainly arrived
at Stralsund, and possibly he may think that the
time has come when he ought to do something for
his million of English pounds.   The grand prize
may be still in the wheel; and, before a week is past,
Hamburgh, dishevelled and drooping as she is now,
may bo shaking the dust from her robes, braiding

her locks with patriotic laurels, and welcoming all the world, like the Roman oracle—*Hic manebimus optime!*

MAY 30.—This day has settled all questions together. I had supped at the house of an intelligent and hospitable friend on the glacis; and after the rambling talk that best befits a supper, discussing the politics and prospects of our beleaguered community, ventilating the characters of the popular men of Germany, and deciding that Hamburgh was an ill-used commonwealth between kings and emperors, allied and hostile; we retired to our chambers for the night. All was calm : the sky was lovely, all star-light and silence. The French howitzer battery gave sign of its restoration, by throwing a few shells, but it was at long intervals. I listened, heard no sound of assault, no *platooning*, which I had now learned to be the only evidence of actual attack; and weariness dropped me into that deep, delicious sleep, which is the perfection of human luxury, and which nothing but weariness can give. But my sleep was not to be like his, who " helps Hyperion to his horse," before day-break I heard the booming of heavy guns; though whether from the French batteries or our own, the sound was too distant for me to discern. However, there were sounds of restlessness in the road in front of the house; and between four and five, musketry began to be audible. It soon became heavy; yet it was so totally unlike the sound of a regular engagement, or even of the fire of regular troops, under any circumstances, that I lay for some time lazily in conjecture. At last this strange, rambling, desultory rattle was evidently approaching, and it became high time to discover what it meant. I threw on my clothes, and saw from my window a number of people hurrying in confusion from the nearest gate of the city; with their bundles on their shoulders, and every appearance of the flight which I had witnessed before. Among them were scattered men in the Hamburgh uniform, evidently in a high state of exasperation, gesticulating, haranguing, and firing their musquets in all directions. I went down among them, and found great alarm among the people, but much more indignation. They exclaimed that they were betrayed, that the city had been sold to the French, that they could have defended it for ever, &c. But on the main point, whether the enemy had actually come, no one seemed to have made up his mind. As, upon this fact, however, all our movements must depend, I gave up the task of extracting information from brains fevered by anxiety and terror, and went towards the gate. There I found a new scene of affairs, workmen delving at fosse and rampart more actively than ever; drums beating through the streets; the guns of the heavy battery which commanded the passage of the islands, beginning to fire: every thing giving signs of a determined defence.

But the truth began to transpire at last. The burgher-guard was disbanded! This had occurred at day-break, by an order from its commandant, Von Hess, stating that " as the Russians had left the city, and the French were in too great force to allow of a rational resistance, there was nothing more to be done; the burgher-guard was at an end." The address closed with some natural expressions of regret at this position of affairs; " a wish that he had died before the coming of such a day; and advice to his fellow citizens, to seek some

spot where they could be secure from the violence
and tyranny of the enemy, and wait for better
times." The firing which I had heard in the morning had been in consequence of the break of the
corps.   The men, outrageous at this termination of
their services, spread themselves through the streets
and roads, furiously firing away their cartridges,
and dashing their musquets against the ground, or
flinging them into the canals, that they might not
fall into the enemy's hands.   Here was, in abundance, spirit, if it had been properly guided.   I
heard no complaints of the commandant.   He was
spoken of as not a military man, but simply an
intelligent and active citizen, whose literary and
personal character had entitled him so far to the
public respect, as to put him at the head of their
volunteers.   But the Russians, Prussians, Swedes,
and Danes, did not come off so handsomely, and
their unconscious sovereigns were visited with some
of the choicest flowers of northern rhetoric.   The
battery on the Grasbroek still continued thundering
away, and though crowds had left the city, multitudes
remained behind, swearing that they knew nothing
of surrender, and that they would not surrender.

No man, but he who has been in a similar scene of uproar, can conceive the difficulty of ascertaining any one fact in this popular combustion. Every soul has a story to tell, and is eager to tell it; but every story is a contradiction of the story heard the moment before. All is now resentment, clamour, calling to arms, and firing ball-cartridges into the air. It is even difficult to ascertain, what might seem the most easily settled of all facts, whether the French are, or are not, actually at the gates, or even within the city. The weight of evidence certainly predominates against their being there, for no one can say that he has seen them; but the testimony of the senses goes for nothing in times like these. Still, from the ramparts no hostile sign is visible. As far as the eye can reach, all is quiet between the city and Hanover. The battalions which we had seen " in grim repose," lying there the night before, have disappeared; neither flag, nor signal waves; and the fields look as undisturbed and untenanted as if they had slept from the beginning of things.

In this strange state the city has continued for full half the day; but there are symptoms, which

to even a less warlike eye than mine, may disclose
some of the truth. A Danish column *has* advanced within a short distance of the city; and in
the direct road to Holstein, sits at this moment a
suspicious-looking vidette, pistol in hand, prohibiting all entry into the Danish dominions. It begins
also to be believed, that Vandamme, with a French
column, is already within a league or two of us;
and thus, that we are to be cooped up between
Danes and French. It is now announced that the
senate is dissolved, and is flying, or has fled; and
finally, that a proclamation is about to be issued,
declaring the surrender of the city.

Noon.—The proclamation has at length appeared; it is brief, and simply recommends that the
people shall be peaceable, " as the Danish troops
are coming to take possession of the city for the
French Emperor." The uproar has begun again upon
this, and all is rage, sorrow, and confusion. But the
execrations fall chiefly on the head of the Danes,
who, as their neighbours, and almost their countrymen, certainly might have acted a more determined
part. But, after all, what can be expected from
those little, trembling governments, which live only

by clinging to the greater powers; a limpet on the bottom of a ship might as well claim voluntary motion. A single act of decision, a single syllable on the part of the Danish government, would clearly have saved a vast quantity of wretchedness to a great allied community, have prevented the beggary and exile of thousands, and what is sure to follow,—instant merciless plunder, and a long course of savage insolence and extortion. But nothing has been able to shake the steady loyalty of the Dane to the stronger side.

The French *are* at hand; and all who are not inclined to fall into their power, are already leaving the city. Numbers of women and children had been sent away, since the times grew more menacing; but now the principal families, and peculiarly those who have made themselves obnoxious by their patriotism,—a character which applies to nearly all,—are pouring through the gates. The disbanded burgher-guard, who, in the French estimate, are all guilty of high treason to the majesty of the sword, have covered the roads since morning, and are taking their way, by hundreds, to join the Hanseatic legion; which is said to have gone somewhere up the Elbe with the Russians; or are going to Lubec, where many of them have commercial or personal connexions.

If those people, with all their worldly interests left behind, feel that it is time to fly; what am I, whose whole interest consists in a few shirts, and a few shillings, that I should stay to drop into the clutch of the gendarmes, and spend the rest of my years in Verdun.

Still, the locomotive spirit is not upon me. The enemy are not yet in *battalia* before the gates; the last paroxysm of the struggle is not come; and I have a feeling, half curiosity perhaps, half sympathy for an honest, brave, and patriotic commonwealth, profligately assailed, and still more profligately betrayed, that keeps me lingering to the last paroxysm. As a stranger, I can have no right to take upon me the blood of strangers in a stranger's quarrel. But if I possessed the right of a native, I know no more seemly way in which a man might take the chances of the field; and none in which he might less regret the expenditure of life and means, than in assisting to avert the fate, or sharing the final calamity of a manly and devoted people.

CHAPTER XXXIV.

RATZEBURG.

JUNE 2.—WE are so far on our way to Pomerania. Hamburgh was no longer tenable, and we left it late enough to entitle us to all the honours that delay could give. Exiles continue crowding along the road; and I have just been listening to the latest news from a party, who having nothing better to do for the evening, have gone into the gardens of the hotel to kill the time by pistol practice, perhaps at the effigy of Napoleon.

Their news decides the point of the occupation of Hamburgh. The Danes first took possession of some of the gates, within half an hour after I had taken my farewell view of the ramparts; but it was not till towards evening that the French appeared. They were chiefly battalions of conscripts, young, scarcely disciplined, and but little fitted for the fatigues of the campaign in Upper Saxony; if a judgment were to be formed from their jaded look after the few hours' march which brought them from Ochsenwerder.

The first to suffer from the victors, was the *Correspondenten*, which has undergone another of the changes of its parti-coloured existence. It now figures as " The Journal of the Department of the Mouths of the Elbe;" for the French cannot endure to leave any thing on earth as they found it. From a cap to a constitution, they have the true milliner's propensity to pull every thing to pieces, merely to put it together again in their own way; a fretful eagerness for change. The old *Correspondenten* has learnt its new language rapidly; it tells its masters' story perfectly *à la Francaise*.

Hamburgh, May 30.—" Yesterday, a brisk fire of small arms was heard all day; and we soon were informed that the French had forced the passes, and were in pursuit of the enemy in the direction of Boitzenburg. Towards evening we saw several battalions enter the city; they took possession of the market place and several of the gates."

May 31.—" Not a moment has passed to-day without our seeing French troops enter the city. At four in the afternoon, their Excellencies the Marshal Prince of Eckmuhl, Governor, and Lieutenant-General Vandamme, reviewed thirty-five battalions of infantry.

" The inhabitants could not recover from their astonishment. It would be difficult to determine what surprised them most; the fine appearance, or the number of the troops. There is indeed a vast difference between what they have before their eyes, and the stories that have been told them of the physical and numerical weakness of those battalions.

" We shall soon give some details of the conduct and manners of the adventurers who have just left us. Those cities which, like ours, have had the misfortune to have those *deliverers* within their walls, know too well how much their presence has cost them. The Russians had just time to save themselves; and were, luckily for us, not able to follow their usual practice of burning and destroying.

" One hundred and seventy pieces of cannon

have been found in the arsenal, and nearly eighty
on the walls. All the establishments are in the
best condition. The works that have been erected
to make Hamburgh a place of arms, are very
considerable; all the officers are astonished at
them, and consider Hamburgh now as a fortress."

My own movements are easily detailed. Immediately on leaving Hamburgh, I went to one of
the little villages in the outskirts, where I expected
to find a conveyance across the frontier. But there
the news had arrived before me, and conveyance
there was none. A German gentleman, on whose
guidance I had depended, was gone some hours
before into Holstein, to escape the French gens-
darmes; I was now left to my own resources; and
my next inquiry was, where horses were to be
hired. The location was easily found, but there
were no horses; it being the practice of the peasantry, on the first sound of an enemy's march, to
fly with their horses to some covert, where they lie
hid until the chance of seizure has passed by; and
the German peasant has had so much experience of this system of robbery, that the first symp-

toms of an enemy put him completely on the alert. The horses were all gone.

But still, as a march through a country to me as unknown as the polar circle, was a measure not to be undertaken, while any hope of better things remained; I inquired whether there were any English gentleman residing in the neighbourhood; as through his influence, and paying tenfold the regular hire, I possibly might effect something. But here again I was unlucky. There was no English gentleman within leagues. But a passing peasant told me that there was an American gentleman, who might be of some use. I was not disposed to draw any distinctions, and to the American gentleman I turned. I had not far to go, for he had been standing within a few feet of me, at the door of his villa. He was connected in some official way with his republic, and if she be polite, I must acknowledge that he was but an unworthy representative. He was a short, thick, supercargo-looking fellow, with that peculiar expression of countenance for which pig-headedness is the only name. My difficulty was stated in a few words; his answer was given in fewer still. With his hands stuffed into the pockets of his pantaloons, and his hat pulled over his vulgar brows, he succinctly told me that " he knew nothing about horses, and could be of no use in the business."

It is possible that fear might have had as much to do with his answer as natural barbarism, for any service to an English subject at that time might have been marked, and I have uniformly found that the same circumstances which awake the courage and civility of an educated mind, turn to fear in a vulgar one. But another American was there, to redeem the honours of his country; a tall, pale, mild-looking young man, who had come up during our short dialogue, and who, on its ending, addressed me, and in a gentlemanlike tone and manner, offered his services. He held some situation under the diplomat, and would have been a very advantageous model for his principal to copy. We sallied forth among the huts without delay, and by his persuasion an old carrier was melted into the confession that he had once a cart and a horse, which, on my promising him a hire, that in other times would have purchased the fee simple of the peasant himself, he " thought he could find."

The young American urged him to the search; both horse and cart were fortunately discovered. I threw my portmanteau in; by the help of a bundle of straw furnished the rough vehicle, and with the thanks to my new friend, which his civility fully deserved, set forward, shelterless, seatless, and springless, on my journey; defying hussars, chasseurs, league on league of fiery sand, and an atmosphere blazing with the fiercest sun of summer.

But my adventure was but beginning. We trotted on spiritedly for awhile, and roamed away among the bushy roads and sandy dells, so long, that I concluded we were fairly out of the jurisdiction of Hamburgh; when, to my surprise, on labouring up a little ascent, I saw the steeples of the city almost directly before me. I addressed a rather angry remonstrance to my driver, who simply shook his yellow locks, and trotted down another road, which seemed to lie in the opposite quarter. But, after another half hour's trotting, another ascent brought us up within nearly the same distance of the steeples as before. Serious anger was thrown away on the old fool, who, besides his being a German carter, which implies the most imprac-

ticable obstinacy under the sky, was probably unable to comprehend my eloquent efforts in the
national language. The situation was a sufficiently
perplexing one. Nothing could be more certain
than that the French were on their way to the city;
for such was now the outcry of every body whom we
met hurrying along the roads; and it was equally
certain that if we continued thus making the circle
of the city, gyrating and flourishing within a mile
of the ramparts, we must fall into the midst of
some of their corps at last. Whether the old carrier were more fool or knave, puzzled out of all his
senses, or calculating the merits with his new masters of giving up a prisoner to them, a stray sheep
from their iron fold; began to raise some doubts in
my mind, and, as a last experiment, I ordered him
to stop, and let me take my way by myself. Columns of dust were by this time rising above the
trees, the sure sign of the march of troops below;
and the air was a various and growing jangle of all
clamours, the creaking of wheels, and from time to
time, the clang of a musket, or the sound of drum
and bugle. It was evident that further deliberation would be out of place, and I was on the point

of leaving my vehicle to its fortunes; when the old man, with the fear of losing his florins strongly before his eyes, importuned me to trust to him for the next five minutes. The florins had certainly sharpened his organ of direction, for he now flogged his horse into a new road, which speedily took us clear of the city. With rejoicing I saw the ramparts sink down into green lines, the steeples diminish to threads, the columns of dust float away into vapours, and heard the clang of the marching battalions, if such they were, fainter and fainter borne away upon the breeze, until it was superseded by the thrushes and robins in the hawthorns, heavy with blossom, that shadowed the road.

But in this land of soldiership, who can count upon escape from military contact? While I was revelling in full security, and indulging my landscape-loving habits in a long range of the valley of the Elbe, which a rise of the road afforded; I was surprised by a sudden confusion of all kinds of sounds full in front, tenfold the former clamour; a huge trampling of hoofs, creaking of waggons, and rolling of gun-carriages; echoes which the ear in times like these acquires a rapid acuteness in dis-

tinguishing. To turn my equipage out of the road
was hopeless, for there was but one; and the alternative must have been a gallop through a succession of fosses and thickets. Besides, a manœuvre
of this order must have brought the eyes of every
man in the coming force upon us ; and the consequence must be capture. So, as next to a successful battle is the honour of a skilful retreat, I
declined the chances of a contest with perhaps ten
thousand bayonets,—for they made noise enough
for the full amount,—got out of the cart, and desir-
ing its old driver, who, as a peasant, could be in no
hazard, to wait for my return ; marched into the
forest without beat of drum. From behind a
thicket I scientifically reconnoitred the advance of
the enemy. They turned out to be *not* French, but
Danes; a huge, long-winded column of baggage and
guns, escorted by cavalry ; and all ordering, shouting, execrating, and bellowing, enough for an
army of fifty thousand men. They were hurrying
to Hamburgh : and they moved on, magnified, like
Homer's gods, in volumes of dusty cloud, that seemed
not unlikely to choke the whole expedition. Yet
Danes, though they were, a rencontre with them

might have had its inconveniences ; for the Danish troops had orders to stop every one whom they met leaving Hamburgh. However, the dust which rendered the road nearly invisible, or possibly the reluctance of the honest Danes, (for their northern blood, if it be chill, is honest,) to do more mischief to their unfortunate neighbours than they could help, saved the wanderers on the road, who had not time to get out of their way ; and I have not heard of their offering offence to any of the multitude.

When this whirlwind had past, I rejoined my cart, which I found still standing where I had left it. The old man had probably given me and the florins up for lost; for he was charmed by our return together, lashed his horse with new vigour, and we went off at a round pace, through a width and waste of sands that might have given no bad conception of the great Zahara.

After about an hour of this travel we reached the confines of one of those nameless divisions of empire which cut up Germany into sovereignties of square miles. I forget the name of the monarch, but at the entrance of his dominions we were met by the sight of bayonets again. A corps

had just marched up to the gate across the road,
where it halted.   But their plump German visages
soon told me that there was no necessity for further circumspection, and we passed them without
difficulty.   They were a company of Prussian
sharpshooters, pushed forward to watch the French.
They were all very young men, and appeared terribly exhausted by their march; they looked half
suffocated with dust and heat.

But now, at least, we were in the land of friends,
we were on the right side of belligerency, and I
desired my charioteer to drive to the first inn which
he could find.

Still the symptoms of war were every where
round us. As we passed along, the distant summits
of the heights commanding the Elbe were tipt with
videttes, a solitary hussar, or sometimes two together, sitting on their horses, crowning the outline
of the hill, like statues against the sky; a curious
and even a picturesque sight, if the " bitter business" of the time could leave room for such specula-
tion.   Along the valley I saw, or imagined I saw,
the movement of troops, by the occasional sparkle
of steel.   But there was a less equivocal evidence

of war, in an enormous blaze, that rose up in broad red sheets, from the conflagration of some village or town a few miles distant, throwing volumes of yellow cloud over the sky, like the crater of a new volcano.

At last we drew up at an inn door, one of those huge, roomy, and gloomy old piles, which still characterise the German roads. But war, or the fear of war, had been here already; and the landlord, with a humiliated countenance, and a profusion of bows, acknowledged that there was not a dinner " for a gentleman" in the house. But all things are good or ill by comparison. Bread and beer were to be got; and those were enjoyments not to be made light of, after a twenty miles flight and fever under a sky that rivalled the torrid zone. They were ordered on the spot; and I never remember to have made a more luxurious banquet. The " *omnia recipiuntur, juxta modum recipientis,*" is true to the letter in matters of taste, whatever it may be in philosophy. No lord mayor of London in the plenitude of his power, no satrap of the west end with the luxuries of half a world squeezed into essences for his table, ever enjoyed his three hours' epicurism with half the zest of my homely entertainment, in the wide, wild room, that let in every wind of heaven round me, and looked, with its grim, smoke-coloured effigies, like a vault of the inquisition.

I am much disposed to question whether any man in civilized life *ever* knows what eating and drinking are. The Englishman, with his five meals a day, certainly precludes himself from all knowledge on the subject. Nature and the Frenchman are at variance for ever; he *can* know nothing of it; his *Almanach des Gourmands* is the direct antipodes to it. The whole continental *cuisine* would have felt flat, stale, and earthly, to the nectar and ambrosia of this Saxon alehouse; and it will be universally found that the grand secret of *gusto* is fatigue and famine, procured by twenty miles forced march over burning sands, and under a burning sun.

I fell into conversation with the landlord on the state of affairs in his neighbourhood. He was a fat, good humoured looking serf, perfectly willing to speak, but with sagacity enough to know the awkwardness of speaking his whole mind, while the

French were within cannon-shot; and nothing could be more guarded than the way in which he contrived to tell me that he wished them fairly in Erebus. This was done not by words, but by indescribable twistings of the countenance, and writhings of the frame; and for even the candour of those I conceive myself indebted to the incurably British accent of my French.

But the times had worked their effect on him too, and no French cosmopolite could speak of events in a more nonchalant tone. " The Messieurs," said he, pointing to their quarters on the opposite side of the river, " have been our neighbours here already, and they will be so again. They will be over here by and by; the Prussians will retire; and the whole will be but *une affaire d'une demi heure !"*

Upon this *demi heure* might depend the extinction of himself, or at least the plundering, and very probably the burning of his house, if the Prussians made any resistance. But the contingencies, formidable as they were, had no alarms for this philosopher of custom. Plunder and burning were

every day matters, and they had lost their pun-
gency.

The old carrier here left me. The sight of the
Prussians had startled him with fears of having his
horse and cart pressed into the patriotic service; and,
if they must be seized, he preferred the French capture, which would keep them in the neighbourhood
of his own village; to the Prussian, which might
march them off to Upper Saxony, Silesia, or the
world's end. We arranged our pecuniary affairs to
his satisfaction, and I let him go.

Yet I soon found that this had been a premature
civility; for, on applying to my cosmopolite after
dinner for horses, he answered me with a smile,
" that he was infinitely sorry, but to find a horse
in the vicinity was absolutely impossible." The
horses had all taken to flight from both French and
Prussian. The intelligence was embarrassing, for
to remain in the inn till next morning would have
been " *mauvaise tactique.*" I remembered the
demi heure, and it would have been more than folly
to wait for the result. A party of Hamburgh exiles passed at the moment on foot, and I joined

them : and in this way we marched along till night-fall, in the direction of Mecklenburg.

I have seldom more enjoyed an excursion. I was in full health and activity. I could have walked for ever. The lightness of the air was delightful. A sense of vigour and elasticity breathed through the frame with every inspiration. When I set out the day was declining, and the transition from the fiery atmosphere and the Hamburgh sands to the cool gushes of evening, made still cooler by the fragrance from the long ranges of low forest and rich pasture through which the road lay, was a new sensation. We were now beyond the reach of any thing but a pursuit of balloons; and, though the peasantry were gathered at the doors of the village post-houses with stories of " a many thousand war-like French," and they were in momentary expec-tation of being fleeced by some of their foraging cavalry, we saw nothing more warlike than ploughmen and milkmaids, for the rest of the day. At length nightfall brought us to a cluster of large stone houses, too undistinguished for a name; where we procured beds. The beds were of the most primitive order, but a twenty miles' walk had rendered us superior to any fastidiousness on the point. The difference between flock and eider-down will be found to depend altogether upon the mode of spending the previous twelve hours. To a man tired enough to sleep upon the pavement, the flock bed is Elysium; and so I found it: I flung myself under my canopy, and, spite of politics and persecution, instantly forgot Napoleon, the Danes, the pursuing hussars, and mankind.

The route to-day has been followed under still easier circumstances: one of our party had obtained a large travelling carriage, in which we gallantly made our way, less like fugitives than gentlemen tourists. Our road lay along the edge of Holstein, that sacred territory which we dared not tread, but which, from the fragments of it within our glance, appeared not much worth treading. The country round us to the horizon was hedgeless and comfortless.

On the continent, every thing that constitutes the life, activity, or even the rural beauty of the soil, gathers into the immediate neighbourhood of cities; the country withers at a distance; she is nurtured alone by her closeness to the town: in

Burke's famous phrase, the daughter "applies her
youthful exuberance to the lips of her exhausted
parent." A league beyond the suburbs of even
the principal cities of the continent, the country,
unlike the perpetual and diffusive luxuriance of
England, grows arid and meagre; vast solitudes
spread over the horizon; a few villages, half ruined,
dotting the plains at wide intervals, enhance the
general aspect of decay; and, but for the passing of
an occasional post waggon, or a dragoon galloping with despatches, the stranger would be disposed
to think that life had departed from the land.
But at length a golden point twinkles at a distance
on the ground, rising like a new-born star; this is
the cathedral spire; other gleams succeed of other
spires; the traveller is approaching a city. Smaller
divisions of the fields, marked by the diversities of
cultivation, begin to colour the landscape; straggling cottages cling to the road; the forest becomes
a grove, the thicket is reduced into a garden; a few
country houses peep out from elms and poplars;
the various rude vehicles of the citizens and peasantry are met on the highways; life thickens up
to the gates. The city is entered; the long, rough,

o 4

rambling streets are crossed; the gates are opened again; every furlong onward makes some deduction from the humanity of the suburb scene, until the fatal league is completed, and we stretch away into the wilderness once more.

Towards noon, the road turned from the melancholy flats of Holstein towards the south, and we passed through some of the appanages of the Mecklenburgh dukedom. The country here, less exposed to the north winds, and considerably varied by the undulations of the ground, exhibited more general fertility. A fine old forest covered us from the sun for an hour's drive; and we then halted to rest the horses at a large, lonely village, which seemed to have grown up with the forest. Every thing in the north of Germany gives an aboriginal impression: the houses are worthy of the first experimentalists in the axe and hammer, and equally worthy of a time when ground was of no value, and the trees of the forest were the property of the first hewer of wood and drawer of water, who would take the trouble to cut them down. The stable of the inn, into which our horses were turned in a drove, to seek their fortune, might have made a riding-house for a regiment of Hulans; and the waste of space, timber, and labour, implied that they all were nothing in the period when this inordinate wooden cavern was reared. This was a considerable village, on a high road; yet except a few loiterers at the inn door, inhabitants there seemed none; or, if there were any, they were probably asleep. Existence stagnates in this country, and the foreigner's three resources are sleep, smoking, and suicide.

But even in this spot, which to all human vision might defy war, on the principle of the " *Cantabit vacuus*," for there was nothing to rob; we found a Prussian patrole, headed by a showy officer, a tall, handsome hero, who came forward to us, pipe in hand, of course, and exchanged civilities. News from Hamburgh, or from any other corner of the world, would have been a prodigious kindness to any man immersed in this slough of despond; but to the Prussian our's had a double interest, as connected with the movements of the French, whose hussars, from the national alertness of the enemy, were every where expected to be soon spreading themselves through the country. In return, we asked for news of our tardy friend, his highness the Crown Prince. The subject was probably an interdicted one. He smiled, and began to talk of the weather.

After some hours' pleasant driving through fragments of forest, and meadows prettily undulated, we at length caught a glance of the Ratzeburg Lake, spreading its lazy and boatless length in the evening sun; here we touched on the dominions of two potentates, or perhaps of three at once: we alighted in the territory of the "Senate and People of Lubec," supped in the domain of Saxe Lauenburg; and shall lay our heads on the pillow under the protection of the Duke of Mecklenburgh. If my topography be wrong, let those who impose on the innocence of travellers bear the blame. The allegiance of the Ratzeburghers must have often found itself a little perplexed in earlier days; but now France and the allies extinguish all the nicer questions. Napoleon is the grand *Ductor Dubitantium* in cases of political scruple; the little sovereignties are hushed like mice in the presence of the paramount lord of claw and whisker; their " metaphysic" claims are swept away, like cobwebs, from the rafters and crevices of the " *Grande Systeme Continental*;" the bayonet is the moralist, the *Code Napoleon* supplies the conscience; and every man hies him to his pillow with but one rejoicing, that he carries his head along with him at night; and one care, that he may find it still on his shoulders by morning.

The town chimes are ringing sweet and silvery over the lake; the lake is slumbering in long reaches of grey and crimson, the last reflection of a lovely sky; the buz of the emigrants coming into the town is subsiding; the breeze comes sleeping through the low groves that fringe the waters; and all the world seems sinking into a Midsummer Night's Dream.

CHAPTER XXXV.

———

POMERANIA.

WE rose early, and saluted the sun as he was coming up, with his chariot wheels fresh glittering from the waters of the Baltic. Ratzeburg had nothing to detain us, and our four strong German horses soon left it low in the horizon. The road was through sand, yet it was firm and smooth, and we whirled along, with the Baltic spreading blue and broad on our left; and a vast plain, rudely cultivated, chiefly with corn, spreading before us, and brightening under the sun. There is no sensation more delightful than that of travelling, under certain circumstances; even in smoothness and rapidity of motion there is a pleasure; the mind is rolled into a state of half reverie, which, without preventing its indulgence in all passing things, sheathes it from all irritation. Our carriage was a

barouche,—unwieldy, old, and which would have
stirred up the supreme scorn of the Kent or west-
ern road; but it was roomy, convenient, and pad-
ded and pocketed sufficiently to have soothed the
nerves and appetites of a much more sensitive
party than its present inmates. It held six, and
it was now, "without o'erflowing, full." The rest
of the panegyric might have been fairly given, the
party, chiefly Germans, being remarkably good-
humoured, unobtrusive, and yet conversible. For
once, Teutchland was not the sole topic; nor the
pipe, the abominable pipe, the sole refuge from
silence. For they could be silent; and the rarity of
this capital qualification, on the Continent, makes
it invaluable where it is to be found. The original
malediction of the foreigner is restlessness; he lives
under an anathema of perpetually doing something.
His governments, and his nature, alike make him an
idler,—I speak not of the few exceptions,—and the
misery of his idleness is to be made endurable only
by eternal trivialities. The Gaul thus chatters
away his understanding; the German smokes and
mysticizes; the whole south of Europe vainly ab-
sorbs itself in sonnetteering, scandal, and maca-

roni. The Englishman is the only individual in existence, who can sit still when he has nothing to do; and hold his tongue, when he has nothing to say; and limitless praise be to him for both. To this pitiful propensity, worthy only of a forest of baboons, is due the theatre and coffee-house haunting spirit, that utterly *un*-domesticates foreign life; a vast quantity of the vice,—for foreign life is intolerably vicious,—and the incalculable waste of the energies, talents, and opportunities, which Providence has given as largely here as elsewhere, but given in vain. To this is due the opera and ballet-fever, the frenzy into which a dancer or a singer throws the public for a hundred square leagues, noble and gentle, prince and plebeian; all crowding for fifty nights together, to see a profligate from Paris, who stands on her toe half a minute longer than all other profligates from Paris; or a syren from Milan or Naples, who eclipses all the violins, and all the vices, of her native hot-bed.

Napoleon has been of service to mankind in his generation, paradoxical as it may seem; he has given this idle swarm something to do. His seizure of the young patricians for his guards of honour, which were nothing but troops of hostages, and which hostages he straightway converted into campaigners; abstracted thousands from the billiard-rooms, the cafés, and the smoking clubs, which, in other days, would have described the whole circle of their existence. The allies infused the same stimulus, *bon gré, mal gré*, into as many thousands on the opposite side; and the result of this involuntary co-operation for the good of Germany is, already, to have thrown a colour of manliness over the pursuits of a considerable number, whose destination was otherwise fixed for nonentities, and who would have been fluttering after the *gens des coulisses*, handling a billiard cue, or dancing mazurkas and polonaises, to the last hour of their last decrepitude.

With those Sybarites the Napoleon regimen was salutary; rather rough, it must be allowed, for the nerves of opera loungers; but incomparably adapted to make them feel that the world was not altogether strewed with velvet and roses; he sent them to drill without delay. Every hero of them rubbed his own horse's heels; the brush and the broom were flourished in hands, of which their owners were once too chary, to submit them to the moon. In garrison they ministered to themselves as well as they might; but, in the field, they took the common chances of soldiership: and no army that ever took the field since the days of Jenghis Khan, trusted to those chances so much as the French; the republican anti-provision principle clinging to Napoleon to this hour. For tents, magazines, waggons, every thing but the actual ball and bayonet, the French armies still trust to the enemy's army or the enemy's country; and when the country is stripped to the nerves, and the army has carried its baggage clear off with it, the French soldier sleeps under the canopy of heaven, and eats grass, his horse, or his comrade. The young guardsmen thus foraged for themselves, plundered for themselves, and fought for themselves; the original law of substitution was completely in abeyance; and their proudest were common dragoons.

But this discipline had its benefits; it redeemed them from the diseased and languid life of utter indolence; it gave them health and vigour, in place of the perpetual sickliness of epicurism; it trained the wan and feeble shoot of opulent degeneracy into a bold and thriving plant; it made the plethoric, pursy and short-breathed son of intemperance a hardy and sinewy figure. It even sharpened the intellect, by employing it; and in the course of two or three campaigns exhibited its work in squadrons, with cheeks of camp bronze, hands fit for either bridle or sword, frames practised and toiled into gallant proportion, and understandings quickened to all the exigencies of their situation; the soldier, as the soldier ought to be.

And on those squadrons, if a turn of fortune should come, will be raised the independence of Germany. They serve unwillingly at this moment, and if the French should make the slightest retrograde step, not a man will follow. They will turn their horses' heads towards their own sovereignties, and be the leaders in the national war. Napoleon has, in fact, committed a prodigious oversight in employing them at all. But all his policy is of the same character. The expedient is made for the hour; and at the hour's end his genius is to be shown in inventing another for the next; all is temporary, headlong, desperate. With him policy rejects the finest of all its elements, and the only one

that entitles policy to rank among the achieve-
ments of the understanding—prescience. But this
is national; the Frenchman's rack and red-hot pin-
cers is *ennui*. The temptation of his fiend is by
fear, not love. He must be stimulated, even though
he be stung. He must have variety, and the can-
tharides and corrosive sublimate of variety. His
spirit is theatrical, and he must have perpetual
scene-shifting. His cutting off his king's head was
not half so much from cruelty, as the love of a scene.
Nothing delights him so much as an event without
a discoverable cause; it is a *coup de théatre!* He
was the natural inventor of the balloon,—showy use-
lessness, brilliant indirection, a tossing among the
storms, a flight at fifty miles an hour, and a conclusion in a thunder-clap. Life is happiness to him
only as it is a convulsion. Napoleon himself, in
that true appreciation of character, which belongs
to his sagacity; and in that graceless style which
Jacobinism has made a national language; has been
heard to say, " I am like the devil; never happy,
but when I have something on my hands." To me
it is utterly surprising, that a Frenchman should
ever plant any tree but a poplar, or build any habi-

tation but a wigwam. In the whole system of Napoleon's administration, I strongly doubt, if a single principle could be found, calculated, *mero motu,* to live a twelvemonth. But the man and the system are made for his sky-rocket people. Give them the flash, the explosion, the brilliant impossibility, the attempt to scale the heavens, and all is done. The sudden downfall is nothing, or perhaps even adds to their rapture. A revolution, a new government, a yearly war, those are the phantoms, which, whatever necromancer will raise, they will worship; and at the same time put their necks under the heel of the necromancer !

We are now housed in Wismar, a little, demure town, which looks as remote from the ways of the world, as if it were planted in Siberia. But this, it must be told, is not the period to see it in its living point of view. Wismar, from one end to the other, is but a large corn-warehouse, and the warehouse is now empty; the farmers in this portion of the Baltic shore making it a depôt for their produce until the season for shipment; and the

depôt having been cleared since the last season,
and now waiting to be filled by the harvest that is
spreading in green billows to the foot of the Silesian hills. The inhabitants, few and idle, live
in the lower floors, the upper are uniformly corn-
lofts. The whole atmosphere is poisoned with the
smell of musty straw. I had no conception that
the innocent corn could be perverted into any thing
so repulsive. Every thing eatable, drinkable, or
visible, is saturated with this heavy and sickening
effluvium. The few inhabitants, I have said, are
idle, but they are not unoccupied; for all day long
they are cracking whips; like the rest of their generation, they find it impossible to be quiet. And
they commence their battle at an early hour: to
my misfortune, I have heard them cracking their
whips since three this morning; and practice has
unluckily made them so perfect, that their whips
produce an explosion little less than a musquet-
shot. A legion of clowns have been thus cheering their heavy hours, parading the streets, with
the effect of platoon firing. The whole population
are probably qualifying for carters, and so far the
practice has merit. But they drive all sleep from

every spot in Wismar, except, perhaps, the church-yard.

———

Yet desolate as this place is, I saw, with the wonder suited to such a phenomenon, an English carriage drive up to the inn-door. As all intelligence from home has some value, whatever be the conveyancer; and as I have none of the usual horror of my countrymen abroad,—that curious, centrifugal force, which drives asunder men who are the fittest companions for each other, whether abroad or at home—I was about to make my approaches; when I saw issuing from the vehicle a warrior, in full costume, Prussian cap, belted coat, and sabre swinging by the side ; fierce and foreign from top to toe ! This was an apparition too formidable to be carelessly ventured upon; and I paused. But on a second glance, the symptoms of heroism were not quite satisfactory. There was a clumsiness in the style of carrying his honours, an *embarras* in the sabre, and even something like a colour of shame and sheepishness in the cheek, as he caught my eye; that argued a novice in the glorious trade.

The problem was soon solved. I recollected in this Tamerlane a young Londoner, whose only campaigns, past, present, and to come, belonged to the counting-house. How he had gained his right to come in such a questionable shape; thus—

> ——————— " in complete steel,
> Revisiting the glimpses of the sun,
> Making day hideous ;"

what court had signed his commission, and sent this fearful personage forth to walk the world in terrorem, and frighten his Prussian Majesty's liege women and children, I had not fortitude enough to inquire; nor do I believe he would have much relished the inquiry, for it was evident that he instantly recognized my look of wonder; and his movement into the hotel proved that he had already attained one step in the science of war—that of making a rapid retreat. I saw no more of the coxcomb.

This propensity to strut in borrowed plumage is the especial heirdom of folly in all corners of the continent. The Parisian *Pekin*, the hero of the Parisian Cockaigne, burlesqued as he is for measuring his tapes and threads in moustaches terrible to the eye, and clanking round his counters in spurs that might stimulate a dromedary, spreads his imitators far and wide; and Europe abounds with tremendous Hulans and ignivomous hussars, who have never wielded more steel than was contained in their shears.

I wish that the country which I love and honour, and which, the more I see of others, I only love and honour the more, had not its *M. Calicots* too. But the passion for military titles, though held by the most invisible thread; the fervour of volunteer and militia men for being called majors and colonels, *coute qu'il coute*, when their largest campaign has been a field-day in midsummer, and their severest service escorting the wives and daughters of their native aldermen home after a ball, sometimes makes John Bull, with all his manliness, a little ridiculous, even at home. In England, however, this fervour seldom breaks out further than on the visage of some precocious apprentice; but John Bull, once turned loose on the continent, is deplorably apt to become an ape. The jaws are suddenly covered with a forest of hair, that might qualify him for a high place in the synagogue; the plain honest broadcloth of his country is manœuvred over with a labyrinth of braiding; the brass-heeled boots and dragoon spur mark him down for a man of war; and he has attained the triumph of his existence, when he has attained the possibility of his being mistaken for a Prussian or Austrian deserter.

Some odd incidents have arisen in consequence. In one of the Italian cities, the Austrian commandant's attention being drawn to the multitude of *militaires,* whom he found suddenly overflowing his streets; ordered an inquiry into the nature of their respective rights to terrify him. His inquiries, however, produced nothing, except that Turk or Tartar never displayed more exuberant moustaches than the individuals in question. His whole staff were " perplexed in the extreme;" they could make nothing of captains and generals of the Wimbledon-Common fusileers, the Cheapside chasseurs, or the Royal Pimlico rangers. The commandant at last struck upon an expedient worthy of more than Austrian sagacity: he swore by Thor and Woden, "that though he could not make them fight, he would make them shave." The order was promulgated, that no man, unless in some actual military rank, should be permitted to walk the streets in moustaches. It had the most miraculous effect. Like Albuquerque's whiskers, the disparagement to their upper lips would have been worse than death, and the greater number of the warriors ordered post horses, and fled from the claws of this tonsorial tyrant without delay. A few, relying on Austrian tardiness, remained. They were seized, shorn without mercy, and sent into the world with clean chins and broken hearts. But the operation was effective in more points than one: the razor, like Dalilah's scissors, extinguished the belligerent propensity in them for life; the warlike principle was fairly cut out; and some of them returned to their country, wiser, if sadder, men.

But a cleverer personage than any commandant that Austria ever produced, Napoleon himself, was sorely beset by a similar perplexity. At his levees, during the peace of Amiens, his chamberlains spent the day in perpetual wonder at the multitude of military poured out by peace-loving England, the *nation boutiquiere;* and in laughter and agony at

their own attempts to master the remorseless barbarism of their innumerable names. Local militia,
army of reserve, volunteers royal and loyal, and
volunteers neither the one nor the other, deluged his
halls, trampled down his field-marshals, and nearly
suffocated the little wonder of the world himself.
The Tuilleries was a blaze of scarlet and bullion;
Where most chose their own commissions, all
might choose their own costume :—all is legitimate
in an enemy's country. Sometimes, in his astonishment, he attempted to talk to them; but patriotism
like theirs disdained to know any tongue but their
own, and he was baffled. He once observed a huge
hero of this calibre stalking with a sabre that out-
clanked the whole drawing-room. Napoleon inquired,
who was the man-mountain? No one knew. He
then approached, and with his most gracious smile,
(and no man can put on a more gracious one) asked
him " from what part of the world he came?"
" De Tipperary!" was the Stentor's answer. The
little Corsican started back at the sound, as if a
bomb had exploded at his feet; collapsed into himself, shrank away, and asked no more questions
for the levee.

Occasional intelligence from unfortunate Hamburgh arrives. The emigration on the first day was immense, amounting to some thousands, perhaps five or six thousand people, of the best of every class. But, as the French battalions began to fill the city, this efflux was stopped, and there was an extreme difficulty in escape. A gentleman with whom I have just had some conversation, was among the last who came away. Some unavoidable affairs had detained him until late in the day; and when at length he hurried through them, and came into the streets, he found that the face of things was changed: every spot was crowded with tired Frenchmen, and the streets rang to the galloping of the French staff; he looked upon himself as undone!

As he was not a native of the city, and was besides well known as having no love for its new masters, Verdun or the scaffold flashed him in the face. Still, like a wise man, he determined to try fortune to the end, got into his tilbury, and boldly drove to the nearest gate. Whether the general order had not yet reached that gate, or the guard were tired, or were drunk, he luckily found no obstruction there. For a moment his heart beat quick, while the yawning corporal stopped him, and asked one or two vague questions; but the conference passed over; the *détenu* bowed with gratitude, never felt before to a soldier of Napoleon; the *vieux moustache* ordered him away with a rough wave of the hand; he drove off delighted, and, like the Lady of the Lake's parting sign—

" Never did his bosom swell,
  As at that *simple, mute* farewell."

In such a place as this, what is to be done but quote verses or make them, *more Teutonico?* Our English translators are bitterly complained of by the Germans, as giving the original material a fashionable coat, a birth-day suit, which affronts the German poetic soul to the lowest depth of its irritabilities. They demand that we should either let their verses alone, or deliver them in the original garb, in their wolfskin state; they demand the ore, as some bold son of the marsh might have smelted it in his rugged brain, and then delivered it out among the clashing of Cheruscan shields for general circulation. The following lines are close to the original in measure, meaning, and almost in words—a study of translation.

SIR HARO'S BRIDAL.

'Twas late, Sir Haro rode away,
To bid the guests to his wedding-day.
When, as he passed the woodland green,
A troop of elfin sprites was seen;
The erl-king's daughter led the band;
She tendered the knight her lily hand;
And, " Welcome, Sir Knight, what haste?" said she;
" Come, join our ranks, and dance with me."—
" I may not dance, I may not stay,
For to-morrow is my wedding-day."

" Nay, come, Sir Haro, and dance with me,
And these golden spurs I'll give to thee;
And a shirt of silk, all costly and white,
That my mother bleach'd in the pale moonlight;
And a ring that, weal or woe betide,
Will bring thee to thy lady-bride;
And a sword, in tournay or in field,
That none shall stand with lance or shield."—
" I may not dance, I must not stay,
For to-morrow is my wedding-day."

" Nay, come, Sir Haro, and dance with me,
And this golden chain I'll give to thee."—
" Your chain, fair maid, would bind a vow:
I must not listen to you now."—

" Come, dance, Sir Haro, if your eye
Would not behold a maiden die.
Come, dance, Sir Knight, unless your heart
Is proof against a poisoned dart."—
" I may not dance, I must not stay,
For to-morrow is my wedding-day."

She struck the knight on his armed breast:
Down to the saddle stooped his crest!
She struck his foaming steed, and cried,
" Now speed thee to thy lady-bride!"
Sir Haro reached his castle gate ;
He scarcely saw his halls of state,
But faint and trembling, tottered on ;
His mother cried, " What heeds my son ?"—
" What heeds thy son ? I've seen a sight,
I've seen the forest fiends to-night."—
" Thou'rt sad, my son," his mother cried ;
" Who shall tell this tale to thy lady-bride ?"—
" I must to the forest dell be gone."—
" Dear son, thou must be back anon."—
" My lady-bride I shall never see :
She shall sleep in the forest-grave with me."

With horse and hound to the forest dell,
Where the erl-king's daughter played her spell,
Sir Haro rode with spur and speed.
But at night came back his weary steed ;

At night came back his weary hound;
But no hunter's cry the bugle wound.
But the bridal troop came bright and gay,
For this was Sir Haro's wedding-day.

The feast was spread, and the dance begun,
" Oh, lady, your knight will be here anon.
All drink to his health!" his mother cried;
And Sir Haro walked in with a warrior's stride;
And before the priest he took his stand;
And he placed the ring on his lady's hand.
But his cheek was withered to the bone,
And his lip was white, and his eye was stone,
And his bridal robe of purple and gold
Hung round him like a coffin's fold.
And that night they slept in their forest-grave:
Thus died the lovely and the brave !

CHAPTER XXXVI.

━━━

STRALSUND.

WE now rolled on through Mecklenburgh, a dreary
country, as flat as Lincolnshire; and, except for
an occasional village, as destitute of human kind
as any of its fens. We murmur at our English
taxes, but, after having made a day's journey in
this dukedom, I shall never be restive again at
any tax that is applicable to highways. It is now
summer, and a most lovely and genial summer;
but driving through the Mecklenburgh roads is
like driving through a field fresh from the plough,
with only the difference, that every new rut seems
deeper than the last, and every one is as rigid as
stone. For a vast extent to the south of the Baltic the country is a plain of sterile clay, with a
general tendency to leave the clay for sand. Labour raises corn of all kinds upon it, for the earth

is always willing, where man is industrious. But the peasantry live wretchedly. In the midst of their wheat they use a deplorable bread of rye: meat is, I believe, seldom eaten by them, if I am to judge from the rare sight of cattle; and in some instances, as Johnson would say, we supplicated even for milk, and supplicated in vain!

We were now travelling through the scene of the gallant Schill's final campaign. He is still perfectly remembered by the people; and as we passed along by some mouldering field-works in the midst of a wild, sepulchral looking plain, they were pointed out as the spot of a fierce rencontre, in which Schill, having found a French detachment, or driven it to take shelter, in the work; attacked it sword in hand, leaped into the trench on horseback, and, at the head of his hussars, took or slew every man.

This entire country was probably once at the bottom of the Baltic. The dead level, the frequent sand, the saline and rude surface, would make an excellent bottom for a great sea lake at this moment. Perhaps the change would not be serious, if the Baltic were to resume its old domain.

The villages are evidently formed on the model of a ship's hold, in every sense; and, if they were turned upside down, might make good sea-boats. The people are as evidently formed on the aquatic principle; and if the most extraordinary quantity of petticoats on the women, and pantaloons on the men, could secure their buoyancy, they might make the circumnavigation of the globe.

Yet what is all happiness but matter of taste? If the honest Mecklenburghers have no likelihood of earthly renown, they have peace; if they produce neither painter, nor poet, nor orator, nor historian, from century to century, they have excellent potatoe gardens, which they value more; if they have not glory, they have pigs; and if they are destitute of books, they have what nine-tenths of the world prefer, brandy. Even in the minor matters of life they are not left destitute; if they have but few specimens of nobility among them, they have storks in every chimney-top, whose modesty, regularity of life, and domestic virtues, may set them in general a much better example; if they have not the court fashions, they have fashions of their own scarcely less preposterous; and if they are deficient in shape

STRALSUND. 323

or grace, no population on the earth enfolds itself
in so much flannel. Withal let it be told, that
they are a remarkably good-humoured race; that
they dance and sing, marry, and are given in marriage, in a mode of their own; that the men are good
soldiers, and the women honest wives; that they
love, honour, and obey their old, odd duke; and
that they toil on their way in quiet and contentment for their ninety or a hundred years, in the
midst of dulness and ditches, that would bring a
London porter to his speedy grave.

At last we gained Rostock, a town of considerable size, but on the decline; a decaying beauty,
which no cosmetic can beautify once more. The
Baltic was the source of its prosperity, and it once
brought a lively trade up to the walls; but the
Baltic is unquestionably gliding away, and it has
left Rostock behind. Why this retrocession of the
sea should occur on the whole length of its southern shore, must be settled by the geologists, who in
these days settle every thing; and who, knowing
much better than Moses how the world was created,
may well moot the point with the surges of the
Baltic. Yet, along this shore there is a singular

P 6

dearth of rivers, to deposit alluvial matter ; earth-quakes, which blow up Messina or Naples once in the half century, and even purify Lisbon, leave the north to its misdeeds ; the Baltic is not a lake, to be sunk into pits, or evaporated into the skies ; it is not like a beleaguered town, to be starved out upon its own magazines ; it is a garrison open to peren-nial supplies ; it is a huge salt-water tank, filled at every turn of the tide.   And yet it is gradually withdrawing ; sand is daily adding to the sand of Swedish and Prussian Pomerania; ships daily shrink further and further from the shore ; and Thorn, and Dantzig, and solemn Konigsberg, and sleepy Lubec, will see their harbours turned into potatoe grounds and promenades, before they will see the Muscovite shave, or Frederic William give his Prussians a constitution.

We found Rostock under advantageous circum-stances—it was the time of the fair, and had more people wandering through its streets than it will exhibit for a twelvemonth to come. It had now even a *table d'hôte*, in which every thing had the gloss of novelty, down to the waiters and the wine.

My chief resource during the day or two that I

lingered out there, was a German book-shop, a
huge lumber-room of literature, in which wisdom
lay baled and parcelled by the hundred weight;
and, between the dust, the dimness, and the intolerable blotting-paper on which the Germans
print, and will print for ever; poring over its
shelves was a labour of some merit. Then the
drums and trumpets of the booths drew the attention. The fair was pretty, lively, and trifling,
with its usual accompaniments of puppet-shows,
sellers of gingerbread, for which some of the Baltic
cities once enjoyed a peculiar reputation—such are
the sources of fame; and Italian pedlars, minstrels,
and jugglers in troops; strange nation, whose gentry
never stir abroad, and whose rabble never stay at
home. Some of those poor people had travelled a
thousand miles on foot since they had first scaled
the Tyrol.

It is harsh to rail at governments, even Italian
governments; but there must be something singularly misconducted in a state of things, which,
in the most luxuriant country of Europe, with
hills and valleys smiling with exuberance, with
harbours on all sides, with a sea directly opening

on the commerce which in every age has made
the gold mine of the nation that possessed it; un-
encumbered by the taxes that cripple the Englishman, and unfettered by that iron military necessity which turns the whole strength of the continent north of the Alps to war, making its kings and
emperors but drill-serjeants on a larger scale, and
its realms but royal barracks; yet drives out annually whole hosts of its people to swell the menialism and pauperism of Europe. The wretched
Italian, with his bright eyes and subtle genius,
keeps up the live stock of human misery, recruits to
par the shoeblacks and chimney-sweepers of France,
the beggars of England, and the mountebanks,
Punches, and pilferers, of all the world beside.

At this fair I made a purchase, a whole *déjeûné*
service of porcelain. Yet let me not be charged
with a too liberal encouragement of foreign manufactures—it cost sixpence; and I carried the whole
home in my waistcoat pocket.

Rostock has a theatre. As may be presumed,
not a creation of that potential voice which bids
the La Scalas and San Carlos rise like an exhalation;
and by the pendant lights of their " blazing cres-

sets of naphtha and asphaltus" from golden roofs
and pictured walls, show many an assemblage not
unworthy of Milton's architect. All here was in
unison with the quiet mediocrity of the town.
But the seats were full, and the spectators appeared to be much interested with the business of
the scene. My imperfect knowledge of the language, and in all lands the stage language is a dialect *per se*, prevented my entering deeply into the
feeling of the performance; but probably there was
not much to feel. All the joys, sorrows, hopes,
and fears of the native stage, seem to have discovered but one mode of escape to the public ear,—
interjection, and that interjection to be uniformly
either *mein Gott*, or *Himmel*. The perpetual *mon
Dieu* and *Ciel* of France, repulsive as they are in
their flippancy to every sense of due reverence, are
scarcely so repulsive as the solemn ponderosity of
those adjurations in the mouth of the German
actor, in every frivolous instance. The entire
amounts to a sense of pain and profanation. The
national stage keenly requires a reform. An in-
quisitor would be pardonable in putting the whole
corporate sins of dramatic authorship in this coun-

try to the thumbscrew and the rack; no severity of the knife would be too severe for extirpating the offences that yearly thus start upon the public understanding; the roughest tyranny would fully deserve to be forgiven for the sake of the purification.

The subject of the play was harmless; the miseries of half-pay,—an intelligible topic, which may meet with sympathies in all lands. But it was curious to find it here : prose and poetry, rags and scenery, illustrating the neglect of the soldier when his services are done, and the wretchedness in which soldiership in general has a tendency to close ; and this, under governments essentially military, and by whose natural policy soldiership ought to be sustained in all its embroidered temptations. What would become of the three black eagles, if they were to be thus summarily stript of their caps and feathers? There was high treason to the majesty of German massacre, in the ragged uniform and consumptive visage of the half-pay subaltern, who sat, to-night, doling out his last loaf and his intolerable story among his children. By whatever appeals to human folly ancient war may have roused man to the assertion of his natural privileges as a wild beast, and

sent him out to tear his species; modern war knows
but two stimulants,—the trumpeter and the tailor.

———

We now entered Swedish Pomerania; equally
wild with the Prussian portion which we had just
left; but a little more diversified by the passage of
the Swedish army. The Crown Prince had arrived,
and was unquestionably on this side of the sea, at
last! But it must be acknowledged that his patriotism " dragged at each remove a lengthening
chain," and that he was determined to keep the
eye of his affections fixed on Sweden as long as
possible. His head-quarters are in Stralsund.
It is notorious that the allies are now crying out to
him hour by hour; he answers them by admirable
rescripts, but there he stands: the grand council of
the beaten sovereignties answer those by more
urgent rescripts; but the whole transpires in the
march of half a dozen regiments half a dozen miles
to-day, to march back to-morrow; another order
for the repair of the fortifications of Stralsund; and
his highness's evening promenade *en fiacre*, to see
that the sun goes duly down. The Germans, who
actually hate the French almost as much as they

dread them, are indignant at this delay. But there
still may be some excuse for this slow auxiliary.
Bernadotte has not quite twenty thousand troops
with him, and if those fell into the fangs of Napoleon, Sweden would be stript of her whole standing army.   The allies are comparatively safe for
a while; for Napoleon cannot follow them, unless
he is inclined to run the risk of having all Germany in insurrection on the slightest reverse; and,
the grand dictator of all, Austria, has not yet made
up her mind.   On the will of Emperor Metternich, and his viceroy Francis, depends the whole
question; Sweden is but a feather in the scale.
The two hundred and fifty thousand soldiers that
a wave of Metternich's hand can pour into the field,
will finish all the labours on both sides at once;
and either crush the allies against the Silesian
mountains, or sweep Napoleon and his fortunes
in a burst of blood and fire over the Rhine.

We reached Stralsund late in the evening: the
town looked large, gloomy, and buried in bastions
and hornworks; all the sights and sounds as we
approached it were military; troops were manœuvring in the fields; the volunteers of the town were

passing in parade before the Duke of Brunswick; and gleams of steel from more remote quarters showed detached corps of the Swedes. The roads were encumbered with carts, bringing materials for the fortifications. A battery, or a battalion, neither of which we were prepared to vanquish, stood in our way to the Pomeranian gate, and forced us to make a long circuit; but this gave us a better view of the novelties of this focus of war and militant princes, aides-de-camp, and ambassadors; and among our other gratifications we crossed the path of his Highness of Brunswick, in his black uniform, riding into the town. He looked in high health and spirits, gallantly reining up his charger till we passed, and was the *beau idéal* of a death's-head hussar. We made our obeisance, which his Highness did us the honour most graciously to return.

––––––––

We are now upon classic ground. Stralsund bore its part in the famous thirty-years' war; of all German wars the most brilliant. Here Wallenstein, a Herculean Goth, a man as much formed for sovereignty as any that ever inherited or conquered

a crown, pitched his standard; and if fortune had
not jilted him at last, might have established some
great northern dynasty, that would be at this day
clipping the pinions of Russia. Its fortifications
were due to Wallenstein, and some of them still
bear his name. The French, in their late possession, blew up the chief defences of the town, a
circumstance in which every inhabitant ought to
rejoice. But Bernadotte's engineers are now
rapidly girdling it again with wall and bastion;
and in another month it will be fit, *selon les régles*,
to be bombarded, stormed, and burned to the
ground. In its present condition, the siege would
be concluded in half an hour, by the advance of a
corporal's guard, and a deputation of the aldermen
to meet it with the keys in their hands. But when
it shall attain the dignity of a fortress, the etiquette
will be, a six weeks' cannonade, with a grand finale of
massacre and conflagration. It is thus that burghers
and their towns must pay for a niche in history.

But the city of Wallenstein has a higher distinction, as the closing scene of one of those gallant
attempts which honour the name of German and
soldier; the enterprise of Schill. On the road

through Pomerania we had felt the interest natural to tracing the steps of the brave ; but here was his last stand,—here he fought from street to street,—here the ground was sprinkled with his blood,—here, even with the most subdued sense of what had been done,—all reminded us of the homage due to the memory of a patriot and a hero.

———

Among the numberless ballads and fragments of verse which the war produced, were several on the death of Schill. Some of those hasty but vigorous performances I gathered at the Pomeranian fair. The lines now translated, give a graphic and characteristic sketch of the hero's final career.

SCHILL.

Er zog aus Berlin ein muthiger held.

Who bursts from Berlin, with his sabre in hand ?
Who ride at his heel, like the rush of the wave ?
They are warriors of Prussia, the flower of the land,
And 'tis Schill leads them on, to renown—and the grave!

Six hundred hussars, in their pomp and their pride
Their chargers are fleet, and their bosoms are bold;
And deep shall that sabre in vengeance be dyed,
Ere those chargers shall halt, or those bosoms be cold.

Then the yager in green, and the dark musqueteer,
By thousands they rose, at the bidding of one;
Then galloped the hunters, no hunters of deer,
And Prussia rejoiced that the chase was begun.

What summoned this spirit of grandeur from gloom?
Was he called from the camp, was he sent from the throne?
'Twas the voice of his country, it came from her tomb;
And it rises to honour him, now that he's gone!

Remember him, Dodendorff! whirlwind and rain
Bleach the bones of the Frenchmen that fell by his blade;
At sunset they saw its first flash on thy plain;
At midnight three thousand were still as thy shade.

Then, Domitz! thy ramparts were flooded with gore,
No longer a hold for the tyrant and slave.
But, Prussia, the day of thy glory was o'er!
And to Pommern he rushed, to renown and the grave.

Fly, slaves of Napoleon, for vengeance is come!
Now plunge in the earth, now escape on the wind;
With the heart of the vulture, now borrow its plume,
For Schill and his riders are thundering behind.

All gallant and gay they came in at the gate,
Where Wallenstein's banner once waved in its pride;
A king in his spirit, a king in his state,
Though now his dark tomb but o'ershadows the tide.

Then dashed the hussar, like a storm, on the foe,
And the trench and the street were a field and a grave;
For the sorrows of Prussia gave weight to the blow,
And the slave of Napoleon was crush'd like a slave.

Oh, Schill—oh, Schill! thou warrior of fame!
To the field, to the field spur thy charger again;
Why bury in ramparts and fosses the flame
That should blaze upon mountain, and forest, and plain!

Stralsünd was his sepulchre, city of woe!
No more on thy ramparts his banner shall wave;
The bullet was sent, and the warrior lies low,
And the dastard may trample the dust of the brave!

He was plunged in the grave without trumpet or toll,
No prayer of his warriors was heard on the wind;
No peal of the cannon, no drum's muffled roll,
Told the love and the sorrow that lingered behind.

They cut off his head; but his triumph is won,
And the love of his country shall weep o'er his bier;
And her high-hearted sons, from the cot to the throne,
Shall honour the dust of the chief that lies here!

When the fight is begun, and the Prussian hussar
Comes down, like a cataract burst from its hill;
Thy glory shall flash thro' the storm like a star,
And his watchword of vengeance be SCHILL, brave SCHILL!

Hamburgh continued, for some months, to be garrisoned by Davoust's corps, and subject to heavy privations and injuries. The French marshal then moved forward to Juterboch, where he was defeated with great loss, by the united Prussian and Swedish force under Bernadotte. As the winter approached, he fell back with his army on the city, which he had fortified strongly, and where he bore a blockade by the Swedes during the winter. In the meantime the battle of Leipsic was fought, Napoleon driven across the Rhine, France invaded, and the Napoleon dynasty at an end. The French garrison of Hamburgh were then suffered to return home. The city has since recovered a portion of its former opulence, and weary of the honour of being besieged, has wisely destroyed its fortifications, turned its huge fosse into gardens, and made its rampart one of the finest public walks in Europe.

THE END.

GILBERT & RIVINGTON, Printers, St. John's Square, London.

Lightning Source UK Ltd.
Milton Keynes UK
UKHW052342050521
383174UK00026B/732

9 781241 423964